The
Emerging
Educator

Working in Early Childhood Settings

EVA STELZER RUDICK

DIANE NYISZTOR

Vanier College

I(T)P® Nelson

an International Thomson Publishing company

Toronto • Albany • Bonn • Boston • Cincinnati • Detroit • London • Madrid • Melbourne
Mexico City • New York • Pacific Grove • Paris • San Francisco • Singapore • Tokyo • Washington

I(T)P® International Thomson Publishing

The ITP logo is a trademark under licence

Published in 1997 by

I(T)P® Nelson

A division of Thomson Canada Limited
1120 Birchmount Road
Scarborough, Ontario M1K 5G4

Visit our Web site at http://www.nelson.com/nelson.html

Canadian Cataloguing in Publication Data

Rudick, Eva Stelzer
    The emerging educator: working in
early childhood settings

1st ed.
Includes bibliographical references and index.
ISBN 0-17-604876-6

    1. Early childhood education – Canada.
2. Early childhood educators – Canada. 3. Day
care centers – Canada. I. Nyisztor, Diane.

LB1139.3.C3R82 1996   372.21'0971   C96-990093-7

Publisher and Team Leader	Michael Young
Acquisitions Editor	Charlotte Forbes
Production Editor	Brad Horning
Project Coordinator	Heather Martin and Evan Turner
Production Coordinator	Brad Horning
Art Director	Angela Cluer
Cover Design	Marko Associates Inc.
Photographer	Robin Tremblay
Composition	Elaine Andrews and Zenaida Diores

Printed and bound in Canada
4 5 6 7 8 9 TCP 09 08 07 06 05 04 03 02

TABLE OF CONTENTS

The Emerging Educator

Chapter 3   A Centre's Orientation 83

Preface

The Emerging Educator is designed for early childhood education students and educators studying or working in the field of early childhood education. This book provides a perspective of day care and outlines the role of the emerging educator within the day-care system. We examine day care from a systems approach. This approach represents a holistic and multidimensional way of looking at an organization. It permits different types of structures and theoretical frameworks to exist in harmony. In light of the interconnectedness of domains of learning and the technological advances of society, it is a good time to apply a systems approach to the day-care environment.

In this book the student is considered to be at the beginning of his or her journey toward becoming an early childhood educator. Both students and educators in the field are introduced to the key members in the day-care system—administrators, parents, support staff, board members, and, the most important members of all, the children. You will study the differences between non-profit and profit day cares and the changing role you might play in each situation, and examine the necessary skills you will need in order to provide quality care and education in the day-care environment.

The book begins with a historical reference to the development of child care and day care in Canada. A good understanding of the roots of our profession enables us to understand the forces behind present-day practices.

Chapter 2 provides an overview of the theoretical and philosophical roots of child care. Chapter 3 describes how to define and use a mission statement as a focal point for merging the theory and educator practice in the day-care environment.

Chapters 4 and 5 take a close look at the interpersonal relations that affect the work of an educator. We provide strategies for the student and emerging educator to develop effective relations with children, parents, educator-trainers, and colleagues.

Chapters 6 and 7 provide details about the legal framework and economic structure of a day care. In Chapter 8 we take the reader through the steps involved in preparing and conducting a job search.

Chapter 9 describes a quality day-care environment. This information is useful for the emerging educator and provides criteria for a high quality day-care environment. A discussion on the relation between provincial and territorial requirements is included.

Finally, Chapter 10 looks at you, the emerging educator, as a professional in the field of early childhood. We describe the ethical issues involved in the child-care profession as well as ways to advocate for better care for the children with whom you will work.

Acknowledgments

We would like to thank our acquisitions editor, Charlotte Forbes, for believing in this project. Heather Martin and Evan Turner provided support along the way. Special thanks goes to Brad Horning, who never found any detail too small or too large for his attention. We would also like to thank the reviewers—Alice M. Taylor (Holland College), Allison Soave (Niagara College), Karen Troughton (Kelsey Institute), Betty Exelby (Loyalist College), and others—who provided feedback to the project.

....

I would like to thank my husband Dan for his support and all his technical help and assistance. My children Michael and Jessica were extremely patient during the process. I also want to especially thank my mother Marion Bankley who provided relentless help along the way. A special thanks to Eva, a friend, partner, and co-author.

Diane Nyisztor
Vanier College

No book is ever written alone. This work was influenced by the positive support of my family. A special thanks goes to my husband Gerry for his constant support and to my children Joelle, Elana, and Lauren whose encouragement cannot be measured. They have read excerpts of chapters and provided useful feedback. I would also like to thank my colleague Diane for her skills and friendship.

Eva Stelzer Rudick
Vanier College

Introduction

This introduction will:

- familiarize you with an understanding of what it means to be an emerging educator;
- familiarize you with the structure and layout of the book.

The Emerging Educator

You entered a program of study that will train you to become an educator of young children. Can you articulate what prompted you to make this career choice? Can you describe what it means to be a teacher or an educator?

Throughout your childhood and teenage years you have experienced many teachers. You may feel you know more about this profession than any other. After all, you have had at least one teacher per year for at least twelve years. This represents many styles within the teaching profession. Perhaps you can identify what characteristics made each teacher special. Can you identify characteristics that you appreciated in grade school or high school that would fit into your perspective for an educator of preschool-age children?

For a moment, think back to the time before you entered the school system. Who took care of you? Who helped you learn about the meaning of life?

....

Reflection

Why do you want to become an educator of young children? How can a training program help you achieve this goal? Identify some personal values that will have an impact on your professional growth. Discuss your answers with some of your peers.

....

This textbook will help you critically examine some of the questions related to becoming an educator of young children. It provides a perspective with which to look at the day-care environment that takes into account the many internal and external influences. We provide a grounding in early childhood theory, a close look at the administrative aspects of a day care from the perspective of an educator, an examination of interpersonal relationships that arise, and a close look at the meaning of professionalism within the field of early childhood education.

How to Use this Book

Objectives. Each chapter begins with a set of objectives. Reading these will help you anticipate the material that will be covered in the chapter. The objectives are designed to prepare you for the new information and material that follows. It provides a reference point for your reading. Upon completion of the chapter, return to these objectives and re-examine them to see if you have met each one.

Advance Motivator. Following the objective box are advance motivators. These are key terms that have special meanings in the field of early childhood education and in this textbook. Examine each key term before reading the chapter. While reading, assign meaning to each term as it appears in the textbook. You will notice that key terms are presented in the order in which they first appear in the chapter. To help you study the material, the key terms are listed in the glossary in alphabetical order.

Reflection Boxes. These are designed to provide stimulating dialogue between students, practicing educators, and course instructors. They can also be used individually as prompts to stimulate journal writing. Dialogues and journals about yourself will begin the lifelong process of learning. This strategy is intended to stimulate learning and help you, the emerging educator, become an inquiry-oriented and reflective practitioner.

Situation Boxes. Case studies are presented in situation boxes. These describe actual events or "situations" that arise during the career of an early childhood educator. Looking at a real situation helps us develop a variety of perspectives and acquire knowledge about real experiences.

Tools. We provide a few tools throughout this textbook that serve as instruments for acquiring knowledge about yourself and the skills you will need as an early childhood educator. These are designed to be useful to both students and practitioners. Compare the answers you give while you are studying to those you give once you are practising in the field.

Summary. Each chapter has a summary that highlights the information presented in the chapter. This is intended to prompt your recall about key points.

Questions and Activities for Further Reflection. These questions and activities will stimulate your thinking and problem solving and help you reflect on the information presented in the chapter. They are designed to stimulate personal reflection based on your knowledge and beliefs.

Self-Test. Each chapter includes a self-test that is designed to facilitate the study process.

Additional Features in this Book

Appendix A. Appendix A is for you to use after your program of study is completed. It outlines many resources, mentioned in this textbook or found elsewhere, that will help you apply for a job and fulfil your professional role as an emerging educator. It will encourage you to think of learning as a continuous process.

Appendix B. Appendix B provides a blank grid that can be used to develop a mission statement. This will be explained in Chapter 3.

Glossary. The glossary includes all the terms that have been high-lighted in the textbook. Concise definitions are provided for each term.

Perspective Taking

Before continuing on to the next chapter, we ask that you try the following exercise in perspective taking. Sit down on the floor. Close your eyes and count to sixty. Now open your eyes. Look around the room but do not look up. What do you see? How is this perspective different from the one that you usually have? An important part of being an educator of young children is to notice things from a variety of perspectives—yours, the children's, and those of the various other people who are connected with the day care.

PART I

A Perspective of Child Care

This section of the *Emerging Educator* introduces the textbook and provides a brief overview of Canadian child-care and day-care history. We look to the past as a means of understanding present day-care needs and perspectives. We use the lens of a systemic structure as the theoretical foundations for this book and as a means of understanding day care in today's society. Chapter 1 lays the foundation for understanding the day care as a system.

In Chapter 2 we provide the reader with a philosophical overview and the theoretical foundations of early childhood education. An understanding of various theoretical paradigms is important for the development of an early childhood curriculum.

Chapter 3 examines the development of a mission statement and the unique orientation of each day care. This perspective provides a means of interpreting the day care from a systemic perspective.

CHAPTER 1

Canadian Child Care, the Day-Care System, and You

In this chapter you will:

- examine the history of Canadian child care;
- identify a systems approach to education;
- examine the components of a system;
- examine the relationship between elements in a systemic approach;
- examine the application of a systemic approach to early childhood education;
- define the day-care system;
- look at the day-care environment.

Advance motivator

Examine the following key terms before reading the chapter. Then, while reading the chapter, try to assign meaning to each one.

intercultural awareness	holism
cultural pluralism	stakeholders
quality child care	goal orientation
system	relationships
reflective practice	resources
inquiry-oriented practice	ecological model
systems approach	mission statement
components	boundaries
embedded	theoretical foundations

Child Care: Contemporary Status and Future Projections

Early childhood education is continually evolving to meet the needs of the children and families within their communities. The 20th century has provided early childhood educators with many challenges. One such challenge is to maintain and nurture the important relationships with the families. However, as we enter the 21st century the family may come in many forms.

Early childhood environments should continue to serve as a support system for these families. A cooperative relationship between educator and parent/guardian is crucial. We must avoid making value judgments about lifestyles. A mutual respect should be nurtured.

Linda Lemesurier, concerned day-care director and advocate

A nurturing, respectful, and educational early childhood environment is achievable when educators, families, and society work together to meet the needs of children. Reflection on the roots of day care in Canada is valuable toward understanding both the present and the future. Current practices often reflect past experiences and trends.

Child care in Canada began over 150 years ago. Over the years many types of child-care services have been offered. These services have been provided through a variety of structures such as religious groups, government agencies, public and private sector groups, or community groups. As part of the North American continent, Canada's child-care history is similar but not identical to that of the United States. Canada's strong ties to England and Europe give this country an early childhood foundation that has its own unique flavour.

Early 1800s to Mid-1900s

Two decidedly different origins of child care in Canada are recorded in the literature. One view notes the emergence of child care as early as 1820, while a second view notes the emergence of Canadian child care to be around 1850.

Pence (1990) suggests that child care in Canada enjoyed a constructive origin. He suggests it began with the Infant School Movement in the 1820s and 1830s. Pence further proposes that studying this origin of child care will provide us with a clear understanding of our contemporary problems and our possible future. The Canadian Infant School Movement began in Halifax and emanated from the Infant School Movement begun some twenty years earlier in Scotland by Robert Owen, a Scottish industrialist. Owen needed to double the workforce for his mills, and the simplest solution was to hire the wives of the men already employed. This meant establishing a kind of **day care** for the children of the families who now had two parents working. This seemingly modern problem took place over 150 years ago. Essentially, Robert Owen established the first workplace day care in history. Owen also set standards for the education and care of young children. His visionary approach was continued by his son. Soon word of Owen's Infant School and pedagogy spread through Great Britain, Europe, and finally North America.

The infant school established in Halifax is the first recorded Canadian child-care facility to be modelled as a workplace day care. Of course, the city of Halifax was not yet considered a part of Upper Canada; Halifax only joined Canada with Confederation in 1867. This may explain why this infant school is not always included in discussions of Canadian child-care history. In the early 1800s early childhood education was part of the political platform of the society it served (ibid.).

Shortly after this fantastic beginning, the admiration for the infant school faded. The family structure began to change with the arrival of the Victorian era. This was perpetrated by a reduced need for women in the workforce and an emergence of a social ethic that emphasized a new family form (ibid.).

This brings us to the second and more generally recognized view that child care in Canada began some twenty or thirty years after the infant school was established in Halifax. Child care began simultaneously in Ontario and Quebec around 1850. The first English-speaking day care was established in 1887. Winnipeg had its first day care in 1906. It was not until 1910 that an infant and preschool centre was opened in Vancouver at the Infants Hospital. The opening of this infant centre on the West Coast of Canada happened nearly 100 years after the first infant school opened on Canada's East Coast.

During this time in Canadian history, child care was predominantly provided under the banner of charitable organizations made up of church groups and women's groups. The Roman Catholic Church represents one church group that exercised a strong influence in the establishment of child day-care services in the early years. For the most part, though, Canadian women during the early day-care history stayed home and cared for their young children. Most children spent their early years at home with members of their families. The greater part of the day was enjoyed in the company of one or both parents, with siblings of different ages, or members of an extended family such as grandparents.

Child day-care services at this time in Canadian history were available primarily to meet the needs of mothers who had to work outside the home and who would otherwise leave their young children alone at home unsupervised. The primary purpose was to provide shelter and custodial care for young children. There was a practice of some day cares serving as employment agencies from World War I to the end of World War II (Vandebelt Schulz 1978; Hendrick 1993). Mothers seeking work would bring their children to the day care in the morning and then wait for the agency to find them daily employment.

Photo 1.2
Early day cares like this one offered basic child-care services to children.

During this time there was a strong emphasis placed "on manners, obedience, cleanliness and religion" (Vandebelt Schulz 1978, 143). Traces of these values can be seen today in many day-care institutions throughout the country.

Financial support for these day cares was in the hands of charitable organizations. Most funding for child-care services came from donations. This reinforced the stigma that child care was not a service of choice but rather a service for families in financial need. In an attempt to dispel this stigma, parents were asked to contribute a minimum fee. In 1850 parents were charged 25¢ a month. By 1932, as subsidies began to decrease and as costs to provide services increased, parent fees rose to 25¢ a day (ibid.).

There were other influences in the early years of Canadian child care. Frederich Froebel (1782–1852) is noted for his influence on the kindergarten. Originating in Germany, his ideas became very popular throughout the Western world. In 1883 Toronto established its first Froebelian kindergarten (Taylor 1990). With the establishment of other kindergartens Ontario became the first place in the world to have kindergarten as part of the public school (Friendly 1994). Froebel designed his program for children who were 3 to 7 years of age. However, in Canada, the methods employed by the Froebelian influence were only accepted for the age range we today refer to as kindergarten. This limited acceptance of the Froebelian kindergarten was due to objections from the Church of England and a social climate that advocated that children should be at home with their mothers (Taylor 1990; Corbett 1990).

Mid-1900s to Present

The Government of Canada's involvement in child care began in 1942 with the passing of the Dominion-Provincial-Wartime-Agreement (Friendly 1994). During World War II there was a great need for women to enter the workforce. With this urgency for workers the federal government entered a cost-sharing agreement with the provinces to establish day cares. The government felt that by establishing day cares, mothers would enter the workforce. The space in these new day cares was predominantly reserved for the children of women whose work was related to the war effort.

This funding ended in 1946 when the government no longer had an urgency for women to be in the workplace. At this time the government also implemented Family Allowance payments. They saw this as an incentive for working mothers to return home with their children. Children during this period began to attend preschool nursery programs instead of child day-care centres. These nursery programs placed greater emphasis on education and less on custodial arrangements. Nursery programs are generally geared for half-day participation as compared with day-care programs that usually involve full-day participation.

In 1966 the federal government introduced the Canada Assistance Plan (CAP). This legislation provided funding for cost sharing of child care between the federal and provincial governments. This cost sharing arrangement is generally regarded as critical in the development of child care in Canada (ibid.). The first province to enter the CAP program was Manitoba. In the late 1970s the introduction of legislated standards and limited funding for each province signalled the beginning of the modern era of child care. A rise in feminism and the increase in the number of women entering the workforce are noted as key turning points in the modern era of child care.

In 1971 Health and Welfare Canada began to collect statistical information on Canadian day cares. In 1971 there were 17,391 recognized day-care spaces in Canada. By 1990 there were 320,288 day care spaces. The increase in day-care spaces levelled off in the early 1990s and we see only a slight increase in 1994 to a total of 324,288 day-care spaces. These figures show an increase of close to 400,000 day-care spaces in a twenty-three-year span. These figures indicate a substantial increase in the amount of children attending day cares in Canada.

Regardless of whether you look at the true origin of day care in Canada as an infant school that provided day care for families with both parents working or shelter for disadvantaged families, child care has always existed to meet the needs of children as perceived by a societal group. This societal group in Canada's early day-care history was represented by either business or religion. We do know that there are two periods in Canadian history when public perception held that children of a young age were best served by being home with mother. These two periods are represented by the Victorian era and the short time span after World War II. We also know that each time women have returned to the workforce in great numbers there was an increase in demand for child-care services. Today, day care exists to meet the needs of all classes of society. It is not limited to meeting the needs of impoverished families. Businesses and communities play a strong role in providing adequate services. Recently, there is evidence of the emergence of a link between child care and government policies.

Where Are We Now and Where Are We Headed?

The provision of child-care services has changed over recent years and is emerging as a provincially/territorially legislated part of the social fabric of Canada. A major point of concern at the present time is that each province and territory operates independently and that there are no national standards of organization.

Today's child-care needs include a growing demand for day care for infants and toddlers. Often infant/toddler programs are offered as part of the regular service provided by a day care. A wide age range, from 6 months to 5 years of age, is visible in day care today. This suggests that an understanding of the developmental needs for the variety of age groups is valid.

There is a renewed recognition of the value of providing on-site, employee-offered child care in the form of day-care services (Martin 1990). This provision helps companies and other organizations attract and keep qualified employees.

Canada today is recognized as a multicultural, multilingual, and multiracial country. There is "consensus among those currently involved in multicultural education that there are certain key components that must be included in the preparation of today's Canadian educators" (Mock 1990, 118). These components include an **intercultural awareness** and a belief in **cultural pluralism**. Intercultural awareness means that you need to become aware of your own values and assumptions in order to understand others. Cultural pluralism suggests that many cultures co-exist in harmony and that we must value our own culture and that of others. It also implies a respect for individual heritage.

The effects of day care on young children vary. According to the literature, good day-care programs have positive effects (Caldwell and Fryer 1982; Spodek, Saracho, and Davis 1991). The introduction of standards and funding into child care represents an important societal statement concerning the importance of **quality child care** for all. Setting of standards and the availability of training programs introduce a new meaning to the terms quality and professionalism in child care.

As early childhood educators, we have known for some time now that while teachers and educators need to change, so does the **system** of child care (Sykes 1994). It appears that educators and teachers in Canada are aware of their roles with respect to this change (Clandinin et al. 1993). Some changes suggest that the future of the field lies in the participation of all members in the system of early childhood education. Early childhood education refers to the body of knowledge that guides the practice of child care and education for children from birth to 11 years of age. It also includes the network of services that exist to meet the needs of children in these early years. Early childhood education includes many services that require an inclusionary approach for social legitimacy. Only as a socially legitimate service can it secure public support (Pence and Moss 1994).

In an inclusionary approach, members of a system work together to ensure that the services provided meet the needs of the population that the system serves. One way to achieve this goal of working together is to engage in **reflective practice**, both at an individual level and as a group working together. Reflective practice involves a constant questioning and reassessing of decisions and actions. A reflective practitioner is one who constantly seeks to improve upon what he or she does from day to day. The best teachers, according to Adler (1993), are those who "are able to systematically reflect on their own teaching" (160). We believe that this reflective process leads to an awareness of one's rationale for making certain choices over others. This method of always questioning your actions is often called an **inquiry-oriented practice**. This leads to a transformation or change in your thinking based on your experiences. This change in thinking leads you to act differently than you would have acted before reflecting on the experience (Adler 1993; Diamond 1991).

This inquiry and subsequent transformation of action is an important part of developing yourself as a reflective practitioner. We remind you that the reflection boxes throughout the book are designed to provide the kind of prompts that will encourage your own inquiry into your emerging practice.

···

Reflection

Do educators have to change the way they care and teach young children, or does the child-care system have to change, or do both have to change? Discuss these questions with some of your peers. Compare points of view.

···

The term system has been mentioned repeatedly. What is a system? What is a **systems approach**? What are the **components** that make up a system? How do these components interact in a systems approach? How does a systems approach facilitate an understanding of day care and early childhood education? Working definitions of the terms system, systems approach, and day care are essential before we proceed.

What Is a System?

A system is an organizational structure. It is a self-contained structure that is defined by individuals who have some connection to the specific system. These individuals can function inside or outside the organizational structure of the system.

What Is a Systems Approach?

A systems approach is a way to look at organizational structures. In a systems approach a variety of structures and theoretical constructs can exist in harmony. A systems approach relies on a **holistic** perspective. Holistic means that many components are considered in relation to one another rather than in isolation. There is an emphasis placed on the interaction between these components.

It is important to establish a definition of the term day care as it is used in this book before describing what the components are and how they interact. Day care in this book refers to a physical location where children are left for part of a day or for a full day. In this location children receive both care and education during hours of the day when primary guardians are unavailable to meet their needs. The day care is a system that is part of or **embedded**[1] in two larger systems—child care and early childhood education. Figure 1.1 provides a diagrammatic perspective of the embeddedness of the day-care system within other systems.

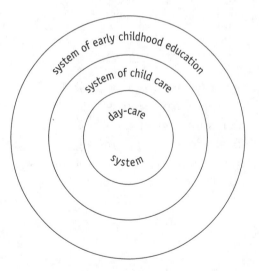

The interaction between one system, here the day-care system, and other systems or individuals in the environment forms the basis of the systems or ecological approach to child care and education.

FIGURE 1.1
The day-care system is embedded in the larger system of child care. Both systems are embedded in the system of early childhood education.

---

[1]The term embedded is commonly used in a systemic framework to mean that one system is found within another larger one. Often, systems are embedded (or exist) in many subsequently larger ones. As stated earlier in this chapter, the day care is a system found within another system, that of child care.

What Are the Components of a System in General and a Day-Care System in Particular?

A systems approach involves many components that work together and are related to one another. Think of a component as if it were an ingredient. If you were to bake a cake, you would need many ingredients to complete the recipe. Each ingredient is as important as the other. You need to know what each ingredient is like and how the ingredients mix together in order to complete the recipe.

Like each ingredient in a recipe, each component must be understood separately in order to understand how it works in a system. The interaction of one component with another helps a system function. The components of a system are **holism, stakeholders, goal orientation, relationships,** and **resources**.

Holism

A systemic approach is based on principles of holistic thinking. Holism implies that information about the particular organization is examined from many areas and from more than one perspective. An example of this in daily living would be the simple act of crossing the street. On a simplistic level you could stand at the corner, look straight ahead, see no obstacles in your path, and cross. On a practical level this is potentially dangerous. Let us look at the situation holistically. You need to consider possible vehicles coming from either your left or right that might drive across your path. You should also consider if any cars are coming from behind, intending to turn the corner where you are crossing. Are there any bike riders on the road who have no intention of stopping? The safest option would be to examine the *whole* picture and not just one part of it.

This holistic view is extremely compatible with the study of early childhood education. Effective programming is usually based on an approach that integrates information, **knowledge,** and experience from many areas. A holistic approach to early childhood education considers "an integrated curriculum that focuses on children's needs and interests and takes into account culturally valued content and children's home experiences" (National Association for the Education of Young Children 1994, 10).

The following reflection provides an example of a situation that, if looked at holistically, must consider the needs of the child and the values of the family and the educator responsible for the child's care. In this example the emphasis on holism includes an approach that is consistent and respectful toward all those involved (Wood 1994).

Reflection

You are a student educator in the day care and you have been placed with a group of toddlers. Your supervisor has provided you with information on toilet training that is consistent with the approach used in the college education training program. The cooperating educator that you are working with is handling toilet training in a way that does not seem consistent with what you have learned. How will you handle this situation? Can you see more than one way to handle this situation?

As a student, one priority is to ensure consistency between you and your cooperating educator. Avoid situations in which children receive mixed messages or are a part of any controversy. One tactic would be to bring up the issue during a meeting with your cooperating educator. Approach this as an information-seeking session. You are the student in a position of learning. You are doing a perception check on the educator's philosophy as well as that of the family's. You should feel comfortable in asking the cooperating educator for clarification so that both of you can work in harmony.

Sometimes, simply taking the time to clarify a situation is extremely beneficial. As a result of your discussion you may find yourself feeling more comfortable with the cooperating educator's way of handling the situation. If you do not agree with the approach being used, try to find a common ground so that you can carry out your responsibilities as a student educator. Listen and avoid passing judgment. If you are still not satisfied at the end of this meeting, speak to your supervisor and ask for further feedback and information. Keep in mind that each individual has a responsibility to provide an approach that is consistent and respectful.

Stakeholders

A stakeholder is any individual or group of people who have a stake or interest in a particular system. Stakeholders in an early childhood education setting usually include children, parents, educators, administrators, support staff, students, board members, funding agencies, and community members. Each individual who has a self-interest in the system is concerned with assuring its success. A stakeholder is guided by his or her interest in making a system work.

Children

Children attending day-care facilities range in age from a few months to 6 years. Older children often require child-care services when regular school is not in session. These services are generally referred to as school-age care or extended day programming and are beyond the scope of this book.

The organization and structure of each day-care system is influenced by the children's ages, interests, family backgrounds and needs.

Parents

Parents using day-care facilities require out-of-home care for their children for part or all of a day. They use day-care services on a part-time or full-time basis, depending on personal needs. Today's day-care system is often dependent on parent fees to meet operational needs. Parents can serve as members of a board of directors. In this way parents become involved in the decision-making process of the day care.

Educators

Early childhood educators are individuals hired to work directly with the children. An early childhood educator is responsible for the programming and organization of activities and routines for the children. Spodek, Saracho, and Davis (1991) suggest that certain personal characteristics are key to becoming a competent educator. These characteristics include a love of children, physical stamina, patience, knowledge of human development, and respect for individual personality. As an early childhood educator you will be called upon to support all aspects of child development.

The educator works in a day care, which in turn represents a part of society. Its very existence results from societal needs. At the same time it provides a service for a part of society—the child. This inter-relationship between the society it serves and the day-care system itself is often referred to as an **ecological model**. Bromfenbrenner's ecological model considers the different layers of the environment that affect the development of the child (Yeates et al. 1994). These layers include the many systems that interact with one another, such as the child's family or peers or teachers.

PHOTO 1.3
Compassion and respect for children are prerequisites for the early childhood educator. These characteristics influence the children in the day care and the overall day-care system.

Administrators

Administrators or directors are responsible for the day-to-day running of the day care. They ensure that the centre is adequately staffed and they provide support to the educators. They are also responsible for the management of the finances and often work with a bookkeeper to control the expenditures.

Support Staff

Support staff refers to all individuals who support the regular working tasks of individuals hired to operate a system. In a day care, support staff include such positions as the cook, bookkeeper, and caretaker.

Students

Early childhood education students spend time in the day cares as part of their training and course work. The amount of time and depth of involvement that a student has with children varies from one training program to another. Educators serve as models for students in their field placement and on-site training.

Board Members

A board member is an individual who sits on the board of directors. There is usually a representative from each of the stakeholder groups on a board. These representatives include staff, community members, parents, or others who have a vested interest. The largest percentage of board members is made up of parents.

Funding Agencies

Funding agencies vary from province to province. Government agencies often allocate funds and grants for the operation of day-care centres. Funding agencies can also include charitable organizations.

Community Members

Community members are individuals who live or work in the community. Day-care systems are surrounded by community people whose services are invaluable. For example, library staff of the local library are considered community members. A visit by a day care to the local library draws on the services of these community members. Community members can become involved on many levels. They can serve as paid visitors or as volunteers.

The Interaction of Stakeholders

Each individual or group has a unique and vital role to play within the day-to-day functioning of the system. Each member is positioned differently in the system and as a result has a different perspective. For example, parents and educators have their own unique and equally valid perspective of the day-care system of which they are each a part. It is also possible for two educators working in the same day care to have different perspectives. It is the **interdependence** of each view that results in the shared view that is system specific. The shared view, on the holistic perspective, is what motivates and drives the system.

The following situation exemplifies the vested interests of four different stakeholders. While everyone is concerned with having a quality outdoor facility attached to the day care, each has a somewhat different perspective.

Situation

Heidi, a 4-year-old girl, looks forward to coming to the day care. She particularly enjoys playing outdoors. She wants the outdoor facility to be fun and available. Heidi has a stake in the outdoor equipment.

Sasha, the educator, is concerned with effective supervision in the outdoor setting. He wants the environment to be safe and needs assurances that he can see all the children at all times. He requires that the playground's design incorporate good visibility of all the apparatus no matter where he positions himself. Sasha has a stake in the outdoor equipment.

Heidi's parents want their child to be happy during the day. They also would like her to get fresh air. The playground seems to make Heidi happy and it is outdoors. They want assurances that the equipment is safe and appealing to their child. Heidi's parents have a stake in the outdoor equipment.

All outdoor facilities must meet municipal construction standards set for permanent and nonpermanent structures. Requirements are set through bylaws that vary from area to area. Bylaws include such things as whether an area needs to be fenced in, the distance a structure must stand from the fence, and what materials are acceptable in the construction of this type of facility. Therefore, the municipality, through its designated representatives, has a stake in the outdoor equipment.

Let us look at the combined view of all the stakeholders in this situation. All agree that the facility needs to be safe. It also should be interesting, fun, and available for frequent and easy access. The educator requires good visibility of all areas of the facility no matter where he is positioned. All these factors need to be considered as part of the parameters that define the outdoor facility. This is because, in the end, the facility must be accepted by all the stakeholders and not by just some of them.

Now, try the following reflection to identify which stakeholder you represent and what your part is in the day-care system.

Reflection

Which stakeholder do you represent? How, in your opinion, will this influence your relationship with other stakeholders? Discuss this with a small group of your peers.

TOOL

Using the space provided, answer the following questions.

Who do you represent in the day care?_____

Using a personal perspective, describe your role in the day care.

_____

_____

Goal Orientation

A system is made up of components that together share the same goal or purpose. All systems are by definition goal oriented. It is the shared goal or vision that unifies all the stakeholders and enables each member of the system to function on the basis of holistic thinking and inquiry-oriented practice.

In the day-care environment the **mission statement** provides the goal orientation. Briefly, the mission statement helps set the directions for stakeholders and serves as the centre's raison d'être. As members of the day-care system arrive at crossroads of decision-making, they consider their choices and make decisions using the mission statement as their guide. The development and application of a mission statement are detailed in Chapter 3.

Systems exist within invisible lines that are artificially created to distinguish where one system ends and another begins. These are called **boundaries** (see Figure 1.2). Sometimes these boundaries are vague and difficult to distinguish. At other times they are clearly defined. Boundaries vary for each organization and are system specific. They represent an artificial enclosure to an environment and are artificially assigned by the members of a given system.

Boundaries are defined by the nature of interactions between members inside and outside the system. There are many routine interactions that generally occur within the boundaries of an organi-

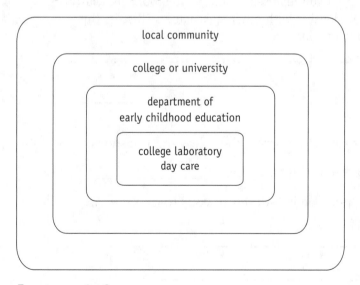

FIGURE 1.2

Example of the boundaries in a college laboratory day care.

zation. For example, educators may meet weekly with the director to coordinate plans and activities. Less frequent, but equally important, interactions occur between the inside and the outside of the system. For example, as mentioned earlier, a day care may use the community library facilities. The director would need to coordinate this and make arrangements with the representative of the library system on behalf of the members of the day-care system who wish to use the library facility. These interactions will be infrequent but necessary for effective communication and functioning of both systems. Understanding the boundaries specific to your day-care environment will provide a clearer grasp of how to interact with members in your sys-tem and those in the external environment.

Relationship

An educational system is driven by human involvement. The relationship of one member to another affects the way a system functions. Individual relationships within a system vary. They are to some extent dependent on the organizational structure. This structure can be referred to as either open or closed. In an **open system** there is more interaction between the boundaries of one system and another than there are in a closed one. A **closed system** tends to operate in a self-contained environment, relying more on its internal structure than on relations with larger or parallel systems. This should not be interpreted to mean that a closed system operates in a vacuum. It does have contact with outside systems. A closed system tends to operate within more clearly defined boundaries and relies less on interaction with elements outside the system.

An open system tends to have a higher frequency of communication with the outside as part of its functional mandate. Non-profit day cares tend to be more open in nature, relying to a greater extent on interaction with the elements that are not directly a part of that particular day-care environment. Board members often include representatives from outside systems, such as community members, organizations that have some responsibility toward funding, and parents. Profit-oriented and privately managed day cares tend to function in the context of a closed system design. A closed system, such as a profit day-care centre, does enjoy a relationship with outside organizations, but there is greater dependency on the internal structure for the purpose of decision-making.

Many relationships are important for a day-care system to function successfully. Educators must interact with parents on a regular basis. It is the educators' responsibility to foster a climate that encourages an open channel of communication. This helps disseminate vital information with respect to the child.

In your quest to become a competent early childhood educator, you will discover that a positive and effective relationship with children, parents, and other staff members is important. As an educator of young children you may be one of the first people a child encounters for long periods of the day outside the home (Feeney, Moravcik, and Christensen 1991). Chapters 4 and 5 are devoted entirely to the types of relationships and the skills required to foster a positive climate through effective interactions.

Resources

Resources include money, materials, community facilities, recycled materials, and the abilities of parents. Money comes from a combination of fees, government subsidies, donations, and fund-raising events. Materials are either bought with allocated funds or are received through donations. Some day cares are situated in locations that facilitate access to community resources. These resources could include a local library, swimming pool, or skating rink that can be used by the children.

Parents provide a unique resource. This varies as the parent body changes. Sometimes in the day care you find a parent who is particularly handy at woodworking. These skills can be used to build shelves, design wooden structures, or simply repair existing areas. A parent who is particularly adept at computer skills can be asked to assist in the design of a newsletter. It is important to tap into the wealth of skills that parents bring to the day care. Involving them will help foster a harmonious environment. Try to get parents to be **advocates** for the centre.

The Dynamic Nature of a System

We spoke earlier of the many interactions that occur in a system. Each component within the system responds to other components of the same system or to components from other systems. Put another way, nothing happens in isolation. It is the very interactions that give meaning to a system and give it a **dynamic** nature. There is a sense of shared decision-making. A systems approach does not rely on a strict hierarchial format where only a director or owner makes decisions. The concerns of the educators, parents, and children are taken into consideration in order to successfully reach the shared view of the system.

One example of interactive relationships can be seen when we take a look at directors applying for financial grants. The director must interact with components outside the system in order to fulfil requirements within the system. The components the director must interact with might include government agencies, outside organizations, or community resources. Figure 1.3 provides an illustration of the many relationships that impact on the decision-making of the educator and the director.

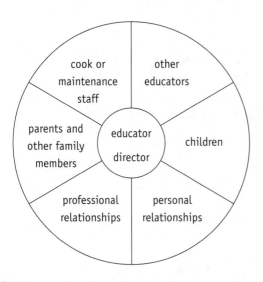

FIGURE 1.3
Some of the many relationships that impact on the educator and the director.

There are many systems of child care, of which day care is one. Understanding your position as a student or as the educator within the systemic perspective of day care and child care is important. Your relationship with other key individuals linked to the day-care environment plays an important part in developing your teaching and care-giving self. A systemic approach considers "children, parents and early childhood educators, and their relationship with the environment in which they work and live" (Yeates et al. 1994, 4).

Applying a Systems Approach to Early Childhood Education

As a student or entry-level educator it is important to understand the nature of the environment of which you are a part. A systems approach to early childhood education will help you situate yourself as a student or an educator and, perhaps later, as an administrator. Using a systems approach toward the environment encourages you to think about "change on a continuous basis" (O'Neil 1993, 11). Change is always present and represents the dynamic nature of a system. A systems approach will also be an effective tool to help you understand the various relationships and interactions that you will engage in with other educators, support staff, administrative staff, children, and parents. For you to become a successful participant within the system, you need to have a conceptual map of it (see Figure 1.4). A systems approach is grounded in holism and an ecological view that is a cornerstone of early childhood education. There is an interdependence between individual stakeholders and the external environment. Work through the following reflection to help you develop an understanding of the interconnectedness of the system.

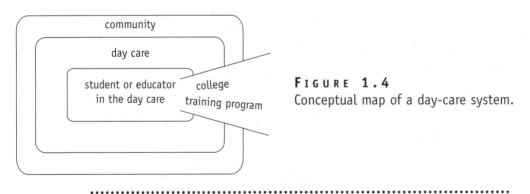

FIGURE 1.4
Conceptual map of a day-care system.

Reflection

Draw a diagram of your position in the day care. Begin with a large circle to represent the day care. Where do you fit? Where do the children fit? What about the director and the parents? If you are a student, include a position for your supervisor.

Applying a systems approach to early childhood education is an effective tool toward the promotion of quality child care. For a system to function well it requires positive relationships between stakeholders, staff training, and a unified interpretation of a mission statement. An environment that fosters positive social interaction tends to facilitate quality care.

Today's educational environment is fast-paced and rapidly changing. It is technological and interactive. A systems approach to education and day care provides a perspective that is compatible with today's information or post-industrial age. As educators in today's world we need to guide and facilitate learning as a lifelong skill. Inquiry into our own practice on an ongoing basis will foster positive relationships with other members within the systems of early childhood education, child care, and day care.

Defining the Day Care

The Day-Care System

We have described the basic principles of a systems approach. Each day-care system is both unique and similar. Uniqueness is determined by its goals, its mission statement, and the families it serves. Day cares are similar in that they exist to meet the needs of parents, children, and society. Each day care fits into the larger systems of child care and then society.

The components of any system include human and physical resources. In a day care there is an important and inseparable relationship between the children, family, day-care staff, and physical environment. All these components interrelate with one another. Although each individual within the system has a unique perspective, the components cannot be looked at in isolation (see Figure 1.5).

Whether you are a student, practitioner, or administrator, you are an important part of the day-care centre. Depending on your function,

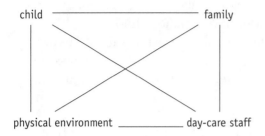

FIGURE 1.5
Family, children, day-care personnel, and the physical environment interrelate in the successful operation of a day-care system.

however, or your position within the system, you will have a different perspective of the day care and your role in it. The example provided below illustrates the changing relationships and the dynamic nature of the system.

Situation

The day care is planning a field trip. Each person plays a different role in the organization and implementation of the field trip. The role you play can be affected by your position within the system. The catalyst for the field trip might come from the director or some of the educators. Depending on the type of field trip, there might be an incorporation of some specific concepts into the curriculum. For example, if a trip to go apple picking is planned, you as an educator might introduce relevant books and read stories related to apples, bus trips, or the harvest of fruits and vegetables in general.

As an educator you are responsible to ensure that appropriate first aid equipment is brought on the trip. Parents are required to give written consent and, oftentimes, will be invited to provide additional supervision. Some centres have a cook on staff. This person could be responsible for planning meals or snacks that are suitable for this type of trip. When there is no cook, the director communicates any specific food requirements to the parents, who, in turn, prepare appropriate foods.

In this example, everyone (parents, educators, support staff, and children) operates with the same purpose in mind. However, each person, depending on their position in the system, has a different role to play.

Is There a Place for a Systems Approach in Early Childhood Education and the Day Care?

Yes. The emphasis of a systems approach on holism, perspective, and goal orientation is valuable to the study of early childhood education. A key element for success in a systemic approach to education is that participants in any given organization support each other's work. Collegial interaction and support are two factors that have a positive influence on the culture of the day-care environment (Wood 1994). Working as a team benefits children, parents, and staff.

Individually, components of a system have one value, but collectively the relationship is both different and greater. In a systems approach you are *in* the system as a participant. Regardless of whether you are a student, educator, or administrator, you are not an objective observer looking in from the outside. Rather, you are inside the system and observing what is happening around you as an active participant. The interactive nature of an educational system suggests involvement of the participants and observers. As a result of your participation and involvement, you are constantly reassessing the best means to attain the goals of the system. This reassessment is an important key to the success of any system, in this case the day care, as the system evolves and goes through various stages, which inform the next and later stages. This may, in turn, lead to the reformulation of an earlier stage (Banathy 1991, 1992). The day-care environment is always changing and constantly revising itself. All this supports the notion of the dynamic nature of the system.

A systemic approach relies on the interdependence of the needs of all those who are involved in the system. Any system operates independently, but it also functions in relation to other systems.

These can be larger, related, or parallel systems. Each member is valued equally. In a day-care system the children's needs provide the impetus for striving for harmony and quality.

Educators meet children's needs through **program content**. This content is built on **theoretical foundations** of early childhood education that serve as frameworks for educators to make sense of their educational existence (Schoenrock 1995) within the day-care system. These theoretical foundations give special meaning to each particular day-care system.

Summary

- Child care in Canada began about 150 years ago.

- The first child-care facility was in Halifax and stemmed from Owen's Infant School.

- Originally, most Canadian child-care facilities were started as charitable organizations.

- The day care exists to meet the needs of children and to provide supplementary care and education for them.

- A system is an organizational structure.

- A systems approach is a way of looking at an organizational structure.

- A systems approach in day care takes into consideration both the internal day-care environment and the external environment.

- The day-care system is embedded in the larger system of child care.

- Stakeholders are individuals who have vested interests in a particular system.

- All systems are goal oriented and function to achieve a common purpose.

- The day-care system is dynamic. It is constantly evolving to meet the changing demands of the society it serves.

Questions and Activities for Further Reflection

1. What attitude would you like to develop within yourself in order to become an effective teacher? Repeat this activity again upon completion of this book. Compare your findings. Have your views changed with an increase in knowledge? Articulate how these views have changed.

2. Observe a group of children and their educator in two different day cares. Describe your perception of the role of the educator in each one in relation to the children. Do either of your observations reflect the type of role you would like to play? What are the similarities and what are the differences?

3. As a student-educator, to whom do you communicate concerns and questions? As a practitioner, to whom do you communicate your concerns and questions?

Self-Test

Provide definitions and examples of the key terms that were identified as advance motivators at the beginning of the chapter. Find the page(s) where information on each term is provided.

On a separate sheet of paper, write down each key term that is completely new to your vocabulary. Revisit these terms at the end of each chapter and assess your understanding of the terminology.

R e f e r e n c e s

Adler, S. (1993). "Teacher Education: Research as Reflective Practice." *Teacher and Education* 9:159–67.

Banathy, Bela H. (1991). *Systems Design of Education: A Journey to Create the Future*. Englewood Cliffs, N.J.: Educational Technology Publications.

Banathy, Bela H. (1992). *A Systems View of Education: Concepts and Principles for Effective Practice*. Englewood Cliffs, N.J.: Educational Technology Publications.

Caldwell, B.M., and M. Fryer. (1982). "Day Care and Early Education." In *Handbook of Research in Early Childhood Education,* ed. B. Spodek, 341–74. New York: Free Press.

Clandinin J., A. Davies, P. Hogan, and B. Kennard. (1993). *Learning to Teach, Teaching to Learn: Stories of Collaboration in Teacher Education*. New York: Teachers College Press.

Corbett, B. (1990). "A Froebelian Perspective on Early Childhood Education." In *Child Care and Education: Canadian Dimensions,* ed. Isabel Doxey, 98–108. Scarborough, Ont.: Nelson Canada.

Diamond, Patrick C.T. (1991). *Teacher Education as Transformation*. Buckingham: Open University Press.

Feeney, S., E. Moravcik, and D. Christensen. (1991). *Who Am I in the Lives of Children? An Introduction to Teaching Young Children*. New York: Merrill Publishing Company.

Friendly, M. (1994). *Child Care Policy in Canada: Putting the Pieces Together*. Don Mills, Ont.: Addison-Wesley.

Hendrick, J. (1993). *The Whole Child,* Canadian ed. Don Mills, Ont.: Macmillan Publishing Company.

Martin, Sue. (1990). "Infants and Toddlers." In *Child Care and Education: Canadian Dimensions,* ed. Isabel Doxey, 193–205. Scarborough, Ont.: Nelson Canada.

Mock, Karen. (1990). "Multiculturalism in Early Childhood Education." In *Child Care and Education: Canadian Dimensions,* ed. Isabel Doxey, 109–125. Scarborough, Ont.: Nelson Canada.

National Association for the Education of Young Children. (1994). "Position Statement." Washington, D.C.: NAEYC.

O'Neil, John. (1993). "Turning the System on Its Head." *Educational Leadership* 51, no. 1.

Pence, Alan. (1990). "The Child-Care Profession in Canada." In *Child Care and Education: Canadian Dimensions,* ed. Isabel Doxey, 87–97. Scarborough, Ont.: Nelson Canada.

Pence A., and P. Moss. (1994). "Towards an Inclusionary Approach in Defining Quality." In *Valuing Quality in Early Childhood Services,* eds. Peter Moss and Alan Pence, 1–9. New York: Teachers College Press.

Schoenrock, Fred. (1995). "Five Reasons to Teach." In *Thinking About Teaching: An Introduction,* eds. G. Taylor and R. Runte, 22–25. Toronto, Ont.: Harcourt Brace.

Spodek, B., O. Saracho, and M. Davis. (1991). *Foundations of Early Childhood Education, Teaching Three-, Four- and Five-Year-Old Children.* Boston, Mass.: Allyn and Bacon.

Sykes, Maurice. (1994). "Creating a Climate for Change in a Major Urban School System." *Young Children* 50:4–7.

Taylor, M. (1990). "The Child-Care Profession in Canada." In *Child Care and Education: Canadian Dimensions,* ed. Isabel Doxey, 65–86. Scarborough, Ont.: Nelson Canada.

Vandebelt Schulz, P. (1978). "Day Care in Canada: 1850 to 1962." *In Good Daycare: Fighting for it, Getting it, Keeping it,* ed. Kathleen Gallagher Ross. Toronto: The Women's Press.

Wood, Chip. (1994). "Responsive Teaching: Creating Partnerships for Systemic Change." *Young Children* 50:21–28.

Yeates, M., D. McKennal, C. Warberg, and K. Chandler. (1994). *Administering Early Childhood Settings: The Canadian Perspective,* 2nd ed. Don Mills, Ont.: Maxwell Macmillan Canada.

CHAPTER 2

Theoretical Foundations of Early Childhood Education

In this chapter you will:

- recognize the influence you have on curriculum and planning;
- identify the philosophers who had an influence on the development of early childhood education;
- identify various theories of early childhood education;
- identify various approaches to curriculum development;
- recognize the influence of the environment, schedules, routines, activities, and opportunities on program goals.

Advance motivator

Examine the following key terms before reading the chapter. Then, while reading the chapter, try to assign meaning to each one.

theoretical foundation	operant conditioning
curriculum	reinforcement
program planning	behaviour modification
maturationist theory	modelling
assimilation	eclectic approach
accommodation	cognitive dissonance
zone of proximal development	key experiences

Emerging Knowledge Base

Educators of young children begin with a base of knowledge that is acquired through direct education and personal experiences. Your base of knowledge grows each time you are exposed to a new experience or a new learning situation.

An interpretation of your teaching and care-giving self is a valid exercise in establishing your knowledge base as an emerging educator. It is important to know yourself, recognize your values, and have an awareness of your beliefs. "Who you are forms the foundation for the professional you will become" (Feeney, Moravcik, and Christensen 1991, 10). Your past experiences with other teachers and educators influence what you believe about teaching and related professions. Your personal beliefs about the role of an educator are important. The way you interpret your role—as educational, developmental, or custodial—will influence the image you portray of yourself as an educator and ultimately influence how others perceive you (Goffin and Day 1994).

A theoretical grounding in early childhood is invaluable in order to function proficiently within the day-care system. As an educator of young children you will be called upon to make choices about the theoretical foundation upon which to build your **curriculum** and **program planning**. Your personal beliefs and acquisition of relevant knowledge serve as a guide. The concepts presented in this chapter provide a basic foundation for current thinking in the field of early childhood education. Further study in this area is recommended throughout your professional career.

Theoretical Foundation

A theoretical foundation in any discipline of study serves to provide direction and focus. Theory serves to enlighten practice. In early childhood studies many theorists and philosophers have had a profound effect on the theoretical foundation of early childhood education. In this chapter we will outline the views of some of the early philosophers. We will also look at a number of the developmental and learning theorists in the field. In some instances you will clearly recognize the influence of a philosophical viewpoint on the development of particular theories.

This outline is meant to provide a basic overview of a theoretical foundation to curriculum development and programming. It is by no means comprehensive and further study in this area is recommended.

Educational Philosophers

Pestalozzi, Froebel, and Dewey are among the first educational philosophers in the field of early childhood education. Many curriculum models today stem from their theories. An educational philosopher is someone who articulates beliefs and values in order to systematize and interpret knowledge.

Pestalozzi

Johann Pestalozzi (1746–1827), a Swiss educator, created a school system based on the principles of child-interaction with the physical, intellectual, and moral environment (Roopnarine and Johnson 1993; Taylor 1990). While it is true that most of Pestalozzi's work was directed toward the grade-school child, Bredekamp (1987) suggests that the seeds of developmentally appropriate practice can be seen in his work.

Pestalozzi considered nature to be an important aspect of the curriculum. His vision of child education included a focus on the whole child. He was an advocate of children learning in groups rather than being tutored on an individual basis. His philosophical approach had a strong belief that children should be nurtured by teachers the way they are cared for at home by their mothers.

Froebel

Frederich Froebel (1782–1852) is considered to be the father of the kindergarten. "Froebel subscribed to the view that childhood represented a noble and malleable phase of human development"

(Roopnarine and Johnson 1993, 7). Froebel saw activity as the basis of knowledge and learning. He placed a strong emphasis on children's experimentation and honoured their play. His philosophical view approached play as an essential part of the educational and learning process.

For Froebel the teacher's role was to provide materials and activities that mould and guide a child's education and learning. Blocks and block play were an integral part of the Froebelian classroom. Today, these blocks and block play are still an important part of most early childhood classrooms. Froebel, like Pestalozzi, saw the teacher's role in child development as nurturing.

The second Froebelian kindergarten to be inaugurated in North America was in Toronto in 1883. As discussed in Chapter 1, this Froebelian kindergarten had a strong influence on the subsequent development of kindergartens in Ontario.

Dewey

John Dewey (1859–1952) is most closely related to the progressive education movement of today. He viewed teaching and learning as a continuous process of reconstruction of experience (Dewey 1966). Problem solving and cooperation are important elements to learning in this philosophical approach to education. Key words in Dewey's curriculum include play and make-believe play (Roopnarine and Johnson 1993).

In Dewey's view a focus on family provided a central concept for the development of curriculum. Children learned about relationships in the home and the construction of these relationships through their families and the families of the other children. Today, the meaning of the word family is more diverse than it was at the time that Dewey formulated his philosophical ideas. Nonetheless, family and related topics are used widely today by early childhood educators as a central concept in planning.

Dewey believed strongly in the principles of democracy and that learning and education should be accessible to all.

Educational and Developmental Theories

Many theories exist about how children learn and develop. Different theoretical paradigms of knowledge have existed over time and these affect the development of curriculum models. An overview of child development and the various theories helps in the development and design of a personal curriculum. A personal curriculum is your framework for the delivery of a sound program of care and education.

Maturationist Theory

The maturationist theory is a developmental theory that is grounded in the ideology of Jean Jacques Rousseau (Brewer 1995). Stanley Hall is considered the founder of the maturationist theory. Arnold Gesell, a student of Hall's, continued and expanded on this work.

> Maturationist theory suggests that the course of human development is primarily genetically determined. Hall believed that each individual in the human race went through a developmental sequence that parallelled the development of the species.
>
> *Spodek and Saracho 1994, 63*

This theory states that children will develop to their full potential within their own time-frame. The **maturationist view** holds that development is governed by heredity. This view suggests that experiences do not have a great deal of influence on individual development. Gesell's research established standards about what most children can do at a certain age and introduced the concept of readiness. The norms instituted by Gesell are still widely used in the education profession. Although these norms have been modified in recent years, there is still one problem associated with them. Many believe that the data obtained to establish norms represent cultural bias (Feeney, Moravcik, and Christensen 1991; Brewer 1995).

For a long time the maturationist approach dominated the field of early childhood education. There are two reasons for this. First, the maturationist study provided useful data that were both observable and measurable, making it easy to quantify information. Second, the early childhood curriculum has a tradition that is rooted in psychology rather than in education.

The tremendous body of research compiled by the maturationists provides educators today with knowledge of various stages of development. It provides relatively reliable information on the various stages of skill acquisition. Its flaw lies in the overgeneralization of norm classification.

Psychodynamic Theory

The **psychodynamic theory**, like the maturationist approach, focuses on developmental stages. A major distinction of the psychodynamic theory is its inclusion of personality development, which is purported to be related to various stages of human development. Sigmund Freud is recognized as the founder of the psychodynamic theory. Erik Erikson is also strongly associated with the further development of this theory.

> The Freudian theory of development assumes a series of biologically determined stages. Each of these stages involves some major central problem whose resolution determines the personality structures that emerge from that stage of development. Each stage can be seen as containing the prototype of a major component of personality.
>
> *Baldwin 1980, 394*

Erikson expanded on Freud's work and conceived eight psychosocial stages of development. "Erikson characterizes the predetermined steps in personality development as a conflict or crisis that arises within the individual and demands resolution" (Langenbach and West Naskora 1977, 72). These conflicts or crises are seen by Erikson as a healthy part of an individual's personal growth (Essa and Young 1994). Social interaction is seen as pivotal in the individual's lifelong development **process**.

The first crisis that an infant is believed to go through in the psycho-dynamic theory is trust versus mistrust. At an early stage of development in a child's life, primary caregivers are encouraged to be responsive to the infant's need for reassurance. There is a strong belief that the emotional climate of infant learning affects the infant's ability to become active, curious, and self-motivated (Honig 1993).

Cognitive Developmentalist Theory

Piaget

Jean Piaget (1896–1980) first conceptualized the **cognitive developmentalist theory** of child development. In this theoretical paradigm the creations of knowledge, learning, and thinking are achieved through an individual's interaction with her or his environment (Brewer 1995; Gordon and Browne 1985). Piaget began his career studying how organisms adapt to the environment. This idea of adaptation fascinated him.

> For Piaget development consists of qualitatively different stages through which each child passes. Each stage is marked by strikingly different perceptions of the world and adaptations to it; each is the product of learning that occurred during the previous stage and a preparation for the stage that follows.
>
> *Lefrançois 1973, 156*

The cognitive developmentalist theory has influenced many of today's curriculum models, particularly the constructivist approach. In this theory the hierarchical stages of development do not progress in a strict linear fashion. Rather, they progress in a spiral where one achievement builds on a previous one and co-exists with it (see Figure 2.1).

Children, according to this approach, go through a process of organizing data or information. Either they take in the information and fit it into knowledge they already have by a process known as **assimilation**, or they have to change the way they think in

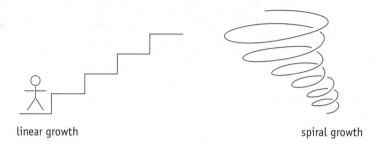

linear growth   spiral growth

Figure 2.1 Linear growth versus spiral growth.

order to accommodate the new knowledge by a process known as **accommodation**.

According to this theory, people perceive and see things differently at different stages of their development. In practice this means that an educator should recognize that children and adults do not perceive events or situations in the same way. Educators need also recognize the valuable influence that the previous experiences in a child's life have on the present cognitive developmental level.

Children from different cultural and social backgrounds come to the day care with a wealth of different experiences. Their backgrounds do have an impact on what they are ready to assimilate or accommodate. An educator would be wise to use the richness of experience that each child and her or his family can provide.

Vygotsky

Lev Vygotsky (1896–1934) was a contemporary of Jean Piaget. While he had no knowledge of Piaget and his work, Vygotsky can still be classified as a constructivist. His work was carried out in Russia behind the Iron Curtain and was not known by Western society until much later.

> In Vygotsky's view the primary focus for educators and psychologists should be on the strengths and capabilities of children.
>
> *Berk and Winsler, 1995, 8*

The focus of this approach is on cognitive development supported by social interaction. Language is a key component in this theory. Learning is mediated with verbal prompts and gentle guidance (Forman 1993). Children who are able to do simple tasks on their own need to be guided and shown how to do the next task or a more complex task by someone who is more of an expert. For example, a young child who has mastered pulling up her or his coat's zipper once the rows of teeth have been connected by the adult can then be shown by the adult how to connect the two sides of the zipper. This part of a child's development is referred to as the **zone of proximal development**. In other words, the zone of proximal development refers to what the child is able to achieve without assistance.

Another important aspect of Vygotsky's theory is the dependence on social interaction. For constructivists following Vygotsky's approach, social situations are seen as ways to maximize cognitive conflict. As mentioned earlier, it is cognitive conflict that leads to construction of knowledge. Social interaction is seen as a method of inducing learning that is superior to merely having a child interact with an object. Recalling our discussion on the philosophical views of Pestalozzi, we can see how his work influenced Vygotsky in the area of social learning.

Educators using this approach focus on individualized learning. The educator must establish the zone of proximal development for each child. This can be achieved through observations of the children in their environment. Educators and children jointly contribute to the development of the child's competence.

Once individual developmental goals are established for each child, the educator designs a highly social environment. The environment should encourage social discourse, the use of language, and group interaction.

Behaviourist Theory

Behaviourist theory was developed in the 1920s. Four well-known theorists associated with this theory are John Watson, Edward Thorndike, B.F. Skinner, and Albert Bandura.

> Behaviourists base their understanding of children on the belief that behaviour can be shaped by rewards and punishments. A theory that organisms will respond to given stimuli based on previous experience with the stimuli.
>
> *Brewer 1995, 5*

Unlike the child development theories, this learning theory is not linked to stage- or age-related concepts. The behaviourist theory of learning identifies the environment as a primary influence on the learner. All behaviour in this view is seen as a function of learning (Feeney, Moravcick and Christensen 1991). **Operant conditioning, reinforcement, behaviour modification**, and **modelling** are words derived from the behaviourist theory. Operant conditioning is the endeavour to control behaviour by increasing or decreasing the presence of the particular behaviour. Reinforcement is one way to control behaviour. It is the process of modifying a behaviour through a reward system. Reinforcement is used to increase a desired behaviour to reduce or extinguish a negative behaviour. Behaviour modification works by introducing a reward to encourage the appearance or disappearance of a behaviour. Behaviour modification is evident in the following example of toilet training. Each time a child uses the toilet successfully, he or she is given a sticker or other reward to show approval of his or her behaviour. When the child eliminates in his or her diaper, no sticker is given.

Another element developed by the behaviourists is modelling. Modelling refers to a practice of demonstrating behaviour or attitudes that one individual wishes another to learn. Children model what they see from other children, educators and other adults. In some cultures modelling is the predominant method for passing on traditions and beliefs. Educators serve as models for young children. For this reason it is important that educators exercise attitudes that they hope will be passed on to the children.

In positive modelling an educator can successfully demonstrate a positive attitude. This disposition is then seen by the children as an acceptable behaviour. As a part of positive modelling, it is important to avoid practising behaviours that you do not want repeated by the children. For example, if you do not want the children to sit on tables, then you should not sit on them either.

Head Start

Head Start is an early childhood program model that began in the United States as a publicly funded program for children from low socioeconomic and disadvantaged groups. We include this model in our discussion of early childhood theories because of its link to university and research institutions. Head Start draws from a variety of learning theories and goes beyond the scope of early childhood. Since it started in the mid-1960s, its goal has been to provide an educational program for both children and their parents. Like Montessori, the Head Start project's aim is to educate parents through nutritional and life skills counselling in order to help them break out of the poverty cycle.

The first Head Start programs were organized by an interdisciplinary panel that included representatives from social services and from the fields of medicine, education, and psychology. A variety of program sponsors from universities and research centres developed

PHOTO 2.1
The behaviourist theory encourages educators to model appropriate behaviour for children. Much social behaviour is learned through play, and children benefit from positive modelling.

different models of curriculum development that would benefit from the availability of public funding.

There is a recent Canadian interest in the concept of Head Start programs. An initiative of the federal government has encouraged Head Start programs for Aboriginal and Inuit populations in Canada. Research into Head Start programs shows that an approach designed to involve the family in education is beneficial.

Implications of a Theoretical Foundation

Understanding the roots of educational philosophers, developmental theorists, and educational theorists in early childhood education provides a knowledge base for the development and design of curriculum models such as high/scope, developmental interactionist, and others. In early childhood education the aim of any curriculum is to plan for the whole child, regardless of the model or approach used. However, different curriculum decisions may be based on different theoretical foundations.

For example, a curriculum may be cognitively oriented, be humanistically oriented, or be a combination of orientations. We believe that decisions for the design of curriculum should be made at the discretion of the people who are directly or indirectly related to each day care and that consistency is an important factor in curriculum design and development.

Educational philosophers and theorists provide information about how children learn and develop. This knowledge is important for any practitioner. In practical terms, knowledge about these theories serves to influence how we act and respond to children. For example, much of what we know today about the predictable sequence of physical development is based on Gesell's norms. These norms inform us that children learn to walk before they can run.

Theories do not determine the content of programs or the things that we want children to learn (Spodek and Saracho 1994). Rather, they describe the philosophical foundation that guide and influence the planning process and the delivery of curriculum content.

Curriculum

A variety of curriculum models have emerged in the field of early childhood education. In early childhood education, curriculum does not refer to the delivery of academic lesson plans as it might in grade school. It refers to a framework for the design and delivery of care, education, curriculum content, and administrative policies (Doxey 1990; Goffin 1994). It is made available through daily plans, activities, or experiences. Daily plans are based on the curricular objectives and are used to outline content that is needed to meet these objectives. Daily plans also articulate, in writing, the sequence in which the learning will occur. This may seem like a daunting task to the novice educator, but experience and practice will facilitate the design and delivery of a curriculum that will lead to a high-quality program.

A **curriculum framework** is influenced by philosophers, developmental theorists, and learning theorists. As an educator you can either blueprint or copy an existing curriculum model or you can borrow ideas from a few models and combine them to create an **eclectic approach**. If you choose an eclectic approach**,** it is important that you recognize which part of your personal curriculum reflects one model versus another. As a novice educator you might find it easier to adopt an existing model until your comfort level develops. After some experience you will be in a position to assess the benefits and downfalls of the model you have selected. Keep in mind that your curriculum decisions should be informed by "an understanding of child development, family dynamics, and the impact of different environmental circumstances" (Goffin 1994, 5).

Curriculum models provide templates for program development. No matter how flexible these models are, they do have boundaries. The initial curriculum models in early childhood education were developed with an educational purpose in mind to serve nursery school programs. These initial curricula were not designed to serve the needs of child-care services that were offered primarily for families in need. Initially, nurseries were established for the middle class and educated factions of society. Soon it was recognized that educational programs could have a positive effect on society as a whole and nursery curricula were set up for disadvantaged children.

A major shift in curriculum models occurred concurrently with the dramatic increase in the number of middle-class women returning to the workforce. This lead to an inclusion of curriculum in day-care as well as nursery-school programs. Parents of children in day care wanted a combination of care and education. The first wave of research on all-day child-care programs did not focus on curriculum but on whether or not these all-day programs were harmful to the children's development (ibid.). Today, research trends include the concept of care, education, and child development, take into account the children's cultural and family background, and look at a broader picture of the influence of full-day programs on children.

As stated earlier, the curriculum models provide the direction for daily plans and activities. "Curriculum developers establish goals, develop experiences, designate content, and evaluate experiences and outcomes" (Spodek and Saracho 1991, x). All curricula have certain elements in common. These common elements include setting long-term goals and medium- to short-term objectives that involve a decision-making process to determine which elements to include; a planning stage that focuses on how and when activities and experiences should happen; an implementation phase; and, finally, an assessment of how and when the children learned (Bredekamp and Rosegrant 1992). What differs in each model is how and why goals and objectives are established, and how they will be implemented day-to-day.

Over the years there have been many influences on the early childhood curriculum that come from diverse conceptual frameworks. Choosing one approach over another helps shape the uniqueness of each day-care system.

Curriculum Models

What is a curriculum model? A curriculum model is a framework that reflects a philosophy of ideas and beliefs about how children learn and develop. Models provide guidelines for educational priorities and methods of instruction (Goffin 1994) to be used in a particular day-care system. Currently, there are many models that exist in the field of early childhood education. This ability for many models to co-exist suggests the complexity and diversity of the field. Some models are based on historical perspectives and beliefs about how children develop. Other models reflect cultural perspectives and the influences of society. Our goal in this chapter is not to impose a curriculum model but rather to provide you with options that allow you to compare the differences. For each curriculum model is conceived with different convictions that are consistent with one's beliefs of child development (Spodek 1991).

The majority of curriculum models have been influenced by a particular theory. For example, the constructivist and interactionist orientation both rely heavily on the developmental theories and the notion of internal motivation. The high/scope model is an excellent example of an interactionist model. Interactionist and constructivist models have a strong theoretical grounding in Piagetian theory. Another example is that of the behaviourist orientation. Curriculum models that rely on a behaviourist perspective view learning as being influenced by reinforcement, external rewards, and punishments. An eclectic approach might use modelling as a form of reinforcement from the behaviourist orientation and a child's free exploration of a rich environment from the constuctivist orientation. In this example, an educator consciously decides to select aspects of more than one curriculum model in order to develop a personal curriculum. We will now examine specific details related to various curriculum models.

Constructivist Approach

According to Piaget, an individual constructs knowledge only when there is a cognitive conflict (Forman 1993). **Constructivist approaches** to curriculum are founded on Piaget's principles of

cognitive dissonance. Cognitive dissonance refers to a conflict in thinking. In order to resolve this conflict a learner must ask questions or solve the problem in order to reconstruct an acceptable interpretation of the situation. This reconstruction of knowledge helps the learner accommodate new knowledge.

Different theorists have used Piaget's theory of constructing knowledge as a basis for developing theories of teaching. A distinction needs to be made here—a theory of how children learn is not necessarily the same as a theory of teaching. Rather, a theory of teaching is usually derived from theories of how children learn. Following Piaget's immense contribution, theorists continued to refine and alter his ideas.

DeVries

This model uses a combination of Dewey's progressivism and Piaget's constructivism. For Rheta DeVries there are developmental levels in everyday situations (ibid.). Children are encouraged to become autonomous and to think for themselves. Unlike Vygotsky, her orientation does not rely heavily on social interaction. However, she does believe in the social construction of knowledge. For her, educators should help children look to themselves for answers. This introspection will help them construct meaningful understanding by resolving cognitive conflicts. For DeVries, like Piaget, children's incorrect ideas about the world are part of their learning process and are the way they construct an understanding of the world (DeVries and Kohlberg 1987) to reflect a unique subjective experience.

Kamii

Constance Kamii's work in early childhood focuses on the development of a child's understanding of physical knowledge. Her beginnings in mathematics education explain this emphasis. A high value is placed on group games.

Kamii, like DeVries, differs from Vygotsky in that she sees the source of cognitive construction as being internal rather than social. For her, children need to discover, explore, and invent their own under-standings (Forman 1993). However, Kamii does believe that once the children have constructed their own knowledge, they need to verbally interact with their peers in order to define this knowledge.

Malaguzzi

Loris Malaguzzi is the founder of the Reggio Emilia approach. This publicly supported system of child care originated in the region of Emilia, Italy, in the town of Reggio. It is an approach to early educa-tion and a system of child care that involves the participation of the entire community.

The curriculum of the Reggio Emilia program is based on a variety of theoretical foundations. For example, it supports Vygotsky's concept that knowledge is socially constructed and Piaget's concepts of assimilation and accommodation. In this approach, chil-dren are encouraged to work in small groups of four to six. Children spend long periods of time developing a project. A project can last one month or longer. These projects are selected based on the chil-dren's interests and questions.

Implications for teaching

This constructivist approach is child centred, creating an environ-ment that encourages and initiates learning in a pleasant atmos-phere. The educator approaches the child's questions in different ways. If the child were to ask a question about the physical compo-nents of an object, the educator would encourage the child to find the answer from examining that object. If the child were to ask a logical-mathematical question, the educator would encourage the child to reflect on the question and to discover the answer (Goffin 1994; DeVries and Kohlberg 1987). In both cases the educator would set up a project that would encourage exploration that, in turn, would lead the child to greater learning in the area of her or his interest. "Teachers, therefore need to be very knowledgeable about Piaget's theory, especially children's pre-operational ways of interpreting experiences, and be able to convert their theoretical understandings into practical knowledge of individual children and developmental progress" (Goffin 1994, 148).

Educators in the Reggio Emilia approach work in pairs, supporting each other and the children. They begin with a group of infants and stay with that group for three years. This helps educators to get to know the children and their families. The educators act as facilitators in the children's construction of knowledge.

Montessori

Maria Montessori

Maria Montessori (1870-1952), a physician by training, was born in Italy. She saw early education as a means to rid society of the social problems of the poor. She believed that education was the best means to improve the human condition.

Montessori recognized each individual as unique. For her, the child was inherently good (Lindauer 1993). She regarded the child as an active explorer and manipulator of the environment. This exploration and manipulation occurred best when the child was at play, which she saw as the work of children.

She believed strongly in the child's interaction with the environment. She further believed that children needed to overcome obstacles, choose their work (play), and follow through with tasks (Montessori 1956). Montessori designed many special materials for the use of young children. She measured the value of each material by examining a child's level of concentration and attention when using it. Montessori schools reflect the founder's belief that children should be exposed to specific materials at the appropriate times, that is, when they are most receptive to absorbing specific learning (Essa 1996). These materials are very much present in modern applications of the Montessori curriculum.

Implications for teaching
This approach is based on individual instruction. In the **Montessori method** each child selects materials based on individual needs. The child is provided with a brief individualized learning session to master the precise use of the material. Once the child becomes

proficient at using the prescribed material, he or she is free to select it to work with at any time.

The role of the educator in this method is often seen as passive (Goffin 1994). Except for brief moments of individualized sessions, the educator is an onlooker. All children are encouraged to work to their full potential. Educators provide a prepared environment but refrain from reinforcing a child's actions. This follows a belief that the reinforcement for learning comes from the child's manipulation of materials in the environment. An educator's respect for the child is critical. Children are permitted to enter the work of other children only when they are invited to do so.

High/Scope Curriculum

David Weikart and Associates

The **high/scope curriculum** is grounded in Piaget's cognitively oriented theory of development (Essa 1996; Lay-Dopyera and Dopyera 1990). The environment is organized around learning centres. Children are viewed as active learners. This program is based on the plan, do, review process and is centred around key experiences.

Planning involves giving the children a time period in which to choose an activity. The activity time is referred to as work time. The terms work and play are used in the high/scope curriculum much in the same way as Montessori programs use them. Children use symbols with their picture on them to designate where in the environment they will be working. The working at their activities is the "doing." The review process is used to provide children with an opportunity to meet with an educator and recall their activities.

Implications for teaching
In this approach the educator works with key experiences that fit into the following eight categories: active learning, language, experiencing and representing, classification, seriation, numbers,

spatial relations, and time. Educators rely on their observations of the children in order to carefully prepare the environment.

Each day, the educator develops a planning board that the children use to decide which activities they will pursue. A child may engage in one or several activities. The educator helps the children think through the plan and then records it. The review process is a time for children to recall their experiences. Each child reports, with an educator's assistance, to the rest of the group the activities that he or she engaged in during the work time segment of the schedule.

Bank Street Model/Developmental Interactionist

Lucy Sprague Mitchell and Barbara Biber

This approach originated from observation studies of young children. It was supported by the writing of John Dewey and still shows traces of this philosophical approach to children (Zimilies 1993). **Bank Street** is in many ways similar to the constructivist approach. There is an emphasis on the quality of the socio-emotional environment of the classroom (ibid.).

This approach was initially designed for educators working with disadvantaged children. Today, the educational goal of this program continues to promote autonomy and exploration. It is often characterized as a child-centred approach. This approach has its roots in the British Infant School Movement.

Implications for teaching

Two major goals of the educator are to help children develop trust and to provide them with a safe and secure environment. This model is responsive to the individual behaviour of the children. It also emphasizes the developmental processes underlying behaviour. It is the underlying process and not the behaviour that is the educational nucleus for the teacher (Goffin 1994). The educator helps children in understanding and constructing their knowledge and provides them with opportunities that promote their growth and development (Spodek and Saracho 1994). The educator or teacher requires a strong educational foundation in the theory of child development.

Anti-Bias Curriculum

Sparks and Associates

This model is based on an **integrated** approach that places a strong emphasis on avoiding the concepts of bias (gender, culture, race, age, and family) within the early childhood education curriculum. This pluralistic orientation emphasizes a respect for cultural differences and a recognition of individual similarities. This view rejects the commonly used "tourist version of multicultural education" (Sparks and Ramsey 1993, 280). An **anti-bias curriculum** focuses on respect and familiarity.

Implications for teaching

The educator in this model pays close attention to the type and diversity of material that is made available to the children. The selection of books would be scrutinized closely with an aim to assure that they avoid bias. An educator builds the curriculum around the family and cultural backgrounds of the children. Individuals are encouraged to develop an awareness and sensitivity to other individuals. The educator pays attention to the children's home cultures and languages and uses these as an integral part of the curriculum.

··

Reflection

Select one curriculum model. Describe what your role as an educator would be if you were to rely on that model for planning. Think about how you would interact with the children in a toddler group or in a group of 4-year-old children.

··

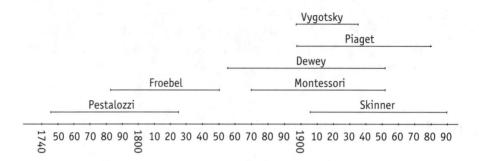

FIGURE 2.2 Time line of philosophers and theorists.

Using a Curriculum Model

Based on the various curriculum models that exist, a student educator or practicing educator will choose a personal curriculum approach. There is a tendency to practice a personal approach that draws specific concepts from a variety of curriculum models. In some instances, practitioners do use one curriculum model exclusively. More often, practitioners will create their own approach based on their knowledge of child development, cultural background, and understanding of different established curriculum models. This leads practitioners to develop programs and plan activities based on their knowledge about curriculum models and sound development of curriculum content. Once an educator makes a choice about a curriculum approach, he or she will formulate a curriculum design. A curriculum design outlines daily and weekly program goals, desired outcomes, activities, schedules, and routines.

Where do you begin? First, it is helpful to recognize that "curriculum is a product of its time. It changes as society changes and as knowledge of children and learning changes" (Feeney, Moravcik, and Christensen 1991, 228). The various curriculum models that were described earlier provide evidence of how thinking changes during different historical periods. You should also recognize that selecting a curriculum as an emerging educator does not lock you into that model indefinitely. As you begin to think about your first curriculum model or your first curriculum design, it is important to realize that the ability to change is an integral part of any curriculum. Your learning will not stop at the end of this textbook or at the end of a course. Your knowledge will continue to expand and this will have an impact on your curriculum decisions.

Each day-care centre has different expectations regarding your role in the curriculum process. Your centre may have particular guidelines and procedures to follow. There are numerous questions you can ask to clarify the expectations in your role as an educator. The following tool can be used as a starting point for or inquiry into your curriculum planning.

TOOL

1. Is there a curriculum model that everyone in the centre is required to follow?

    _____ yes _____ no

2. Do the educators work together as a team and decide on a particular curriculum model or does each educator develop his or her own model?

    _____

3. Do I need to submit plans for approval, and, if so, what is the format of these plans?

    _____

    _____

The process and design of your curriculum will vary depending on the outcome of these questions. Some centres require all educators to implement the same approach or model. If you work with other team members in deciding on a particular model, some research will be required on your part so you know with which model or approach you feel more comfortable. You will also need to know how you are expected to present your plans. Curriculum designs differ, depending on the age group of the children with whom you are working. Curriculum planning for infants and toddlers is significantly different from planning for preschool children. Usually, infant planning is carried out for each individual child. In working with preschool children, plans tend to be designed for the group as a whole.

Curriculum Process

We will demonstrate a curriculum process based on the experience of one educator. Derek was hired in August to begin work in September. He had been hired to work with a group of seven 3-year-old children in a workplace day care. The centre encouraged all educators to use an appropriate curriculum model. Each educator could select his or her own model, but it had to be submitted along with long-term goals to the director for approval before planning could begin. Before graduating from an educator-training program, Derek established his philosophy of how children learn and develop. He knew that his planning must stem from his personal philosophy and be in harmony with the centre's mission statement.

Derek believes that planning should begin with the children and that it is important for him to know as much about the children as possible. To achieve this goal, Derek first spent time with the director of the centre asking questions about the families and cultural backgrounds of the children. He then spent time with the educator whom he would be replacing, and he spent time observing the children in their environment. This gave him the needed information for the development of plans, schedules, routines, and activities.

Besides an inquiry-oriented practice, Derek needed a review of the literature. He decided to implement the cognitive developmental approach. As was discussed earlier, this approach focuses on the whole child and has its foundation in Erikson's emotional development, Piaget's cognitive development, and the developmental norms of Gesell (Hendrick 1990; Goffin 1994). With a framework in place, Derek began to think about developing long-term goals for his program and for the children.

Long-term goals take into consideration theories of child development, the individuality of each child, and the mission statement of the centre. In Derek's case, "goals may be stated as a final product or as a continuing process" (Langenbach and West Neskora 1977, 126).

One goal that Derek articulated related to cooperation. Each goal can and, in fact, should have several outcomes. Some of the outcomes related to cooperation might be to have the children play cooperatively with their peers, or to build common structures during block play, or to have two children work together to assemble a large puzzle. Another activity that involves the development of cooperation is parachute play. There are a variety of parachute games that enhance cooperation (Nyisztor and Stelzer Rudick 1995).

Based on his knowledge of developmental theories, Derek knew that the play of 3-year-old children often involves parallel play situations. He considered how to design activities and experiences that would feed into his curriculum decisions and achieve his desired outcomes. He knew that it is developmentally appropriate to begin to design opportunities and activities that foster the emergence of cooperative ventures. Based on his desired outcomes, Derek made decisions about his program content. Table 2.1 recaps Derek's curriculum process.

The curriculum process requires educators to invest time, demonstrate flexibility, and make changes once they begin to work with the children. It is sometimes helpful to organize a flexible program for the first few weeks.

1.	Consulted with the director to clarify expectations.
2.	Consulted with other educator(s) to learn more about the children and about the curriculum that was being followed.
3.	An approach was selected. In Derek's case the developmental interactionist approach was chosen.
4.	Spent time observing the children.
5.	Began to write program goals and outcomes.

TABLE 2.1 Recap of the steps in Derek's curriculum process.

Curriculum Content

Curriculum content includes the substance of what is to be delivered through the plans and daily experiences that together deliver a given curriculum. Consideration of what plans and experiences should be included is based on knowledge of development and learning theories as well as on personal observations of the children with whom you are working.

We would like to propose the curriculum planning model approach in Figure 2.3 as a working model and one that can be used with any curriculum model. A planning model is not a curriculum in and of itself, rather it is a tool to structure the use and implementation of a curriculum model.

Our proposed planning model will work with virtually any existing curriculum model and takes into consideration long-term goals, developmental objectives, and content objectives. While we do not discuss behavioural objectives in this chapter, content objectives can be written as behavioural objectives in order to articulate the delivery of activities and experiences for young children. Developmental objectives are based on various theories and norms that have been established over the years. Further study in the area of developmental objective writing is warranted in order to generate

STEP 1
Identify the day care's mission statement.

STEP 2
Establish a personal or group philosophy.

STEP 3
Articulate developmental objectives.

STEP 4
Establish long-term goals. Can be group specific, or for the day care as a whole, or designed for one individual.

STEP 5
Set objectives. These are group specific and must meet both long-term goals and developmental objectives.

STEP 6
Design opportunities, activities, experiences, routines, and transitions.

STEP 7
Implement opportunities, activities, experiences, routines, and transitions.

STEP 8
Evaluate and return to step 3.

F I G U R E   2 . 3
Curriculum planning approach.

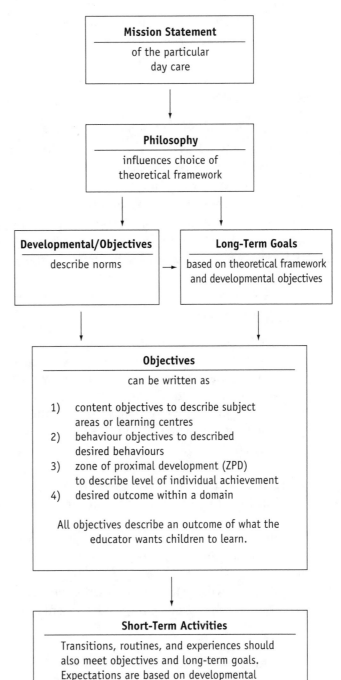

Mission Statement

of the particular day care

Philosophy

influences choice of theoretical framework

Developmental/Objectives

describe norms

Long-Term Goals

based on theoretical framework and developmental objectives

Objectives

can be written as

1) content objectives to describe subject areas or learning centres
2) behaviour objectives to described desired behaviours
3) zone of proximal development (ZPD) to describe level of individual achievement
4) desired outcome within a domain

All objectives describe an outcome of what the educator wants children to learn.

Short-Term Activities

Transitions, routines, and experiences should also meet objectives and long-term goals. Expectations are based on developmental objectives.

these objectives. We suggest that you read further on any of the curriculum models presented in this textbook.

Observations

An educator needs to spend a considerable amount of time observing and recording the activities that the children engage in, the way they manipulate objects, and the way they handle routines and transitions. Observation records, once completed, need to be interpreted. Interpreting observations for the novice educator can often be a challenging task. Experience will improve this practice. It is through the interpretation of these observations that you are able to add substance to your curriculum content.

....

Situation

Sauline was working with a group of 4- and 5-year-old children. During a three-week period she observed several children consistently playing with the wooden train set and building roads with the blocks for the vehicles. Based on this observation Sauline decided to incorporate transportation into her program plans. She began by organizing a train ride for the children.

....

Many perspectives can be used to help determine how you will develop the content to meet your curriculum. For example,

- Perspective 1: Content can originate from the children, their interests, and their ideas.

- Perspective 2: Content can originate from child development theories that focus on the whole child.

- Perspective 3: Content can originate from the community in which the day-care centre is located.

- Perspective 4: Content can be developed from an integrated approach.

- Perspective 5: Curriculum content can be developed through an eclectic approach.

Content can originate from the children, their interests, and their ideas. This implies developing curriculum content based on extensive observations and interpretations of those observations. For example, if you observe several children in your group continuously playing with the wooden train tracks, you could deduce that these children have an interest in trains and possibly in transportation. One idea might be to develop additional and alternative activities dealing with trains. Another idea would be to extend the topic of transportation.

Content can originate from child development theories that focus on the whole child. If child development is used as a source of curriculum content, then familiarization with Gesell's norms of physical development is essential. You would design and plan activities based on these norms. For example, if you are working with 2-year-olds you would not plan an activity that involved skipping.

Content can originate from the community in which the day-care centre is located. Each community has its own facilities and services that a day care can use. "You can help children begin to build an understanding of the community as a social system by focusing on the interrelatedness of the people who live and work in your area" (Essa and Young 1994, 216).

Content can be developed from an integrated approach. A thematic approach is an example of an integrated approach. Themes can be the centre around which appropriate activities are planned. This allows "teachers to integrate several different subject areas into meaningful and worthwhile experiences for children" (Feeney, Moravcik and Christensen 1991, 234).

Curriculum content can be developed through an eclectic approach. This technique would draw on more than one perspective. For example, an integration of the developmental level of the children and the cultural and social influences within their communities would generate the curriculum.

Once you have made decisions about the perspective from which you will develop content, you are ready to plan a program. Program plans include activities, opportunities, the environment, schedules, and routines.

TOOL

Write a content objective.

_____

_____

Design three different activities or experiences that will help children achieve this objective. Your activities and experiences should use very different materials and focus on different aspects of child development.

1 _____

2 _____

3. _____

Program Plans

Educators take different approaches in the organization and preparation of the **program plans**. Some develop their schedules and routines and then design their activities. Other educators work on the environment first. A bank of activities is usually generated once the scheduling and the environment have been organized. Either approach is manageable and is generally related to educator style. We will begin our discussion with a closer look at the environment.

The Environment

Consistency between the curriculum approach and the environment is crucial. If the curriculum approach advocates that children increase their independence and autonomy, then the environment must reflect this by providing material that is easily accessible to the children.

The environment must meet the needs of all the children individually and as a group. The environmental requirements of the infant and toddler's room will be different from the requirements of the 2- or 4-year-old's room. In their book *Early Childhood Environment Rating Scale* (1980), Harmes and Clifford provide an excellent tool for the evaluation of an early childhood environment.

One way to obtain ideas about environmental design is to visit different centres. These visits will enable you to see firsthand some innovative and creative environments. Some day cares, as part of their professional development, allow their educators two half-days a year to visit other centres. Most national early childhood conferences organize day-care visits for delegates attending the conference. These visits are always an enriching experience.

The responsibility for setting up the environment will vary. As a student or new educator you may begin working in an environment that is already established. It is important to exhibit respect for the children by working in this established environment for awhile before making changes. If you are team teaching, any arrangement of the environment should be a joint effort between you and the other educators. Regardless of the process established in setting up and arranging the environment, it is important to invite "learning through exploration and discovery" (Read, Gardner, and Mahler 1993, 19). Learning centres or activity centres are often designed to encourage exploration. Table 2.2 lists some common centres and areas that an early childhood environment should provide.

It is essential that all children feel that the surrounding environment is their place. This effect can be achieved in a variety of ways. For example, displaying the children's names and pictures in the roomor having the children bring something in from their homes that they would like to leave at the centre, such as a favourite book or a picture to hang on the wall. When children become involved in the process of arranging the environment, they often create setups that we would never think of arranging.

dramatic play area	block area
area for painting/easels	science centre or discovery centre
book corner or centre	private area (space for one child)
water play	carpet area
sand play	tabletop area

TABLE 2.2 Common elements found in an early childhood environment.

Organizing and establishing the environment should reflect the mission statement, curriculum approach, goals, and outcomes. If we select the goal that Derek initiated concerning cooperation, the environment would be designed to maximize play situations that encourage children to work together. The material would also include items that require working together to complete a task. A cooperative environment attempts to minimize competition, and the stress that is associated with competition should be nonexistent.

Once the environment is arranged, keep in mind that as the children grow, develop, and change so will the environment. Parents can be very supportive and a valuable resource in the design and set up of the environment. Many day-care parents donate materials and pictures, make curtains, or paint shelves. It is essential that you tap into all of these resources.

PHOTO 2.2 Including a water table in the day care's environment encourages exploration of a variety of materials in a cooperative environment.

Schedules

Schedules should be flexible. They serve as a guide rather than as a control over you and the children. Establishing a schedule usually involves negotiation and discussion with the director and other educators in the day care. Often many facilities in the centre need to be shared, such as the gross motor area, the outdoor play area, and sometimes the kitchen for lunch time.

The organization of the schedule may also need to be developed on a seasonal basis. For example, many day cares like to end the day with outdoor play and for many months of the year this is a prominent feature of the schedule. However, when the daylight hours become shorter in the fall, playing outdoors at the end of the day in darkness is not necessarily an ideal situation. Therefore, a schedule may need to be changed to allow the children outdoor time earlier in the afternoon.

One way to organize the schedule is to break it down into time blocks. There needs to be a balance between active and quiet time blocks. An active time block allows for movement and self-selection of materials and activities. Self-selected activity implies that the children choose from a number of available environment areas and materials. A quiet time block refers to periods of the day when the children's movements in the classroom are limited. Snack time or storytelling are good examples of a quiet time block.

Infant rooms often do not function with the group schedule but on individual schedules, as infants need to be on their own timetable. It is also not uncommon for these schedules to change on a daily basis. They need individualized care and they benefit from a schedule that is in sync with their own body rhythms. Table 2.3 contains a sample schedule for toddlers and Table 2.4 provides a sample schedule for a group of 3-year-olds.

Toddlers and 2-year-old group are together till 8:30 a.m.
(times are flexible, but the time block sequence is followed)

7:30 a.m.	free play in the 2-year-old room
8:30 a.m.	bathroom and diapering
8:50 a.m.	free play time in the toddler room
9:30 a.m.	snack time bathroom and toiletting
10:00 a.m.	gross motor time (gross motor room)
10:30 a.m.	story time
10:45 a.m.	outdoor play
11:30 a.m.	bathroom/toiletting, diapering
11:45 a.m.	lunch time
12:30 p.m.	story time
12:45 p.m.	nap time
2:30 – 3:00 p.m.	wake-up time, quiet activities, and bathroom and diapering
3:00 p.m.	snack time
3:20 p.m.	outdoor play
4:00 p.m.	bathroom/toiletting, diapering
4:20 p.m.	free play
4:30 p.m.	2-year-old children join the group

TABLE 2.3 Sample day-care schedule for toddlers.

Family grouping 8:30 (times are flexible, but the time block sequence is followed)	
7:30 a.m.	free play
8:30 a.m.	free play time
9:30 a.m.	clean-up time
9:45 a.m.	snack time
10:00 a.m.	circle time/story time
10:30 a.m.	gross motor time
11:00 a.m.	outdoor time
12:00 p.m.	lunch time
12:45 p.m.	story time
1:00 p.m.	nap time
2:00 – 3:00 p.m.	wake-up time, quiet activities
3:00 p.m.	free play
4:00 p.m.	snack time
4:20 p.m.	outdoor play
5:30 p.m.	family grouping

TABLE 2.4 Sample day-care schedule for 3-year-olds.

Now that you have had an opportunity to look at two different schedules, try the following reflection.

....

Reflection

What are the similarities and differences in these two schedules? Explain what is similar and what is different in each schedule.

....

Routines and Transitions

Routines are part of the curriculum. Goals and outcomes can be integrated into the routines. Routines include snack and lunch times, naps, and transitions. During snack and lunch times, for example, curriculum goals of autonomy and independence can be achieved quite effectively. Children can be encouraged to pour their own drinks. They can help serve and clean up after eating. In this way, the outcome of the children's actions meets specific program goals while they engage in routine activities.

A transition is the period between time blocks. It is a span of time when you move the children from one time block to the next, for example, between outdoor play and lunch time. Transition times need to be well thought-out and planned and can often pose problems for novice educators. For example, the transition between free play and group time is more than just the moment that announces the end of free play. It is about helping the children learn about anticipating events by giving them a few moments notice before the end of free play. It includes the clean-up time before group time. You might use clean-up time to introduce a new song. All of these steps need to be carefully thought-out. When planning a schedule, you should review it to see how many transitions there are. Keep transitions to a minimum to help the schedule run smoothly.

PHOTO 2.3
Outdoor time is an important part of a day care's schedule. It challenges the educator to facilitate a smooth transition from the indoor activity to going outside.

Activities and Opportunities

Activities and opportunities are times to achieve program goals and outcomes. Once program goals and outcomes are established a useful exercise is to brainstorm as many activities as possible. Children can help generate activity ideas.

···

Situation

Erika is in her first year as an educator. She is placed with 4- and 5-year-old children. She is experiencing some difficulty in generating activities for the children. Most of the children have been at the day care since they were 18 months old and she is concerned about whether she is being too repetitive and not providing enough diversity.

With this concern in mind, she decided to involve the children more actively in the planning of activities and developed a routine. Every Thursday while the children were lying on their cots at nap time, she would spend a few minutes and ask each child what activities they would like to do during the next week.

Erika found this to be a very enlightening experience. She took their suggestions and developed program ideas from them.

···

Activities are usually developed for many formats. Self-selected, teacher-selected, teacher directed circle time, gross motor time, and outdoor play are some examples. Self-selected activities that are initiated by the educator allow the children the opportunity to choose from a predetermined collection of material. For example, in teacher-selected experiences the educator chooses particular board games for the children to play with. In self-selected activities that are initiated by the children, the children choose what is available from all of the materials in the day care. In the example of the board game, the children would decide what board game they wanted to play. In either type of self-selected activities or teacher-selected activities the children can work on their own or with other children. Opportunities for self-selected activities can and usually do occur during free play, gross motor time, and outdoor play. In these situations the children ultimately have the choice as to whether or not they want to participate and for how long.

Teacher-directed activities involve the direct participation of the educator. Teacher-directed activities occur at different times during the schedule—at circle time, during free play, or in activity time blocks. When teacher-directed activities occur during free play, they allow the children the flexibility of joining in or doing something else. When they are done in activity time blocks, then all children must participate as a group, and some children find this difficult. One example of a teacher-directed activity is cooking. A cooking activity during free play involves the educator working with and guiding a small group of children through the activity. One important factor to remember when planning a teacher-directed activity during free play is that there will be times when all children will want to participate and this may require the activity being repeated.

It is essential that activities be developed from the simple form to the more complex form. This means breaking down the activity into its simplest form and building from there. Various levels of complexity should be offered at any one time. For example, cutting can be introduced at its simplest form, progressing to the more complex tasks. Start by tearing paper, followed by cutting plasticine, to cutting shapes and designs (Nyisztor and Stelzer Rudick 1995).

As we discussed, the schedule requires a balance in the type of time blocks. There should also be a balance in the programming between self-selected and teacher-directed activities. It is essential that children have options and choices in what they will do during the day.

We can use Derek's curriculum plan to construct the following schedule:

Free Play: Board game—Sleepy Old Grump; large floor puzzles that require more than one person to complete; poster board stretched out on the wall with paints set out so that children work together on the same project; a large piece of white fabric stretched over the table with glue, sequins, and scrap fabric for the children to make a common tablecloth; block centre open; and dramatic centre set up as a grocery store.

Snack Time: Open snack set out for a 30-minute time block at a table that accommodates four children at a time.

Circle Time: Memory game. Several objects are placed on a tray. After everyone has had a chance to look at them the tray is covered with a towel. All the children have to try and remember what was on the tray. One child at a time is selected to take the object off the tray as it is guessed. If there are any objects remaining, the group can ask that child questions about the properties of the unselected objects, such as "What colour is the object still on the tray?" Story—*Mortimer* by Robert Munch.

Gross Motor Time: Cooperative hoops. Set out one hoop per child. Play music. When the music stops all the children must find a hoop and freeze in it. Before resuming the music, take away two hoops. Again when the music stops, the children must find a hoop and freeze in it. This continues until all the children must squeeze at least one part of their body into one hoop.

Outdoor Play: Parachute activities followed by free choice. Bring a bean bag and a few hoops outside for the children to practice throwing and tossing. As soon as a child completes his or her toss, she or he must retrieve the bean bag and give it to another child to try.

Lunch Time: Followed by naptime.

Free Play: Memory game of concentration; construction toys; bean bag toss; continue the mural painting and tablecloth; block play.

Snack Time: Children sit together. Educator stimulates conversation about the events of the day. Educator encourages dialogue between the children. Sample questions: "Tell me what you did today with a friend?"

Outdoor Time: Walk to the park.

Derek's plan reflected his curriculum approach. He planned for co-operative activities. This was delivered through board games and floor puzzles where children could work together to achieve a common goal. He also introduced activities in the morning that were carried over into the afternoon session. This provided program continuity.

It becomes evident that there are many theoretical approaches and frameworks that can be used in planning and programming for the children. The key to success is understanding the implications of each and selecting a format that reflects your beliefs and meets the situation of your workplace environment. Keep in mind that a curriculum is dynamic. It changes to accommodate new knowledge and is applied differently to different children in different situations.

One other factor that influences an educator's choice of curriculum approach is the centre's orientation. It is important to work within directives that are inherent in the centre's mission statement.

Summary

- There are several child development theories and learning theories that influence curriculum development.

- The development of a curriculum creates the direction for daily plans and activities.

- Curriculum models and approaches prescribe a philosophy of ideas and beliefs about how children learn.

- Curriculum designs will vary depending on the age group of the children.

- Observation of the children is a key factor in the design of activities for the children.

- Program plans, activities, and experiences are vehicles for delivery of a curriculum.

- The environment should be organized and well designed.

- Schedules need to be flexible.

- Program activities and experiences should reflect the centre's mission statement or philosophical approach.

Questions and Activities for Further Reflection

1. What are some of your personal beliefs about how children learn?

2. How will your beliefs about how children learn influence your curriculum design?

3. Review the curriculum approaches, find one that you would like further information about and select one of the reference texts for further study.

4. Select one curriculum model. Articulate the points you agree with and disagree with in the approach. Give a rationale for your answers.

5. Choose a curriculum model. Develop a set of activities and experiences based on this approach.

Self-Test

Recall each of the theories. Write a one- or two-sentence explanation that describes the theory. Include the name of the theorist(s) who articulated each particular position.

R e f e r e n c e s

Baldwin, A.L. (1980). *Theories of Child Development*. New York: John Wiley and Sons.

Berk, L.E., and Winsler, A. (1995). *Scaffolding Children's Learning: Vygotsky and Early Childhood Education*. Washington, D.C.: National Association for the Education of Young Children.

Bredekamp, S. (1987). *Developmentally Appropriate Practice in Early Childhood Programs Serving Children from Birth Through Age 8,* ed. S. Bredekamp. Washington, D.C.: National Association for the Education of Young Children.

Bredekamp, S., and Rosegrant, Teresa. (1992). "Reaching Potentials: Introduction." In *Reaching Potentials: Appropriate Curriculum and Assessment for Young Children,* eds. S. Bredekamp and T. Rosegrant. Washington, D.C.: National Association for the Education of Young Children.

Brewer, Joann. (1995). *Introduction to Early Childhood Education*. Boston: Allyn and Bacon.

Canadian Child Care Federation. (1994). "National Guidelines for Training in Early Care and Education." *Interaction* Vol. 8:6–9.

DeVries, Rheta, and Lawrence Kohlberg. (1987). *Constructivist Early Education Overview and Comparison with Other Programs*. Washington, D.C.: National Association for the Education of Young Children.

Dewey, John. (1966). *Democracy and Education*. New York: The Free Press.

Doxey, I. (1990). "A Basic Canadian Curriculum." In *Child Care and Education: Canadian Dimensions,* ed. Isabel Doxey, 143–155. Scarborough, Ont.: Nelson Canada.

Essa, E. (1996). *Introduction to Early Childhood,* 2nd ed. Albany: Delmar Publishers.

Essa, Eva, and Rosemary Young. (1994). *Introduction To Early Childhood Education.* Scarborough, Ont.: Nelson Canada.

Feeney, S., E. Moravcik, and D. Christensen. (1991). *Who Am I in the Lives of Children?* New Jersey: Merill Publishing.

Forman, G. (1993). "The Constructivist Perspective to Early Education." In *Approaches to Early Childhood Education,* 2nd ed., 137–155. New York: Merrill.

Goffin, Stacie. (1994). *Curriculum Models and Early Childhood Education: Appraising the Relationship.* New York: Macmillan Publishing Company.

Goffin, Stacie, and David Day. (1994). *New Perspectives in Early Childhood Teacher Education: Bringing Practitioners into the Debate.* New York: Teachers College Press.

Gordon, A. M., and K.W. Browne. (1985). *Beginnings and Beyond: Foundations in Early Childhood Education.* New York: Delmar Publishers Inc.

Harmes, T., and Clifford R. (1980). *Early Childhood Environment Rating Scale.* New York: Teachers College Press.

Hendrick, Joanne. (1990). *Total Learning Developmental Curriculum for the Young Child,* 3rd ed. New York: Macmillan Publishing Company.

Honig, A.S. (1993). "The Erikson Approach." In *Approaches to Early Childhood Education,* 2nd ed. eds. J. Roopnarine and J.E. Johnson, 47–70. New York: Merrill.

Langenbach, Michael, and Teanna West Neskora. (1977). *Day Care Curriculum Considerations.* Columbus, Ohio: Charles Merrill Publishing Company.

Lay-Dopyera, M., and J. Dopyera. (1990). *Becoming a Teacher of Young Children,* 4th ed. New York: McGraw Hill.

Lefrançois, Guy R. (1973). *Of Children: An Introduction to Child Development.* Belmont, California: Wadsworth Publishing Company.

Lindauer, S.K. (1993). "Montessori Education for Young Children." In *Approaches to Early Childhood Education,* 2nd ed. eds. J. Roopnarine and J.E. Johnson, 243–59. New York: Merrill.

Montessori, M. (1956). *The Child in The Family.* Chicago: Regenry.

National Association for the Education of Young Children and the National Association of Early Childhood Specialist in State Departments of Education. (1990). "Guidelines for Appropriate Content and Assessment in Programs Serving Children Ages 3 Through 8." In *Reaching Potentials: Appropriate Curriculum and Assessment for Young Children,* eds. S. Bredekamp and T. Rosegrant. Washington, D.C.: National Association for the Education of Young Children.

Nyisztor, Diane, and Eva Stelzer Rudick. (1995). *Moving to Learn: A Guide to Psychomotor Development in Young Children.* Toronto: Harcourt Brace.

Read, Katherine, Pat Gardner, and Barbara Mahler. (1993). *Early Childhood Programs, Human Relationships and Learning.* Fort Worth, Texas: Harcourt Brace Jovanovich College Publishers.

Roopnarine, J., and J. Johnson. (1993). *Approaches to Early Childhood Education,* 2nd ed. New York: Merrill Publishing Company.

Sparks L., and P. Ramsey. (1993). "Early Childhood Multicultural, Anti-Bias Education in the 1990s: Toward the 21st century." In *Approaches to Early Childhood Education,* 2nd ed. eds. J. Roopnarine and J.E. Johnson, 274–94. New York: Merrill Publishing Company.

Spodek, Bernard. (1991). "Early Childhood Curriculum and Cultural Definitions of Knowledge." In *Issues in Early Childhood Curriculum,* eds. Bernard Spodek and Olivia Saracho. New York: Teachers College Press.

Spodek, Bernard, and Olivia Saracho. (1991). "Introduction: Concepts of Early Childhood Curriculum." In *Issues in Early Childhood,* eds. Bernard Spodek and Olivia Saracho. New York: Teachers College Press.

Spodek, Bernard, and Olivia Saracho. (1994). *Right From the Start.* Boston: Allyn and Bacon.

Taylor, M. (1990). "Foundations of Early Childhood Education." In *Child Care and Education: Canadian Dimensions,* ed. Isabel Doxey, 65–86. Scarborough, Ont.: Nelson Canada.

Zimilies, H. (1993). "The Bank Street Approach." In *Approaches to Early Childhood Education,* 2nd ed., eds. J. Roopnarine and J.E. Johnson, 261-73. New York: Merrill Publishing Company.

CHAPTER 3

A Centre's Orientation

In this chapter you will:

- define the term mission statement;
- examine the purpose and implications of a mission statement;
- identify steps needed to develop a mission statement;
- study the effects of a mission statement on the organizational structure of the day care;
- identify a variety of grouping styles available in day-care services;
- identify different operational hours that are possible in the day-care environment.

Advance motivator

Examine the following key terms before reading the chapter. Then, while reading the chapter, try to assign meaning to each one.

mission statement	brainstorming
outcome	divergent thinking
profit centre	convergent thinking
non-profit centre	matrix
participative management	same-age grouping
elements of a system	family grouping
clientele	mixed grouping

The Mission Statement

As a practitioner, it is both useful and important to know how to use and establish a mission statement. What is its impact on you? In this chapter we look at some general implications of a mission statement and more specific issues related to you and the day care.

The mission statement, written in one or more sentences, briefly outlines the focus of an organization. The goals or aims of the day-care system are defined through its mission statement and identify what an organization is about. In a day-care system this statement is the driving force behind the design and delivery of a curriculum. As we noted in the last chapter, the development of curriculum models is based on a theoretical foundation. However, curriculum models also need to be in harmony with the mission statement of the particular day-care centre.

A mission statement must be both broad and specific. It is designed to enable stakeholders to operate with some degree of freedom while providing a focus for decision-making. Sadly, the mission statement is often little understood or rarely in the forefront of daily considerations once it is established. Reasons for this could be that the mission statement does not provide a measurable standard, is not quantifiable, or it does not provide specific enough information about an educator's role—for example, how can an educator demonstrate the he or she has earned his or her pay?

Two sample mission statements are provided in tables 3.1 and 3.2. We will refer to these again in our discussion on developing the mission statement.

> To provide a secure, nurturing environment that promotes the education of young children where family members are asked to actively participate in the day-to-day operation of the day-care services provided for the children.

TABLE 3.1
Sample mission statement from a cooperative day care.

> To provide a safe environment and a challenging education for children from all cultural backgrounds whose parents work for the greater part of the day. To provide parents with information concerning the daily activities of their children.

TABLE 3.2
Sample mission statement from a profit day care.

Each of these mission statements caters to a stakeholder group that is slightly different. In Table 3.1 we can see that the stakeholder group includes families where at least one family member can contribute time to the centre during its operating hours. This statement would be suited for a cooperative day care where at least one family member does not work full time. Table 3.2 is an example of a mission statement that would be geared toward a family in which all primary caregivers are busy during the operational hours of the day care.

Although a mission statement is about process and goal orientation, it does become a yardstick from which to measure performance. It provides criteria with which to evaluate the efforts and effectiveness of a system. If the mission statement of a system reflects what it "is committed to, it is also an agreement to be held accountable for working towards" (National Association of Secondary School Principals 1987, 24). Goals "set by stakeholders will reflect their needs, interests, concerns, and priorities. These in turn will be influenced by values and beliefs" (Moss 1994, 4).

It is difficult to quantify such things as a nurturing environment or challenging education. These are goal statements that provide guidelines and parameters for the achievement of these goals. A mission statement is not measurable in exact or quantifiable terms. It is a description of qualitative goals that reflect the complexity of a total setting. The mission statement helps the system focus on a process that occurs over time (Finch 1988). It leads the way to articulating desired **outcomes** that are delivered in the form of the plans and activities that make up a curriculum.

The mission statement can be thought of as the central idea(s) from which curriculum is designed and programs are developed. Stakeholders use this central idea as a guide to derive goals and establish outcomes for the many elements within a day-care system. According to Bredekamp and Rosegrant (1992), all effective educational programs have clearly stated learning objectives that educators will help children to develop through a planned curriculum. These objectives are adjusted regularly to meet children's needs while remaining in harmony with the mission statement.

The most inclusionary approach to the establishment of an ecological view that supports its mission can be seen in the Reggio Emilia model. In this model the entire community is involved in the development of a system of "early childhood services based on a common value system and pedagogical philosophy" (Pence and Moss 1994, 173).

Figure 3.1 exemplifies how the mission statement expands outward into the design and establishment of goals. Desired outcomes, in turn, stem from the goals. Notice how desired outcomes can meet more than one goal. In fact, an educator would strive to have many outcomes stem from each goal and have one outcome fulfil more than one goal. By understanding the mission statement and its implications, you will become a more effective educator.

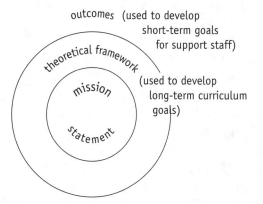

outcomes (used to develop short-term goals for support staff)

theoretical framework (used to develop long-term curriculum goals)

mission statement

FIGURE 3.1
The mission statement is at the centre of decision-making.

Who Is Responsible for Developing the Mission Statement?

The responsibility for the development of the mission statement varies depending on the type of day-care system involved. In a

profit centre this responsibility usually falls to the owner(s). The type of mission statement that is devised will reflect the needs of the potential market. An owner generally begins with a philosophy of his or her own early childhood beliefs, but ultimately the goal orientation must be compatible with the needs of the potential market.

This process is very different in a **non-profit centre**. In this case, representatives from the community or parent system are of critical importance if the mission statement is to be viable. Instead of an owner looking for a market in which to provide a day-care service, parents who comprise the market hire individuals to organize a day-care service to meet its needs.

The Purpose and Implications of the Mission Statement

A mission statement serves as a point of origin for many decisions within and outside the system (Banathy 1991; Taylor 1989). It is a broad statement that establishes a common goal: a key factor in defining any system. A well-defined mission statement, effectively carried through to all levels of planning, yields positive results in the day-care environment.

There are always alternative ways to achieve goals. Using a mission statement to establish purpose contributes toward an environment where alternative ways of handling situations can exist in harmony. The mission statement ensures that the actions of the day care's stakeholders influence the ultimate goal or shared vision of the organization. A mission statement provides an orientation for individuals within a system and for the system as a whole. It is probably one of the most important declarations that a day care must make to function effectively. In effect, it is the statement that steers the system in a given direction. It enables members involved in the system to identify their rationale for certain actions. If everyone works toward the same goal, then differences in style and approach are tolerated more easily. This fosters a climate of acceptance.

Using a mission statement paves the way for **participative management**, a style of management that involves employees and clientele in relevant decision-making (Taylor 1989). To be successful, time needs to be built in for participative management. In practical terms this means holding a meeting at the beginning of the year to review the mission statement and plan accordingly, holding regularly scheduled meetings throughout the year to discuss ongoing planning, and holding meetings at the end of the year to reflect on how well the members of the system have met the stated objectives. This process is a cornerstone of reflective practice.

In a day care the mission statement serves as an underlying principle of planning. "Planning is the foundation on which other managerial functions are built" (ibid.), and plans should be in harmony with the mission statement. The mission statement informs many decisions, from hiring to establishing a curriculum framework. It serves as a manifesto from which to design policy. As a stakeholder your understanding of the day-care's mission facilitates your ability to meet objectives. Day-care systems are constantly being evaluated by outside groups, such as prospective parents, local colleges, or perhaps governing agencies. With a mission statement in place, you can provide these groups with a sense of what your particular centre is about.

Not every day care is for everyone. Educators, parents, and other groups need to ensure that the mission statement is compatible with their ideals. The mission statement becomes the system's language of operation. When criteria are clear and visible for all to see, there is a sense of openness and trust. This leads to a healthy climate of operation. "Finally, the presence of a clear mission argues for more consistency of behaviour" (NASSP 1987, 25).

Developing a Mission Statement

As a student or educator you might ask yourself, *Why is it important that I understand how to design a mission statement?* The answer is simple. Understanding the process involved in developing a mission statement will help you understand how to use it and recognize its implications in the day care. Regardless of who is responsible, it is important to note that the process of goal setting in a day care will determine what the goals will be (Moss 1994, 2).

While it is true that most centres you enter will already have a mission statement, the contemporary status of day care suggests a renewed interest in rewriting the mission statement. The contemporary status of day care refers to the current status of day care, which reflects the current needs of families and modern lifestyles. You may well be invited to be part of this process. Furthermore, understanding the existing mission statement will help you recognize what constitutes quality at a particular day care.

There are two broad categories to consider that are helpful in formulating a valid and effective mission statement: 1) the **elements of a system** that are common to the type of organization or institution you are developing the mission statement for, and 2) the elements that are unique to the particular system under scrutiny.

In practical terms this means that all day cares have some common elements (NASSP 1987). For example, they exist to serve the needs of parents and children or to promote learning in a nurturing environment. Day cares are also designed to meet the specific needs of a community, workplace environment, or philosophical approach. An example of specific needs is an on-campus university facility. In this scenario a day-care facility is provided to meet the needs of a group of faculty and students who require child-care services that are flexible in terms of hours and centrally located to all the buildings of the university.

Reflection

Examine the mission statement of a day-care centre. Identify the words or phrases that highlight characteristics common to all day cares. Identify the words or phrases that represent characteristics that are unique to the day care.

Some day cares operate as independent systems, while others are embedded in a larger system. A day care that is embedded in another system will have elements that are common to both the day care and the larger organization.

Whether using an existing mission statement or designing a new one, there is an ongoing reflection process of both the common and unique elements of the system. The mission statement must serve its clientele. Identifying the clientele is key to the success of any organization. This must be done prior to or in conjunction with the designing of a mission statement.

How to Determine the Clientele

One of the major stakeholders in any organization is the **clientele**. In a day care this group includes parents and children who benefit from the services that the day care has to offer. Identifying the clientele in a child day-care facility is a challenging task. A new centre has to begin from scratch and an existing centre has to verify that the clientele is still the same as when the mission statement was originally established. Keep in mind that communities and their needs change. Therefore, you may find yourself re-evaluating your clientele from time to time. This may lead to an adjustment of your mission statement.

A day care exists to provide a service to a specified group of people. In recent years "we have seen an increase in the acceptance of early childhood education as an essential service for our society" (Spodek, Saracho, and Davis 1991). Regardless of whether you represent a profit or non-profit day care, identifying the specific group that will use the day care is an important task. The mission statement informs the clientele about the nature of the day care and informs the educator about the direction for planning for the clientele.

The following questions will assist you in defining your clientele. The column on the

PHOTO 3.1
Children are an important part of your clientele.

left poses specific questions to help you determine the clientele and help you determine whether your system is an independent one or one that is embedded in a larger system. The column on the right provides points to help you reflect on the questions.

Questions	Reflections
1. Is this day care part of a larger organization such as a community centre or workplace environment?	1. If the answer is yes, go to question number 2. If the answer is no, go to question number 4.
2. Does the larger system in which the day care is embedded already have a mission statement?	2. If the answer is yes, you will need to secure a copy of it and ensure that your mission statement is congruous with that of the parent system. For community-based day cares, go to question number 4. For workplace day cares, go to question number 3.
3. What are the hours of the workplace?	3. This question is provided to help you consider such issues as shift work, staggered arrival and departure times, and lunch times. If your mission statement is to service the needs of all employees, then the answer to this question will affect the operational hours of the day care. On the other hand, if the day care only services those employees working in the daytime hours, your mission statement will be different.

Questions	Reflections
4. Who in the community are you trying to serve?	4. There are many community members you may want to serve. Perhaps you are trying to meet the needs of those who live in the vicinity or those who work in the vicinity. You may want to offer some specialty program that will attract a specific interest group. You may be operating a university-based day care that caters to students and faculty who have flexible and varied schedules.
5. If you are a community-based centre operating in the suburbs, you will need to ask about travel time from the parents' workplaces to the day-care centre.	5. If the parents are working quite far from the day care, you need to plan to open earlier in the morning and stay open later in the evening. This is an important consideration when establishing policies related to picking up the children at the end of the day.
6. A day care may be located close to local elementary schools. Will you be serving the school-age children in an after-school program if they have siblings in your day care?	6. The answer to this question is very important. Often, parents will select a day care that is located close to a school if this means that they can count on some continuity in a child care.

Questions	Reflections
	A family with more than one child may enjoy the ease of picking up all the children in the same location. There is an added comfort in knowing that siblings are together in a safe environment.
7. Will you include an infant group or will the day care begin at the toddler age?	7. If you choose not to include infants in your day care, you may limit your clientele to those with older children and no younger children who need day care. On the other hand, infant facilities require a different staff ratio than toddler facilities.

Your day-care centre may or may not have a mission statement. Regardless, it is essential that you have a clear understanding of the clientele. Once this is accomplished you are ready to develop the contents of a mission statement.

Developing the Contents of a Mission Statement

There are a number of steps involved in developing the contents of a mission statement.

Procedure

1. *Identify stakeholders.* This means identifying who will be involved in the day care. The answer includes the clientele

(ranging from parents to children), educators, the director, community members, and anyone who has a vested interest in the day care. An important step in the process of identifying the stakeholders is to look at the relationship the day care will have with the community at large and with other organizations.

Once you identify the stakeholders in the day-care system, you need to actively recruit representatives from each group and form a working group that will define and write the mission statement. Members of this group will include parents, community members, educators, and members of the workplace. The group should be small enough to facilitate regular meeting times. Keeping a regular and consistent schedule will help foster a climate of trust and creativity. At the same time, the group needs to be large enough to reflect the needs of all the stakeholders. Once the group is formed and the meeting times are established, you can begin a **brainstorming** session.

2.   *Brainstorming.* Initially, all members of the working group are invited to brainstorm. Brainstorming is a technique that was developed by Osborne (1957). It is important that each stakeholder participates in the process. This is not a time to pass value judgments. Everyone's contributions are important. This is a time to share beliefs and philosophical ideologies. This process is often referred to as **divergent thinking**. The brainstorming session helps orient the thinking of the group. It brings all the representative stakeholders together while building a mission statement.

The process is simple. Jot down ideas, thoughts, and words on a piece of paper as they emerge. A typical brainstorming session might generate the types of words in Figure 3.2. At this point, leave out action verbs that could be used to identify outcomes. Verbs will be added when drafting the mission statement (step 8). Action verbs include words such as foster, encourage, facilitate, and develop.

safety	qualified staff
caring	outdoor space
educational	educational material

FIGURE 3.2
Words from a brainstorming session.

3. *Narrowing.* Narrowing should not be carried out at the same meeting as brainstorming. Before the narrowing process begins, a period of reflection is important. During this time, members of the working group go off on their own and think about which ideas and values are most important to them.

When your working group reconvenes, begin by eliminating the words and sentences that are repetitive, redundant, or are of lesser importance than other words or phrases. Keep in mind that the completed mission statement is no more than one or two sentences. Narrow your selection to a maximum of twenty words or ideas. This process of **convergent thinking** is far more challenging than it may appear at first.

4. *Interview a range of stakeholders.* Each member of the working group involved in building the mission statement should interview as many individuals who could be served by the day care as possible. They can ask such questions as: What do you believe is important to this day care? What do you value? What do you want to get out of the day care? What should the day care provide?

Provide a rating sheet with each of the key words and phrases that the working group has selected. Have interviewees rate key words and phrases from most important to least important. While interviewing stakeholders, try to remain neutral. This is a difficult task when you, too, have a vested interest in the outcome.

5. *Examine the responses, organize the data, and identify areas of agreement.* Compare the responses of those interviewed. Look for similarities. Organize the data in a hierarchical order. The purpose of this activity is to identify the whole range of possible missions for the day care. It is important that the working group does not focus on one particular statement too early in the process (NASSP 1987). Consider all statements fairly.

6. *Identify the major points of agreement.* Use the interviewees' responses to again narrow the choice of words and phrases. This can be done by listing common words or phrases that the group

chooses. At this point the group should still have a substantial number of key concepts, ranging from ten to twenty points. If there are more than twenty points, the group should vote on which ones to eliminate.

7. *Prepare a **matrix***. A matrix is a grid that will help you organize and develop your ideas. List the agreed-upon key words and phrases across the top of the matrix. These need not be listed in any particular order. For example, let us say that the group agreed upon two key words, child-centred and play-based. These words would appear across the top of a grid as shown in Figure 3.3.

	child-centred	play-based

FIGURE 3.3
Sample key words placed across the top of a matrix.

The second step is to use the same key words and place them in the left-hand column in the reverse order of how they are written across the top. By combining the words across the top with the words on the left-hand side, a working matrix is generated. See Figure 3.4.

	child-centred	play-based
play-based		
child-centred		

FIGURE 3.4
Placing key words in left-hand column in reverse order to create a working matrix.

Once the working matrix is prepared, each member in the group is given a copy. In order to complete the matrix, each member of the working group reviews the matrix independently and pairs the concepts he or she thinks work best together. These individual choices are then discussed in the group. Figure 3.5 is an example of a completed matrix. Let us examine how this was done.

A member of the group working independently would begin by reading the first word at the top of the left-hand column. In our sample it says *language-based*. The members would then read each word across the top of the page and rate the word *language-based* in relation to the words at the top of the page that he or she believed best linked with this concept. In our sample, the member felt that *cognitive-orientation* should be paired with the term *language-based* and marked the number (1) in the box where the two concepts intersected. This procedure is repeated until each set of words in the left-hand column is paired with one set of words across the top.

Once each member has completed the matrix, the group gets together to compare notes. Each member pulls out two or three words from the left-hand column that intersect most often with a word across the top. A close look at the sample matrix in Figure 3.5 indicates that this member showed a preference for linking words from the left-hand column to the words *child-centred, relaxed environment,* and *cognitive orientation.* This member would consider these concepts important enough to include in the mission statement. The group then identifies the common concepts and agrees upon which ones should be included in the mission statement.

An analysis of Figure 3.5 would indicate that the group placed a strong importance on a child-centred mission statement. The number (1) appears most frequently in the column directly under this word, indicating that this is a high priority. The terms *cognitive-orientation* and *relaxed environment* have the next most frequent rating. While the team might value the notion of a *cooperative environment* the term did not receive any ranking in this matrix. Therefore, the mission statement would not use that particular word in defining the centre's goals or objectives.

	child-centred	play-based	safe	nurturing	cooperative environment	health & nutrition	relaxed environment	anti-bias	cognitives orientation	language-based
language-based									(1)	
cognitive orientation		(1)								
anti-bias	(1)									
relaxed environment	(1)									
health & nutrition				(1)						
cooperative environment	(1)									
nurturing							(1)			
safe		(1)								
play-based									(1)	
child-centred							(1)			

FIGURE 3.5
Sample matrix used in the development of a mission statement.

8. You are now ready to *draft a mission statement*. Completing a matrix may seem tedious, but it is important that the group reach a high rate of consensus. Agreed-upon concepts are put into one or two sentences that form the basis of the mission statement. If "a significant portion of the group does not accept a statement, its members will not use it as a guide for their own behaviour" (NASSP 1987, 17). A blank matrix is provided in Appendix B. You can use it to help you develop a mission statement.

9. *Reflect on the implications of this draft.* Developing a mission statement that will be valuable is a process that takes deliberation and time. Once the first draft is prepared, give educators, support staff, and parents time to reflect on its implications and a chance to express their views and concerns before finalizing the mission statement. After reflecting upon the implications and receiving feedback, the draft can be modified as necessary.

10. *Finalize the mission statement.* It is prudent to review the purpose of the mission statement on a regular basis. This is critical if the mission statement is to continue to serve its purpose. Ultimately, the mission statement will be finalized by the owners or executive of the board of directors. The statement should reflect the needs and concerns of the working group.

Fostering Specific Skills in the Day Care

Developing a mission statement is an important step in identifying what particular skills you want the day care to foster. A matrix will help your group identify skills that are important to the day care.

Ask yourself questions about the importance of friendship, academic readiness, independence, and a sense of cooperation. Different stakeholders will demonstrate different perspectives.

There may be times when a day care's mission statement already exists and is not compatible for all who apply to the day care. For example, a parent may want to have his or her child involved in an academic setting. However, the centre may have a play-based curriculum. How do you meet these two objectives? Make your mission statement clear to parents who apply to your day care. Explain in advance what skills you hope to foster. The mission statement should give parents some indication as to whether a centre relies on a philosophy that is predominantly teacher directed or open-ended. The parents' values and needs should be in harmony with the day care they choose for their children.

If as a practitioner you do enter a centre that already has a mission statement, look at it and ask yourself, *What kind of skill development is implied, what kind of programming will help meet this goal?* The mission statement in Table 3.1, for example, implies that the parents' cooperation is an important component of the day care's operational mandate. You will have to ask yourself if this type of parental involvement in the centre's programming would be agreeable to you.

Who Should Know About the Mission Statement?

Everyone involved with the centre should be informed of the mission statement. This includes parents, students, educators, members of the board of directors, members of the larger system in which the day care is embedded, and support staff. Many centres have a broad philosophy. A philosophy is a general statement of belief. It can assist in the design of a mission statement, but, unlike a mission statement, it is not goal oriented.

In conclusion, a mission statement needs to be dynamic. This infers that it is open to change when it can no longer drive the system. At the same time, it serves as a guiding force in the development of the day care on a long-term basis without being too constraining. If you see that your mission statement is no longer working, you will need to re-examine and evaluate its effectiveness. This may indicate that it is time to change the existing mission statement. The mission statement describes a commitment of the organization and should be shared by all those who are stakeholders in the particular system.

Academic and practical training in the field of early childhood education are critical to the success of any child-care service. Your training background and the mission statement of the day care where you choose to work should reflect a degree of harmony.

How Does the Mission Statement Affect the Operation of a Day-Care Centre?

There are a wide variety of early childhood settings in North America. A mission statement often serves as a catalyst for decision-making about such issues as grouping style, physical environment, the number of children being served, and hours of operation.

Grouping Style

Our discussion of grouping style focuses on three organizational strategies. The first involves putting children of the same chronological age in the same group. We refer to this as **same-age grouping**. The second style places children of different ages together. This is classically referred to as **family grouping**. A third arrangement is to group children chronologically for a designated part of the day and use family grouping for the other part of each day. We call this **mixed grouping**.

For whichever style you work with, there are a few noteworthy points. Grouping and group size may be influenced by the day care's mission statement. Group size will influence your curricular decisions. Consider the following reflection.

....

Reflection

Read the following two excerpts from different mission statements. What grouping style would you plan for each statement? Provide a rationale for your decision.

Children shall be provided with an environment that most resembles a family setting.

Children shall be given an opportunity to socialize with other children of the same age.

....

Another factor in determining grouping style is staffing arrangement. A family grouping lends itself to having more adults in the same room at the same time. This can satisfy an educator's need to spend time with peers.

Some day cares choose grouping styles based on what is appropriate for a specific age group of children. For example, younger children like to sit closer to the educator while older children tend toward greater independence for large parts of the day (Spodek, Saracho, and Davis 1991). This means that younger children need a smaller educator to child ratio. It may also indicate that family grouping can be successful since the proximity to the educator during group time varies with different age groups. In a family group setting you may choose to position yourself so that you are closer to the play area where the younger children congregate. The older children, with their greater degree of independence, will feel free coming to you when they need help even if they are not sitting right next to you.

Physical Environment

The physical environment refers to all indoor and outdoor space that is available for use by the day care on a regular basis. Some of the elements related to the environment that are important to consider are room size, furniture and equipment, proximity to bathrooms, and movable and fixed play materials.

Some day cares are housed in their own building. Others are housed as part of a larger organization, such as in an office building, hospital, or school. Still others may be in shopping centres or private homes. A day care that is self-contained in its own building has a clear picture about the physical elements that are available. This is different in a structure where a day care is part of a larger organization, such as a community centre. In this case, the day care shares the environment with other groups that are also part of the community centre. For example, there may be a gym and a playground that the day care can use on certain days. On other days it may not be available to the day

PHOTO 3.2
Storytelling in a same age grouping fosters an environment where adults spend quality time with the children.

care because the centre is using it for play groups or fitness classes. Negotiation is needed to ensure that the environment is suitable for all.

Different climates also influence the design of the physical environment. The following situation describes how the physical indoor environment of a day care was modified to accommodate the children's needs during the long winters.

Situation

The board of directors of a local community centre in Montreal began designing a new workplace day care. Long winters made it difficult for the children to play outside for long periods of time. This situation limited convenient use of the outdoor space and playground equipment. To compensate, the board decided it would be important to include a large indoor space in the design of the day-care facility. This decision was made in order to promote physical fitness and motor development on a year-round basis. The room that was ultimately designed was well equipped with a large climbing apparatus, balls, and wheeled toys.

Number of Children Being Served

The number of children being served varies from centre to centre. Some centres serve only a small number of children, having one group for each age, while others may have two or three groups for each age. A mission statement may help determine the size of a centre. For example, a centre's mission statement that says "to provide an intimate family environment", would tend to be smaller in size than one that says "to meet the needs of all children in the community between the ages of 6 months and 5 years."

In large centres, issues of sharing outside space and special facilities may arise and require a great deal of coordination between various members of the system. The following situation demonstrates how one centre coordinated outdoor activities.

Situation

There was one outdoor space provided for eight groups of children. The space was large enough to accommodate four groups of children at any given time. A staggered schedule was set up that allowed the younger groups of children to use the space earlier in the day and the older groups later in the day. Lunch for all children was planned around the use of the outdoor space.

Hours of Operation

The hours of operation will vary, depending on the type of service being offered. Nursery schools and preschools have traditionally offered half-day programs where the younger children might attend in the morning and older children in the afternoon. A trend in recent years has been to offer extended hours based on changing needs and lifestyles. Same age-grouping, family grouping, and mixed grouping have all become common. In combining same-age and family grouping, children may spend the morning with other children of the same age while spending the afternoon in a multi-age group setting.

The hours of operation of day-care centres also depend on the location and needs of the communities they serve. Workplace centres operate under two different sets of parameters: either they are open shorter hours than community-based centres or they are open on a twenty-four-hour-a-day basis. This will depend on the type of workplace environment and the hours of operation of the company. A company that has shift work may require round-the-clock day-care service while a company that has traditional business hours will have other needs.

For example, a workplace day-care centre where the company closes at 4:30 p.m. might only stay open until 5:15 p.m. Community day-care centres in suburban areas traditionally have longer hours as they must consider travel time for the parents. Rural day-care centres and centres in the north frequently have shorter hours, once again reflecting the needs of the parents and the community.

The two tables below provide examples of the hours of operation within two different workplace day cares. Table 3.3 represents a company that manufactures computer parts. Executive and secretarial services are open from 8:00 a.m. to 6:00 p.m. while production runs on a twenty-four-hour basis with three operational shifts. The day care constantly re-evaluates its availability. Currently, there appears to be a small need between 7:30 a.m. and 9:00 a.m., a greater need between 9:00 a.m. and 4:30 p.m., and a slowing down between 4:30 p.m. and 6:00 p.m. Few employees in this company require overnight service. As a result the company decided on the following schedule:

day care opens	7:30 a.m.	All age groups, except the infants, are placed together in one large room. Educators rotate this early shift and work together.
full service	9:00 a.m.	All the educators are in by this time and children are divided by age group.
group size changes	4:30 p.m.	Many children begin to leave. Two groups are placed together in order to operate efficiently with less staff.
closing	6:00 p.m.	One staff member is responsible for closing time. This responsibility rotates between staff members.

TABLE 3.3
Example of hours of operation in the day care of a computer parts manufacturing company.

The nature of shift work varies from setting to setting. Table 3.4 represents a schedule in a hospital setting. The hospital has three consecutive round-the-clock shifts: 8:00 a.m. to 4:00 p.m., 4:00 p.m. to midnight, and midnight to 8:00 a.m. Due to complications related to staffing, this particular day care has chosen to meet the needs of only the 8:00 a.m. shift.

open	7:30 a.m.	All educators arrive at the same time. All groups are open and children go to their respective rooms.
most children are picked up	4:30 p.m.	Most staff leave at 4:30 p.m. Two or more rooms are grouped together.
closing	5:30 p.m.	One staff member is left in charge of closing. This responsibility rotates.

TABLE 3.4
Example of hours of operation in a hospital day care.

In conclusion, the day care is represented as one system that functions within the system of child care. It also operates in relation to other systems, such as that of the family and workplace. This systems approach represents a viable way to study the day care and its interdependence with the environment.

Training and Early Childhood Education

As an educator of young children you will have a significant influence on the day-care system. Your training and experiences will be an invaluable part of what you will have to offer other members of the system. You will bring to the day care your views, ideas, and knowledge about working with children. Drawing on a combination of your **knowledge**, **skills**, and **disposition**, you will make suggestions and provide ideas toward creating a quality environment for the children. It will be important to understand the mission statement of the day care you will join. In this way your training will complement the day care's statement of purpose.

There are a diversity of training programs available to early childhood students across Canada. These training programs differ from province to province. Two- and three-year college diploma programs and three- and four-year university programs are available. Some provinces/territories offer courses through distance education while others offer courses through Prior Learning Assessment (PLA). PLA allows students with previous early childhood experience to challenge early childhood education courses through the development and presentation of a portfolio. Most programs place a strong emphasis on the practicum/fieldwork component of the training program and see it as an integral opportunity for students to integrate theory and practice.

The design and variety of training programs are often linked to the provincial requirements and regulations. There is a growing belief that the establishment of national standards will have a positive effect on the quality of child care. In May 1995, prompted by this belief, the Canadian Child Care Federation (CCCF) adopted National Guidelines for Training of Early Childhood Educators.

These Guidelines include an emphasis on type of study, personal reflection, and communication. Some of the established guidelines are cited by the Canadian Child Care Federation.

> Specialized studies in early childhood care and education form the framework for supporting professional theory and practice.

> Knowledge of human development and an appreciation of the role of the family serve as the foundation for promoting each child's optimal development.

> *Canadian Child Care Federation*, Interaction, *1995, 7-8*

The first excerpt clearly values the importance of specialized training. Specialized study is the backbone for translating theory into practice, knowledge into action. Your ability to translate theory into practice plays an important role in developing your teaching and care-giving self. What constitutes "specialized studies" is not clearly delineated in the guidelines. The guidelines do mention a number of areas that should be included, for example, knowledge of child development. Child development courses are essential and they form the foundation and basis of any training in early childhood education. Knowledge of child development ensures a provision of appropriate activities that are geared to the developmental level of each individual child.

Another important topic covered under specialized training is acquiring a grasp of the role of the family. Different cultures may have different views of this role and each situation may require a different application.

Your training program serves as a foundation for acquiring relevant knowledge and developing practical skills as an early childhood educator. In practicum/fieldwork experiences you can practice and develop skills as they relate to your knowledge of early childhood. With the guidance of your cooperating educator, supervisor, or director you will be able to bring together your knowledge and skills. This will assist you in your work with the children and help you assume your responsibilities as an early childhood educator. Your training will provide you with a framework and foundation from which to begin and continue to develop in your chosen field.

Summary

- A mission statement helps an organization focus. It serves as a basis for establishing the stakeholder group and as a basis for planning.

- Participative management involves all stakeholders in the process of decision-making.

- The day-care's clientele refers to members of society who are served by the day care.

- Brainstorming is part of a process known as divergent thinking.

- Convergent thinking refers to a process of zeroing in on specific points.

- Everyone in the day-care system should be informed about the mission statement.

- There are three ways to group children: same-age grouping, where all children of the same chronological age are together; family grouping, where children of all ages are placed in the same room for the whole day; and mixed grouping, where children of the same age are grouped together for one part of the day and with different ages for another part of the day.

- All indoor and outdoor space, as well as available equipment, make up the physical environment.

- Hours of operation of a day care vary according to need.

Questions and Activities for Further Reflection

1. You are a student/educator in a day care. Is there a mission statement? If there is a mission statement, ask to see it. Determine the implications for planning based on this mission statement. What parental goals would be most compatible with the mission statement of the centre where you are placed for a practicum or where you are working?

2. You are about to apply for your first job in a day care. Identify one criterion that you would like to see included in a mission statement. Explain your choice.

3. You are an educator in a day care where the mission statement is contradictory to your beliefs. What action could you take?

4. What kind of grouping style do you believe you would enjoy working with and why?

5. How will a day care's mission statement effect the way you implement your training?

Self-Test

Select all the key terms that relate to the development of a mission statement. Describe how each term effects the development of a mission statement.

References

Banathy, Bela H. (1991). *Systems Design of Education: A Journey to Create the Future.* Englewood Cliffs, N.J.: Educational Technology Publications.

Bredekamp, Sue, and Teresa Rosegrant, eds. (1992). *Reaching Potentials: Appropriate Curriculum and Assessment for Young Children.* Washington, D.C.: National Association for the Education of Young Children.

Finch, Janet. (1988). "Ethnography and Public Policy." In *Education, Training and the New Vocationalism: Experience and Policy.* Milton Keynes: Open University Press.

Moss, P. (1994). "Defining Quality: Values, Stakeholders, and Processes." In *Valuing Quality in Early Childhood Services,* Peter Moss and Alan Pence, 1-9. New York: Teachers College Press.

National Association of Secondary School Principals. (1987). *Developing a Mission Statement for the Middle School.* Reston, Virginia: National Association of Secondary School Principals.

Osborne, A.F. (1957). *Applied Imagination.* New York: Charles Scribner's Sons.

Pence, A., and P. Moss. (1994). "Towards an Inclusionary Approach in Defining Quality." In *Valuing Quality in Early Childhood Services,* Peter Moss and Alan Pence, 1–9. New York: Teachers College Press.

Spodek, B., O.N. Saracho, and M.D. Davis. (1991). *Foundations of Early Childhood Education: Teaching Three-, Four-, and Five-Year Old Children,* 15–31. Ma.: Allyn and Bacon.

Taylor, Barbara. (1989). *Early Childhood Program Management: People and Procedures.* Ohio: Merrill Publishing Company.

P A R T **I I**

Working and Communicating in the Early Childhood Setting

Chapters 4 and 5 provide an in-depth look into the various interpersonal relations that occur within a day-care system. Chapter 4 focuses on the relationships between adults and children. Specific communication techniques are provided for the educator to use during the normal course of daily interactions with children. Chapter 5 highlights the many relationships that are part of the daily life of an educator in the day-care system. The focus of Chapter 4 is relationships between adults who are directly and indirectly involved with the day-care system. Various techniques of communication are discussed in both chapters.

In these chapters the reader is asked to examine personal beliefs and values. We believe that this personal examination is critical in order to develop a broader understanding of others.

CHAPTER 4

Interpersonal Interactions: Between Adults and Children

In this chapter you will:

- differentiate between interpersonal and intrapersonal skills;
- examine techniques of interpersonal interaction between adults and children;
- recognize the importance of cultural awareness as a part of interpersonal communication;
- identify skills that are specific to enhance positive communication between adults and children;
- identify techniques for dealing with separation anxiety;
- identify strategies for developing a positive self-concept in children.

Advance motivator

Examine the following key terms before reading the chapter. Then, while reading the chapter, try to assign meaning to each one.

interpersonal skills   disposition
intrapersonal skills   facilitator
interpersonal competence   family notebooks
interpersonal self   separation anxiety

Interpersonal Relationships

Constructive and effective relationships stem from an aptitude to understand and communicate with people as well as to understand ourselves (Covey 1989; Gardner 1993). A web of interpersonal relationships exists among members within each day-care system and among members outside the system. Effective interpersonal relationships foster a positive atmosphere between you and other stakeholders within a system. Relationships are based on interactions with others and through personal internal actions. Skills used to interact with others are known as **interpersonal skills** while skills used to maximize a personal understanding of yourself are known as **intrapersonal skills**.

As an early childhood educator you rely on interpersonal skills to communicate with the various stakeholders in the system, such as children, parents, other educators, the director, and members of the board of directors. In this chapter we will examine the importance of interpersonal skills and look at how you can achieve competence in this area. Particular attention is given to the relationships between adults and children. Chapter 5 expands the concept of interpersonal competence to include adult-to-adult relationships.

Interpersonal interactions between adults and children show that while adults influence children, so do children influence adults. Children are active participants in setting the tone of interpersonal relationships with the adults with whom they interact. Within the day-care system many adults, including students, educators, and parents, develop interpersonal relations with children. Other adults within the day-care system who also interact with the children include the director, support staff, and even possibly a college or university student/supervisor. During the early years, the primary guardian is usually the primary adult with whom the child interacts. When children are placed in day care, the secondary adult is usually the educator in charge of the group.

As the educator (or perhaps student) placed in the classroom with young children, you have a responsibility to ensure that interpersonal relations are positive and effective. There are many techniques and skills of communication that are available to help you with this task. First, let us look at a working definition of interpersonal skills.

Interpersonal Skills: What Are They?

As individuals we strive for **interpersonal competence** in our work and personal lives. Each one of us has a certain innate skill in this area. In order to become more competent we need to establish where we are starting from and what skills we wish to develop. A skill is an ability to do something well. Having the skills to be interpersonally competent means that you have ways or methods of achieving this goal. Skills are represented as a measurable output of your knowledge and can often be seen in terms of performance.

Through personal skill development we achieve interpersonal competence. An example of a skill used to develop interpersonal competence "includes knowing how to adjust your communications according to the context of the interaction, the person with whom you are interacting" (Devito 1995, 13). For example, if someone speaks to you in an angry tone, you may have a tendency to respond in a hostile manner. This would not prove effective. A better tactic would be to adjust your reaction and provide an outwardly calm response. This will serve to diffuse the heated situation.

It is important to understand interactions and how they can influence others. We all have different styles of interpersonal interactions and we all develop different interpersonal relationships. Our goal within the day-care system is to work in harmony with others.

Understanding yourself and your intrapersonal skills is a good starting point for developing effective interpersonal skills. In Chapter 1 we looked at a small part of this equation. We looked at understanding our belief system and our values through reflection. This understanding of our self must be taken a step further in order to develop the interpersonal skills we need to work with children.

Developing interpersonal skills is a lifelong process. As we mature we change our views and our interactions. Your comfort level in any given situation will also influence how you interact. You may possess the necessary skills for a given situation. However, if you are feeling uncomfortable and unsure of yourself in a new situation, you may find it difficult to demonstrate those skills. It is not uncommon for early childhood students to feel uncomfortable or unsure of themselves at the beginning of a practicum experience. This is due to the fact that new situations often affect our anxiety level. As our comfort level increases, so does our ability to utilize our interpersonal skills. Another example of a situation in which many students experience difficulty is class presentations. You may know the techniques necessary to give a good presentation, but you may not be able to achieve this goal because you are nervous. With practice, your nervousness decreases and you may be more successful in using the skills you have when giving your presentation.

Each time you react to a situation you acquire experience that alters your theoretical paradigm of that situation and, in turn, improves your skill in responding to it. It is wise to reflect on and evaluate your actions. Reflections should focus on personal feelings and beliefs to help you better understand your choices and methods of interactions.

Here are techniques that you can develop to improve your interpersonal interactions:

- be open to new information,

- be open to different points of view,

- be patient,

- be careful of first impressions,

- exercise flexibility,

- be culturally sensitive,

- respect individual personalities, and

- demonstrate empathy.

Be open to new information. Be receptive to new information that may be offered to you. Sometimes we are overcome with a desire to disregard information, especially if it is information that troubles us. One way to handle such situations is to say, "Let me think about this" or "I will need some time." In effect, what this does is give you some time to think about what is bothering you. This reflection can be done on your own where you can honestly examine your feelings about why the new information does not feel right. Rarely are we confronted with information that has to be responded to immediately.

Be open to different points of view. It is easy to get stuck on our own point of view. We become comfortable and become attached to our way of looking at things, although a different point of view can be helpful in solving a problem.

Be patient. Let children finish their conversations when they are talking or asking questions. We have a tendency to finish sentences or to respond to someone before the speaker has had a chance to finish. We often know the question, but we need to have patience and allow children the time to finish their thoughts on their own. Having patience as an educator also means giving children adequate time to get dressed for outdoor play. When you demonstrate patience, you avoid the tendency to rush or hurry children. This results in a calmer atmosphere.

Be careful of first impressions. Keep first impressions tentative. Often our first impressions are based on previous experiences and not on what is happening at the moment. Reserve judgment for a later time.

PHOTO 4.2
Children model their educator's behaviour. If an educator displays patience when children are completing their assigned tasks, the children will be calmer and happier in their interactions with each other.

Exercise flexibility. This means being able to adjust to situations as they happen. Recognize that life does not always go ahead as planned or according to a strict schedule. Your ability to adjust easily to these changes can have a positive impact on the way you interact with others. For example, if you are rigid in your behaviour, the atmosphere will be tense.

Be culturally sensitive. There is often more than one way of handling a situation. Cultural differences can influence the way we value certain things. Recognize that individuals from other cultures may do things differently. This does not mean that one way is better than the other, it means that it is different.

Respect individual personalities. We are all unique. Demonstrating respect of children's individual personalities allows them to feel good about themselves and who they are.

Demonstrate empathy. Be understanding of and compassionate to others. This means accepting other points of view and other perceptions of a situation as valid.

A good place to start improving your interpersonal skills is by examining yourself. How you react is based on who you are.

Understanding Yourself

A step toward interpersonal competence begins with an understanding of yourself. "Understanding ourselves—what we feel and why we respond as we do—is very important" (Read, Gardner, and Mahler 1993, 12). This ability to look within and to understand our beliefs and values is what Gardner (1983, 1993) refers to as the **intrapersonal self**. Intrapersonal refers to our personal dialogues and reflections with ourselves. "The place to begin building any relationship is inside ourselves" (Covey 1989, 187). This helps us to become secure and independent. Only true independence can lead to interdependence, a position that enables us to build "rich, enduring, highly productive relationships with people" (ibid.).

Reflection

Take a few minutes to think about yourself, your beliefs, and the way you interact with other people. Consider how you interact with children in various situations.

"The complex system of beliefs, values, and attitudes that define our self-concept determines the beginning point for our interactions with others" (Wilson, Hantz, and Hanna 1995, 63). Beliefs are a part of our self-concept. Individuals may share the same belief, for example, that it is important for children to be polite and respectful of adults. However, our expectation in terms of what constitutes polite and respectful behaviour may vary.

An understanding of ourselves, our self-concept, our beliefs, and our values influences the way we respond to situations and the types of relationships that we develop. It is who you are that influences how you respond to situations. Who you are is based on personal experiences and interactions with others.

Attitudes form an important part of your belief and value system. Attitude can be partly described as a disposition, the temperament of your actions. Disposition, however, is more than just attitude; it is prompted by an internal force. Disposition takes into account your underlying makeup and your tendency to act. Although actions are based on a particular disposition, we believe that this underlying makeup can be adjusted through conscious effort on the part of the individual. For example, as adults we can foster our disposition to continue learning and applying the knowledge and skills we acquire (Katz 1987). As educators, we can foster a child's disposition to learn, be curious, and be creative.

Culture

Interpersonal skills are also affected by culture. Interpersonal competence is culture specific (Devito 1995). As individuals, we learn about and develop our interpersonal skills in relation to our culture. When it comes to personal understanding and "personal knowledge, the culture assumes a determining role" (Gardner 1983, 274). For example, in Western culture it is typical to use questions as an important tool for obtaining facts and information. In the Inuit culture individuals do not ask many questions; they spend their time observing and seeking out the answers through observation. Westerners have a tendency to ask questions in order to encourage conversation. Silence is difficult. However, silence is a part of Inuit conversation. It is an important part of the communication process. Inuits are comfortable with silence.

All humans are capable of learning skills that are needed to function effectively in more than one culture. It is important to recognize the skills that you have because of your cultural background and to identify the ones that will be needed when you are functioning in your own or other cultures.

Language is a tool of culture and culture lives within language. It is difficult to separate the two. According to Pool (1994), culture is a world view and a way of interacting with the world. Pool further suggests that translating from one language into another does not translate the way of thinking, only the words. For example, there are many countries that use Spanish as their language. Each, however, has its own unique culture. The same word in different countries may have a different innuendo, a slightly different meaning.

As early childhood educators we need to become aware of other cultures and learn to interact with children based on our understanding of their culture. We must accept that our interactions are limited by our understanding. The depth of our understanding of other cultures is based on our perception and interpretation, which are grounded in our perspective. We view other cultures through our own lenses. Realizing this paradigm will help us further understand other cultures and possibly avoid being judgmental in the development of our attitudes. For instance, you might assume that your conversation with an Inuit individual is not going very well because he or she is not asking very many questions. If you recall our description of the Inuit culture, you will understand that silence is a part of the conversation.

Interacting with Children

Learning to interact effectively with children is an important part of early childhood training. It is strongly emphasized during the practicum experience. Educator–child interactions have a significant influence on the development of the child's self-esteem. Children need to develop positive self-esteem. Their self-esteem stays with them into adulthood. One of the ways an educator or student in their practicum placement can influence a child's self-esteem is by being supportive. Strategies that do not provide needed support lower a child's self-esteem.

Another supportive interaction to develop with children is trusting relationships. Trust is a very important principle in the child's development. Erikson regarded trust versus mistrust as the first part of a child's moral development. If children are expected to develop secure and trusting relationships with the educators that care for them on a daily basis, then the educators need to model consistent and reliable behaviour. It takes time to develop a trusting relationship. This becomes difficult for some children who may be in centres where staff changes frequently. Consider the following situation.

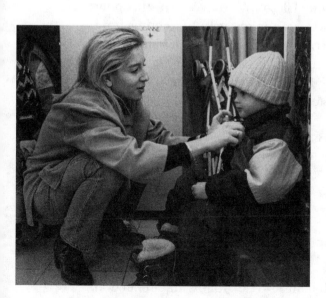

PHOTO 4.3
Trusting relationships are important components in a child's development. Mutual trust and respect between the educator and the child create positive interactions and reinforce positive self-esteem for both.

···

Situation

> Marie Eve began attending day care at 18 months of age. She had a very difficult time separating from her mother. The educator initiated a morning routine with Marie Eve's mother that helped Marie Eve deal with the separation. This routine was quite simple. Each morning, after Marie Eve's mother left the day care, the educator took Marie Eve to the window to wave goodbye to her mother. This procedure worked well for Marie Eve and helped her and her mother in the move toward separation. Marie Eve's mom and the educator knew that this was a procedure that would eventually be phased out.
>
> Within three months of Marie Eve beginning the day care, her educator left the centre. When the new educator began working, Marie Eve again began to have difficulty separating from her mother. Marie Eve had to begin once more to develop a trusting relationship.

···

It is situations like Marie Eve's that can make it difficult for both children and parents in the day-care environment. Children need to develop a sense of trust as this becomes a basis for their development of friendships (Bruzzelli and File 1989). If you are the new educator coming into this situation, you might ask the mother how separation was dealt with by the previous educator. Providing continuity for the child is a useful step toward positive relations. The simple skills of communicating with parents will help you establish the routines and habits that existed before your arrival.

Once children have been able to develop trusting relationships, the educator's interactions can focus on encouraging and fostering autonomy. An example of this is waiting patiently while the child washes the paint brushes at the sink or when one child serves a snack to the other children in the group. Give the child time to do the task on his or her own to encourage autonomy.

Interactions need to be positive, consistent, and frequent. All too often we negate children's feelings. The following reflection provides an example of how we often negate children's feelings.

Situation

Read the following situation and try to determine what is wrong.

Sarah was playing in the playground with Zena. The two girls started to run around the perimeter. Sarah tripped and fell on the pavement, scraping her leg and knee. She began to cry. The educator went over to see what was the problem. She looked at Sarah's leg and knee and told her, "You're fine, your leg is okay, it's just a little scrape."

How do you think Sarah feels when she hears the educator say this to her? The educator is not acknowledging Sarah's feelings at all. The educator is telling Sarah how she feels. This invalidates Sarah's true feelings. Sarah may in fact be fine, but she should be given a chance to express herself. How else do you think the educator could have responded?

Consistency is essential for children. Consistency can be offered through their routines and schedules and in their interactions with the educator. Children need to know what to expect in their daily routine. They also need to receive the same message every day about their behaviour. If jumping on the cots is not acceptable, they cannot be allowed to do it one day and not the next. When children have consistency in their schedules they are able to predict what will happen next and this allows them to feel secure in their environment. Consistent interactions will help them develop consistent behaviour and trust.

Educator–child interactions should be frequent and reflect a balance of group and individual relations. Group interactions seem to occur naturally during snack time, lunch periods, and circle time. Educators often find it useful to set daily goals to ensure that individual interactions occur. You might, for example, set a personal goal to have a minimum of at least one individual interaction with each child in your group every day. Educators experience individual or group interactions in many ways: during discussions, through singing, when giving directions, and when providing guidance through verbal exchanges to redirect inappropriate behaviour and encourage appropriate behaviour.

Quality interactions can be achieved when educators are able to create an effective balance between the time spent interacting with the children and with the other educators. For example, it is common for an educator who works alone with a group of children to gravitate to other educators for conversation during outdoor play. These interactions and exchanges of peer conversation are valuable as long as they do not interfere with educator–child interactions.

Our interpersonal interactions with children play an important role in the development of their pro-social skills. Your interpersonal relationship with the children needs to demonstrate that you value peer interaction. "Teachers, through sensitive interactions in many situations, can enhance children's social knowledge and hence their sense of trust in friends" (Bruzzelli and File 1989, 73). Children need opportunities to interact with peers with limited adult intervention and supervision to develop their pro-social behaviours. Through modelling, coaching, praising, question asking, or direct teaching about effective social behaviours or peers' reactions to them, adults can successfully develop peer interactions with children.

Communication

What is communication? Communication is a process that involves both sending and receiving messages. Communication skills are essential to function effectively in our multicultural society. Educators come from different cultures, and through communication an understanding between individuals will develop. "The whole climate of interpersonal relationships in an education centre can be affected by an individual's ability to communicate" (Machado and Botnarescue 1993, 144). Verbal language is an obvious method of communication. However, there are more subtle or less obvious forms of communication, such as body language and facial expressions.

Communication with Children

Effective communication between children and their caregivers is vital in providing a positive environment. According to Vygotsky, communication with others is a key "ingredient in the young child's expanding capabilities" (Pflaum 1986, 11). As discussed in Chapter 2, Vygotsky's theory is a good example of how communication skills represent one of the many interpersonal skills needed for successful interactions. There are a number of points to consider that will enhance educator–child communications.

- Talk to children at eye level.

- Use a normal speaking voice when communicating with the children and speak as if you were having a normal conversation.

- Use everyday language.

- Listen when a child is speaking.

- Respond clearly to the children.

- Avoid correcting a child's grammar during conversation.

- Recognize when communication is not as effective as you would like it to be and take action.

Talk to children at eye level. This means crouching down or sitting on a chair so that you are speaking to the child face to face. When you stand and bend over to talk to the child, you suggest a position of power. This is neither respectful nor comforting to the child. Your

PHOTO 4.3
Trusting relationships are important components in a child's development. Mutual trust and respect between the educator and the child create positive interactions and reinforce positive self-esteem for both.

body position makes the difference between being approachable versus being intimidating.

Use a normal speaking voice when communicating with the children and speak as if you were having a normal conversation. A relaxed tone helps children feel comfortable. By modelling appropriate ways to communicate, you are more likely to encourage them to communicate with you in the same way.

Use everyday language. This helps children learn vocabulary that is relevant to a variety of situations. Oversimplification of language does not foster appropriate acquisition of language skills. Using words that are too complex isolates the listener. Use language that is both appropriate and relevant to the particular situation. This helps children match vocabulary with experiences. It also builds their verbal and linguistic communication skills.

Listen when a child is speaking. Listening is an important aspect of communication. If you want children to listen to you when you speak, you should model this behaviour and listen to them when they speak. Listen with the intent to understand. This means that you avoid interrupting children when they are speaking and that you listen for their feelings at the heart of their message. This shows the children that you respect them. Learning how to listen effectively is a skill that requires practice.

Respond clearly to children. Use simple and clear language to respond. Your responses to children's conversations should match what they are saying. Articulate your words and use proper grammar. You are a language model for the children with whom you are communicating.

Avoid correcting a child's grammar during conversation. Rather than correct a child's grammar during the course of conversation, you should model the correct grammar in your response. At some point in your response you might paraphrase what the child has said. In this way you keep an open and positive line of communication between you and the child. The child will not feel intimidated to talk to you the next time. Furthermore, the child will learn proper grammar through your modelling.

Recognize when communication is not as effective as you would like it to be and take action. This implies that the responsibility for effective communication lies with the adult. It is up to you to make things work. Keep in mind that communication is needed for the conceptual growth of the child. The educator has the responsibility of maintaining effective communication.

Early childhood educators are working with children during years when their language is developing. Educator's have a great influence on and responsibility in the development of children's language and communication skills. Early childhood educators must be aware of language development. Many children may enter the day care with a different mother tongue than that of the majority of the children. Educators need to be aware of and sensitive to these situations.

These key points about communication are general guidelines that you will need to modify or adjust, depending on the age of the child with whom you are working. For example, if you are working with an infant, your communication style will be different than if you were working with 4- or 5-year-olds. You will spend a good portion of your time communicating with the infant on an individual level. Each time you change the infant's diaper, you might talk to him or her about what you are doing, or you might play with his or her toes, or you might talk about the picture that is hanging near the changing table. The infant will communicate with you through expressive sounds and body language. With a group of 4- and 5-year-old children, however, your focus may be to encourage the children to engage in conversation and your role will be to act as a facilitator. A facilitator generally listens more than he or she talks (Creaser 1993). As you gain more experience in working with children of varying ages, you will learn how to adjust your communication skills to match the developmental levels of the children.

Communication between Educator, Child, and Parent

Within the day-care environment, a triad of interactions exists among the child, educator, and parents. In an ideal system the triad

(Figure 4.1) meets to "foster communication and share perspectives" (Cohn and Gellman 1988, 3).

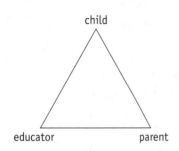

FIGURE 4.1
Triad of interactions.

Good child—adult relationships are important to have. It is important that interactions flow easily among those involved. The optimal situation requires a solid relationship among the child, primary guardian, and the educator. The child needs to receive the same messages from all adults involved in his or her care. When primary guardians or parents are properly informed of situations, members in the triad can respond and deal with the child in the same way.

Interactions at the Beginning of the Day

Whenever children are dropped of at the day care, they and their parents should be greeted by warm and friendly faces. It is the educator's role to help smooth the transition from the home to the day care and assure the parents that they are leaving their children in a warm and safe environment. The following two scenarios provided in Table 4.1 are examples of a parent and a child being greeted at a day care. Which one do you feel is more reassuring?

SCENARIO # 1

Stewart is brought in at 8:00 a.m. His mother is in a rush to get to work. She brings Stewart to the door and hurriedly says goodbye. Mark, the educator, is playing in the block area with two children who arrived earlier. The block area is directly opposite the room's entrance way. Mark calls out: "Hi, Stewart, come over and join us." Stewart's mother leaves. Stewart, still a bit sleepy, stands at the door and gazes down the hallway watching as his mother walks away. The educator again invites Stewart to join him and the children.

SCENARIO # 2

Stewart is brought in at 8:00 a.m. His mother is in a rush to get to work. She brings Stewart to the door and hurriedly says goodbye. Mark, the educator, is playing in the block area with two children who arrived earlier. The block area is directly opposite the room's entrance way. Mark tells the children he is playing with that he will be right back. "I am just going to say hello to Stewart and his mom." Mark gets up and walks over to the door. "Hi, Stewart. Hi, Mrs. Smith. How are you both today?" The mother might respond, "I am really in a rush. I am going to be late for work." The educator responds, "I understand, don't worry." Mark then speaks to Stewart, "Let's go over and see what the other children are doing?"

TABLE 4.1
Sample interactions between parent, child, and educator at the beginning of the day.

In both scenarios the educator greeted the parent and the child. However, scenario #2 uses a more advanced level of interpersonal skill. The child is integrated into the group and the mother is reassured that Stewart will be well cared for. There is the opportunity in the second situation to invite the parent into the room and to sit on the floor to play with her child. Even though she cannot stay, this would further reassure and comfort her.

Situations dealing with infants are a little different. Infants cannot verbalize their feelings. It is your responsibility to go to the door, greet the parent and child, and physically take responsibility for the child's care. This may mean something simple like taking the child in your arms and holding her or him for a few moments. Physical warmth and affection are good tools to help a child feel comfortable and safe. An open line of communication between the educator and parent will help share information about how the infant is feeling in the morning. For example, the educator might ask what kind of night the infant had. The parent's answer will help the educator better understand the child's mood during the day.

Interactions at the End of the Day

The end of the day is a good time to make personal contact with the parents. Children greet their parents with enthusiasm and excitement. Parents are happy to see their children. They are also tired at the end of a long work day. Chances are that you, too, are tired. Still, it is your role to help make a smooth transition. Once again it is time for personal contact. You might say: "Hi, Mrs. Smith, would you like to come in for a few minutes?" Parents will not always accept your offer, but sometimes relaxing for just a few minutes with their child is a helpful way to make a smooth and stress-free transition.

The end of the day is a good time to give parents an anecdote related to the day and their child. All parents like to hear something about what the child did during the day. This is a good opportunity for positive feedback.

Children often spend more than seven or eight hours of the day in day care. This represents a time span that is often greater than an educator's shift. This means that the educator who is with the child at the end of the day is not necessarily the same one that was there in the morning. It may also mean that the primary educator has gone for the day. Furthermore, as children begin to leave at the end of the day, groups may be merged and the educator who is left in charge has really only spent a few hours with any given child. Parents may have questions that they wish to direct to the primary educator. The primary educator may have points they wish to communicate with the parents. A good way to handle this is through **family notebooks**. This is a notebook in which parents and educators can leave informal comments, ask questions and receive answers, or read an anecdote about the child and his or her day.

Educators can also develop strategies that promote child-to-parent communication about the events of the day. One way to increase the communication links between child and parent and day care is to create a photo album. This is an album with a collection of photographs that have been taken during various activities. Children on a rotating basis get to take this home and share it with their parents. Children enjoy telling their parents about their friends and this is a great way for parents to learn the names of the other children. Another idea is to create storybooks from the stories children have written. These books go home with a different child each night so that the child can read the story to the parent or the parent can read the story to the child.

Interpersonal Skills Used to Deal with Separation Anxiety

Separation anxiety requires thoughtful interpersonal actions between the educator, parent, and child. Separation anxiety is an apprehension that the child experiences when being separated from the primary caregiver. Separation anxiety is more common during the child's first few times at the day care. As the child becomes accustomed to the environment and develops a sense of trust, he or she will feel less anxious in anticipation of being left by the parent or primary caregiver. Still, separation anxiety can be stressful for the parent, child, and educator. There are numerous approaches to handling this.

It is the educator's role to establish coping strategies to deal with this stress. In selecting a coping strategy it is important to recognize a few basic tenets. Children need to feel secure, safe, and supported. Assess whether the child's anxiety is due to fear of leaving their parents or fear of the environment. Your role is to ensure that the child feels comfortable in the classroom environment and in your care. Your ability to communicate with a child will increase his or her feelings of safety and security (Feeney, Moravcik, and Christensen 1991).

The following reflection may assist you in determining the most effective coping strategy for your particular situation.

•••

Reflection

Ask yourself: What do I believe is at the heart of the anxiety the child is feeling in relation to separation? How do the parents react when their child clings to them? Do I believe that parents should leave quickly? Should parents be invited to come into the room and spend some time with the child, helping him or her integrate into the classroom environment?

Your actions will vary, depending on your belief system. For example, if you believe parents should leave quickly, then you would reflect this in your attitude. You might go up to the parent, take the child by the hand, and say goodbye to the parent.

On the other hand, if you believe that the parent should help the child make the transition between the home and the day care, you would go up to the parent and child and invite them in. You might even suggest that the child show the parent some new book that is out on the shelf. Once the child appears to be settled in, you can join the child and the parent, making both feel comfortable.

Whichever approach you rely on to handle separation anxiety, we suggest you encourage parents to be clear and definite about when they will leave (Hendrick 1990). Parents should be instructed to let their child know when they are leaving.

In conclusion, adult-to-child interactions play a vital role in the development of a child's self-image. As an educator, it is important to develop the techniques and skills needed to interact with children effectively. The next chapter explores how interpersonal skills can positively influence adult interactions and lead to greater interpersonal competence.

Summary

- Interpersonal skills play a vital role in promoting meaningful relationships among the various stakeholders within the day-care system.

- Developing an understanding of yourself (intrapersonal relations) helps in achieving positive relations with others.

- Numerous techniques of communication between you and the children support meaningful interpersonal relations between you and the children.

- Some techniques to enhance interpersonal relations with children include being supportive, honest, and fostering autonomy.

- Communicate with children at their eye level. Use a normal speaking voice and use everyday language.

- Good interpersonal skills involve listening when others speak.

- An important part of good interpersonal relations with children is to maintain a positive relationship with their parents.

Questions and Activities for Further Reflection

1. Some of the parents of the children in your class have volunteered to help in the classroom. They are eager and delighted to participate. When the parents arrive, their children are happy to see them. Jason's parents are consistently unavailable to volunteer. He comes from a single-parent home. His mom works full time and his dad lives out of town. Jason feels sad every time another child's parent volunteers in the class. Design effective strategies for handling this situation.

2. Make a list of practical things you can do as an educator to prepare a parent volunteer.

Self-Test

Identify techniques to create an atmosphere of positive communication between you and the children, you and the parents, you and other educators. Provide examples of how you would implement these techniques in a day care.

References

Bruzzelli, C.A., and N. File. (1989). "Building Trust in Friends." *Young Children*, 44:70–75.

Cohn, M., and V. Gellman (1988). "Supervision: A Developmental Approach for Fostering Inquiry in Preservice Teacher Education." *Journal of Teacher Education,* 2–8.

Covey, S. R. (1989). *The Seven Habits of Highly Effective People.* New York: Fireside Books.

Creaser, B. (1993). "Teachers As Observers of Play: Involving Teachers in Action Research." In *Growing Teachers: Partnership in Staff Development,* ed. Elizabeth Jones, 106-116. Washington: National Association for the Education of Young Children.

Devito, Joseph. (1995). *The Interpersonal Communication Book,* 4th ed. New York: Harper Collins College Press.

Feeney, S., E. Moravcik, and D. Christensen (1991). *Who Am I in the Lives of Children?* New York: Merrill.

Gardner, H. (1983). *Frames of Mind,* 10th ed. New York: Basic Books.

Gardner, H. (1993). *Multiple Intelligences: The Theory in Practice.* New York: Basic Books.

Hendrick, Joanne. (1990). *Total Learning: Developmental Curriculum of the Young Child.* New York: Merrill Publishing Company.

Katz, L. (1987). "The Nature of Professions: Where is Early Childhood Education?" *Current Topics in Early Childhood Education,* 7:1–15.

Machado, Jeanne M., and H.M. Botnarescue. (1993). *Student Teaching: Early Childhood Practicum Guide,* 2nd ed. Albany, New York: Delmar Publishers.

Pflaum, S. (1986). *The Development of Language Literacy in Young Children.* Ohio: Bell and Howell Publishing.

Pool, Annelies. (1994). "Aboriginal Languages—Can They be Saved?" *Above and Beyond: The Magazine of the North,* Summer 1994.

Read, Katherine, Pat Gardner, and Barbara Mahler. (1993). *Early Childhood Programs,* 9th ed. Fort Worth, Texas: Harcourt Brace Jovanovich College Publishers.

Wilson, G.L., A.M. Hantz, and M.S. Hanna. (1995). *Interpersonal Growth Through Communication,* 4th ed. Madison, Wisconsin: Brown and Benchmark Publishers.

C HAPTER 5

Interpersonal Interactions: Among Adults

In this chapter you will:

- recognize informal and formal modes of communication;
- identify practical tips for communicating with parents;
- examine techniques to design a parent–educator interview;
- look at the relationships that develop between educators;
- examine communication with your supervisor;
- identify your role in relation to the director;
- examine the educator's role in relation to the board of directors.

Advance motivator

Examine the following key terms before reading the chapter. Then, while reading the chapter, try to assign meaning to each one.

cultural pluralism	newsletters
informal communication techniques	parent information meetings
formal communication techniques	mentor program
parent conferences	

Dynamics of Interpersonal Relationships with Adults

Relationships among adults essentially rely on many of the same interpersonal skills that you develop in working with children in the day-care system. Many stakeholders in the system are adults and you will develop different relationships with each of them. These relationships significantly influence the way in which the system functions.

Adult interpersonal relationships are built on a foundation of inter-cultural awareness and cultural pluralism. In a pluralistic society the stakeholders within the system may come from many cultures. Effective interpersonal relationships evolve as we co-exist and work in harmony with one another.

Flexibility and communication are key ingredients in developing and maintaining positive interpersonal interactions and provide the groundwork for good interpersonal relationships. In the previous chapter we discussed communication as an important tool for positive interpersonal relations with children. This tool is also important in adult relationships.

Communication is a tool used to transmit and interpret messages (Wilson, Hantz, and Hanna 1995). Part of this interpretation is based on a two-way relationship. In order to develop a positive relationship, equal responsibility is accorded to the person delivering the information and to the person receiving the information. If you are delivering the information, you need to be clear about what it is you want to communicate. Be sure that your message is in sync with your tone and body language. Sometimes when we speak we do not send the intended message. Unfortunately, once a message has been sent, it is irreversible. Sometimes we overreact or come on too strong in a situation and we often regret it later. You can try to rephrase what you said or apologize for your reaction, but you cannot erase what has been done (Devito 1995).

Listening is an integral part of communication and the other side of the relationship. "The best message is useless if no one is listening" (Harris 1995, 83). Effective listening involves giving your full attention to the individual who is speaking to you. It can also involve feeding back the information to clarify that you have heard and understood the information correctly.

It is vital to create an atmosphere where communication is descriptive or supportive as opposed to evaluative or threatening (Devito 1995). Communication that requests information or describes an event is usually not threatening. If we feel challenged by a communication, however, we tend to respond by defending ourselves. The atmosphere surrounding the delivery of information has a significant role in the way individuals respond to one another.

As a student or novice educator you will be a newcomer to the day-care team. How can you best integrate into the day-care system? You will need skills to maximize relationships with parents, other educators, the director, and your supervisor.

Relating to Parents

As an educator your relationship with parents begins the moment a parent registers a child at the day care. While it is true that the practitioner has more frequent and constant interaction with parents than a student does, the student should not avoid involvement. There are some basic similarities that both the student and the practitioner have when interacting with parents. Whether you are an educator or student trainee, it is important that you take initiative in relating to parents. When you interact with the children on a daily basis, consider the uniqueness and individuality of each child. The same should be true in our interaction and communication with parents.

PHOTO 5.1
Students learn communication skills by interacting with educators in the day-care environment.

Investing time to cultivate relationships with the families of the children that are in your group is wise. The sharing and exchange of information can work toward developing a strong tie between the home and the day care.

Special events at the day care encourage families and educators to socialize. Such an event could be the summer barbecue, the spaghetti fundraising dinner, a cross-cultural dinner, or the day-care centre's anniversary celebrations. These events encourage the social gathering of children, parents, and staff. They provide opportunities to meet other members of the child's family. Knowing the child's family broadens your relationship with the child. These opportunities are the beginning of informal communication experiences with families and parents. A positive relationship with families and regular communication with them avoids situations where communication is reserved for problems or negative instances only.

Spodek, Saracho, and Davis (1991) break down communication techniques with parents into two broad categories. These are **informal** and **formal communication techniques**.[1] Informal techniques happen on an ongoing basis. As the term implies, they are not planned. They do not involve a specified topic or agenda, but they do represent a very important and regular form of communication between the parent and educator/student. Interactions at the beginning of the day and at the end of the day provide important opportunities for these informal interactions. At the beginning of each day an educator can ask parents how the morning went at home. At the end of the day an educator can provide an anecdote about an event in the day. Family notebooks are also helpful tools to enhance informal communication between the parents and educators.

Formal communication techniques are planned. They have a set or predetermined agenda. They usually involve a specified topic.

---

[1]In our writing, the term formal communication techniques has the same meaning as the one presented by Spodek, Saracho, and Davis (1991). However, we have expanded the use of the term informal communication techniques. We refer to *Foundations of Early Education* for further information.

These do not occur as frequently as informal communication techniques. They represent an important part of the communication process between parents and educators. Formal communication techniques include **parent conferences**, **newsletters**, and **parent information meetings**.

Informal Communication Techniques with Parents

The Student's Interactions with Parents

As a student the first time you meet a parent or family member is when the child is dropped off at the day care. Students are at times uncertain or shy in this situation. Should you, for example, stay where you are within the classroom or get up and greet the parent? It is common practice for your cooperating educator to introduce you to the parent or family member. Regardless of whether you are introduced by someone else or you do your own introductions, you can introduce yourself by saying:

Hello, my name is _____.

I am a student from _____ and I will be
(give name of teaching college you attend)
with   your   child   every   _____   until
(day, or on specific days of the week)
_____ ”
(provide length of time of your practicum experiences)

In this way you reassure parents by letting them know who you are and what days you will be there. Following this first introduction, you will be in a position to greet the parents each time you work at the centre. Once you have introduced yourself, you are ready to interact with parents as if you were a cooperating educator. The *as if you were a cooperating educator* means that you will take on the same responsibilities as a cooperating educator would. However, you need to keep in mind that parents may sometimes ask you difficult or sensitive questions. When this occurs, resume your role as a student and direct the parents to the educator in the classroom. This demonstrates your respect for the educator and your sensitivity to the parents.

The Educator's Interactions with Parents

As an educator your goal is to achieve positive relationships between you and the primary guardians. These relationships are key to the success of the day-care system and allow you and the parents to work together on behalf of the welfare of the child.

Open communication is essential for positive relationships. You may feel nervous about communicating with parents, and it is entirely possible that they feel the same way about communicating with you. Your role as the educator is to initiate these informal conversations and begin the communication process, despite your feelings of discomfort. You may feel that for awhile you have a one-sided relationship because it may take some parents more time than others to feel comfortable in the relationship. A parent may, for example, prefer using the family notebooks rather than having a face-to-face conversation with you. You may need to adjust your expectations and realize that you will not develop the same type of relationship with each parent.

Beliefs about family structure also influence communication. It is important for an educator to keep in mind that there are different kinds of family structures. There are single-parent families, two-parent families, and blended families. It is important that as an educator you examine your own values with respect to these structures so that you do not pass judgment on families that may exist in a structure that is different from your beliefs. Be honest with yourself and respectful of differences. This will facilitate positive communication. You may also find that you communicate more comfortably with one parent than the other. This is acceptable, but you must show the same respect to both parents. Situations may also become complicated in families where the parents are divorced. In these situations it is important that you speak to the director to find out how the situation has been handled previously and to find out which parent is the primary guardian. This information will guide you in your interactions with each parent.

In situations where children change from one day-care group to another, parents often rely on their relationship with their child's initial educator for support. Changing from one group to another is also a transition time for the parents and they may need the educator's support to help make this transition smooth and easy. For example, the initial educator might offer to have the child spend the first half hour of the day with him or her and offer to take the child to the new group later in the day. This period of transition could take place over one week.

Informal communication can help avoid tensions that can develop between educators and parents. Some of these tensions occur because the educator has not met the parents expectations. The greatest expectation is that the child will receive the educator's full attention.

In any of these situations, use active language when speaking with parents. For example, begin sentences with "I will..." or "Let us look at alternatives...". In this way, you state that you, as the professional, are willing to take action. This approach helps build a good rapport with parents that, in turn, becomes the building block of a positive relationship. Showing a willingness on your part to look at more than one solution to any scenario shows good faith. Positive inter-actions between educators and parents are vital steps in avoiding many potential problems that could arise. The following situations provide an example. The first situation is from the educator's perspective and the second situation is from the parent's.

....

Situation 1

Kelen was working with a group of 2-year-old children. They had an unusually hectic afternoon. During free play time, one of the children in the group became quite sick. Kelen's co-educator took care of the sick child, leaving Kelen alone with the rest of the children. Several children were playing at the water table when Kelen noticed an excessive amount of water on the floor. She assumed the water had been spilled. She and the children began to clean it up. A short while later she again noticed water on the floor. This time she realized that somehow the plug in the water table had become loose and the water was leaking. She tried unsuccessfully to put the plug back into the water table. The children thought this was just great. They were excited to help Kelen wipe the water off the floor. While mopping up, many of the children got their clothes wet. One of these children was Justin.

Once the floor was dry and the water table put away, Kelen began helping the children change out of their wet clothes. As she was helping two of the children change their clothes, Justin's mother arrived. Justin had not yet changed his clothes. His mother was angry, but Kelen didn't offer her an explanation.

....

Kelen had spent a busy afternoon with the children and under the circumstances felt that she had handled the situation appropriately. How would you have handled the situation? How could Kelen have reacted more clearly and assertively to improve the situation?

....

Situation 2

Justin's mother arrived to pick him up. When she arrived Justin was playing with the blocks (he had been waiting for his turn to get changed). His mother noticed that his shirt was wet. She became upset wondering how the educators could let him play in a wet shirt? Didn't she know that his shirt was wet? She went over to Kelen and told her that the next time Justin had a wet shirt, she wanted it to be changed right away!

....

How do you think Kelen felt when Justin's mother spoke to her this way? When Justin's mother arrived should Kelen have said something to her about the events of the afternoon? Should Justin's mother have asked some questions to clarify the situation before assuming that Kelen did not know that Justin was wet? How do you think Kelen should respond to Justin's mother?

Formal Communication Techniques with Parents

Parent Conferences and Interviews

Parent conferences and interviews are designed to inform parents about their children's progress. Parents are interested and eager to know what their children do during the part of the day when they are not present. These represent a time when practitioners can meet their "obligation to respond to parents' requests for information" (Spodek, Saracho, and Davis 1991, 153). Conferences and interviews serve as "private, uninterrupted opportunities for conversation and there is no chance that the child might overhear himself [or herself] being discussed" (Hendrick 1990, 390).

If you are team teaching, you will need to determine with your co-educators the structure of the interviews. Will you do all the interviews together? Will you divide up the parents? Or will you do some separately and some together? These are important organizational questions to answer before planning the interviews.

The following tips are provided as a guideline for planning a parent conference or interview. As a student you may find it helpful to observe an interview or a conference with a cooperating educator.

- Be prepared; plan in advance.

- Maintain a time schedule.

- Use language that is easy to follow.

- Be specific; give examples.

- Listen when the parent is speaking.

- Rephrase the parent's comments to be sure you understood.

Be prepared; plan in advance. There are a variety of things you can do to prepare for the conference or interview session. During the regular day, keep a sheet of paper and pen handy. Many interesting anecdotes occur during the course of the day. When time permits, jot down a few notes that will remind you of your observation. During nap time, or at the end of the day, take a few moments to transfer the information into a file folder on the particular child you observed. These types of anecdotal comments provide spontaneous and meaningful information about the child.

Maintain a file folder or other form of record-keeping device for each child. Include such items as anecdotal records, photos of the child actively engaged in play situations, or samples of the child's art work. Review your notes prior to meeting the parent and bring the notes with you. Parents appreciate it when you have put thought and effort into preparing for the conference. This demonstrates that you have an interest in their child.

Maintain a time schedule. Keeping to a time schedule is not always as easy as it sounds. Some parents may have more questions or comments than time permits. In cases where their concerns seem to necessitate further discussion, suggest setting up a second meeting at a later date. With experience, you will become better able to manage the time more effectively. Initially, you may want to keep a watch on the table to keep you on track. When there is one minute remaining, you can say something like "to wrap up" or "in conclusion."

Use language that is easy to follow. Avoid using jargon. The use of everyday language makes it easier for parents to identify the points you are trying to raise. Everyday language helps set up a comfort level between you and the parent. If you use a technical term, follow it up with a concrete example of what you mean.

Listen when the parent is speaking. In order to hear what the parents are saying, it is important to let them finish their thoughts. Do not interrupt parents while they are speaking. To do so gives a negative impression. Also, we are better at absorbing what others say when we listen attentively.

Rephrase the parent's comments to be sure you understood. We are all concerned with the child's well-being. Rephrase the parent's comments to ensure that each of you has the same understanding of the issues that have been raised. Begin by saying, "Is this what you meant?" and state your paraphrased version of the parent's comments.

A final note. Some educators find it difficult to report to the parent in person. Making the parent feel comfortable and at ease will also help you relax. Be ethical and be kind. Remember, you are talking about someone's child. "Parents identify closely with their children and criticism often implies criticism of the parents as well" (Spodek, Saracho, and Davis 1991, 155). Be sure to present a balanced description, including both strengths and weaknesses.

If, after an interview, you think that the parent is left feeling uncomfortable or with some issues still unresolved, remember that it is important to follow up on those issues. This can be achieved through an informal meeting the next day or by arranging a second interview.

Newsletters

Newsletters serve many functions. Each group or the day care as a whole can put out a newsletter. A newsletter communicates news about events in the day care and highlights activities, new songs, or particular skills that are the focus of the day-care's programming (Hendrick 1990). Newsletters can serve as reminders that, with a change of weather, parents need to send sun-block, rubber boots, or other relevant items with the children. Recipes of some of the foods that the children particularly like can be included as well.

A newsletter can serve as an excellent public relations vehicle (ibid.). You can use it to direct parents to articles relevant to day-care activities or parenting. As parents become more knowledgeable and learn specific terminology about early childhood, your communications will improve.

Parents can also use the newsletter to inform other parents about community workshops related to child rearing or community events that could be shared by children and parents.

Parent Information Meetings

A parent information meeting is a good way to provide current knowledge related to the well-being and development of children. It provides a forum for social interaction between parents. Parent information meetings need to be well planned, informative, and, at the same time, relaxing. During the meetings many centres include a slide show or a video of the children engaging in a variety of activities. These types of presentations gives the parents firsthand ideas of how their children spend their time at the day care.

You may choose to plan a meeting that focuses on one topic related to the development of children—for example, the benefits of reading to children and how this fosters a positive attitude about reading and reading achievement (Brock and Dodd 1994). Provide parents with articles that support your belief that reading is beneficial. You might want to set up a lending library and encourage parents to take home a book for the evening to enjoy with their children at bedtime. To meet the needs of today's diverse families, educators need to "work with parents to provide books and materials that are tailored to their lives and cultures" (ibid. 16).

These parent information meetings can involve guest speakers who address specific topics of interest or concern to a group of parents, such topics as parenting skills, dealing with behaviour problems, nutrition, and sibling rivalry.

An educator or student can take a variety of steps to create a relationship that is meaningful and will contribute to the development of positive communication in the day-care system. See Table 5.1.

Encourage parents to participate in special events or special projects.

Encourage parents to arrive early enough so that they can help settle their child in for the day.

When parents arrive early, invite them to spend some time looking at the activity areas that their child is interested in.

Invite parents to participate in field trips. Keep in mind that volunteers need to have guidelines to define their responsibilities. This will help them be competent and feel confident.

On occasion, offer evening workshops on topics of interest and relevance to the age and stage of development of the children at the centre. Offer workshops on health education. Parent meetings are useful tools for sharing information with parents and for gleaning information from them.

As a student, participate in these meetings. Come prepared. If you have already spent some time interacting with the children and there is something particular you wish to discuss, share it with your cooperating educator first. This shows a degree of respect for the educator with whom you are working.

As an educator or student educator, subscribe to appropriate journals or magazines.

When you come across articles of interest and relevance make them available to the parents

Encourage parents to spend an hour in the classroom for a special occasion. Tell them to spend this hour engaging in activities with the children.

TABLE 5.1
Ways of involving parents in the day care.

Even though parents and educators are not always in agreement, there needs to be a time when both parties can listen to each other.

Use the professional skills of parents for special event days in the centre, involve them in some form of activity. Every parent has a skill to offer. Invite parents to volunteer in the classroom. Keep in mind that not all parents will have the time for this. Also, some parents are better suited to direct involvement with the children than are others. As an educator you can take certain steps to help make this a positive experience. Choose something that can capitalize on the strengths of the volunteer (Hendrick 1990).

Most important, let parents know the positive influence they can have on their children's emotional and intellectual well-being. All parents, after all, want what is best for their children. An open channel of communication with parents avoids an authoritarian approach. Use cooperative efforts for the best relationship possible.

Interpersonal Relations with Other Members of the System

Relations between Students and Supervisors

You are practising to be an educator/teacher of young children. At the same time, you are a student. You may have many teachers for many different courses. Your practicum supervisor is the person that comes to observe you in the field while you are training. Your supervisor guides you through your practicum or pre-service experience. Although your supervisor comes and goes and does not observe you throughout the day, this person is an important part of the training team. The supervisor serves as a conceptual link and liaison between the university or college faculty and the field of early childhood (Knowles, Cole, and Presswood 1994).

The student in pre-service training is part of a university or college training system. The supervisor is an integral part of the system of the training institution. The supervisor provides feedback to the student. The supervisor also makes clear the intent of the training program to the director and cooperating educator in the day-care system.

The cooperating educator functions as a part of the day-care system. The student becomes a bridge between the day-care system and the training institute. This means that you, as a student, need to contribute actively to the discussions in both the day-care and training system. This helps you develop a "shared understanding of teaching-as-dialogue" (Creaser 1993, 115).

As a student you are often busy trying to *do* the work you need to do to complete your practicum. It is often difficult to focus on doing the practical tasks and attending your seminars. Nonetheless, it is important to attend seminars. Use these sessions as an opportunity to talk about theory and practice. Link personal experiences to theoretical concepts that you have studied in class. For example, share experiences of play episodes as catalysts for discussion (ibid.). Plan teaching experiences based on your theoretical knowledge. Your participation will enhance your relationship with your co-students and your supervisor.

Use supervisory sessions to ask questions and explore ideas. Inquiry and problem posing lead to a successful understanding of one's own actions. Use the experience of your supervisor to guide your growth and development. Come prepared to supervisory sessions. Being prepared will lead to a positive and fruitful relationship with your supervisor. Accept your supervisor's comments as challenges for growth rather than as negative criticism. It is sometimes helpful to articulate some of your expectations or concerns related to supervision early in your placement. This will lead to a more effective relationship.

Interactions between Educators

Interactions between educators will vary depending on the structure of the day care. In some centres educators work on their own or with a group of children; in other centres educators work with one or two co-educators. How quickly your relationships develop is greatly influenced by whether you are working alone or with others. Remember that as a new educator it will take time for your relationships to grow and for you to be accepted and trusted as part of the team. Having new educators in the day care means change, and it takes time to adjust to change. Some of the stress that comes with accepting a new staff member relates to our own insecurities. We are often apprehensive about how this new educator will relate to the children, to the parents, and to the other educators. What if they like the new educator better? This transition phase is made easier when other staff members have been involved in the selection and hiring and are eager to have you on aboard.

Some day cares have begun a **mentor program** for new staff members. The mentor orientates a new staff member to the centre and introduces them to parents and other members of the system. Mentors can help you with the many questions you have or they can provide suggestions in difficult situations. Often new educators feel more comfortable asking their mentor questions rather than the director of the centre. A mentor is usually a peer educator while the director is often perceived as an authority figure. Having someone available to answer your questions makes the transition into a new environment much smoother.

Co-workers are involved in both informal and formal communication situations. Informally, they can tell you specific information about the children or remind you of special events. Some centres use a communication notebook, in which important information is written on a daily basis. Formal communication between co-workers occurs during staff meetings.

Staff meetings involve the educators and the director/owner of the centre. Many centres have staff meetings once a month. Some centres have these meetings during nap time and hire substitutes to watch the children. Other centres may hold the meetings after work or in the evening. The agenda for these meetings is usually prepared by the director in consultation with the educators. Staff meetings are ideal opportunities for educators to share and exchange ideas and to generate new ideas together.

A positive environment between co-workers contributes to high-quality day care. Children and parents can sense when a group is working as a team. Teamwork implies that "duties are rotated, schedules are coordinated and resources are shared" (Wagg 1995, 26). Your attitude will play a role in influencing these interactions. A positive and accepting attitude will foster a healthy work environment. How you relate to others, communicate, and solve problems forms a meaningful model for the children with whom you are in contact (Feeney, Christensen, and Moravcik 1991). If, as a team, you are successful in attaining a goal, it is important for you to celebrate. "Celebrating is the most often overlooked yet most powerful aspect of team-building" (Wagg 1995, 29). Interacting socially with co-workers can enhance your relationships with them.

Difficulties will arise between co-workers and it is essential that you deal with these situations professionally. During difficult situations you need to call upon your interpersonal competency to guide you. To avoid potential problems, communicate issues promptly with co-workers. Educators who work with the same children but at different times of the day need to communicate and work closely together. The following example illustrates this point.

....

Situation

Tony was experiencing difficulty at the end of the day when it was time to go home. When his mother would arrive to pick him up, he would tell her that he was not ready to go home or that he had not had enough time to play. His mother would usually give him a few minutes to play before he had to get dressed to go home. As soon as he would leave the classroom, he would either run around the centre or go into another classroom to play. He seemed to do everything possible to avoid getting ready to go home.

Helma, who was with Tony at the end of the day, was not his regular educator. Helma was very uncertain as to how to handle the situation. Helma felt very strongly that before she would or could do anything she needed to speak with Tony's educator about the situation. She was not sure if the mother wanted to handle the problem herself or if the mother wanted her help. Did the mother expect Helma to handle the situation?

....

These were important questions that had to first be discussed with the other educator before they could be discussed with the parent.

As educators it is important to arrange time to share more than planning. There is great value in arranging meetings to share insights and episodes. This collaborative inquiry can serve as a powerful vehicle for professional growth (Creaser 1993).

Interactions between Educators and the Director

The director is the manager of your day-care system. He or she is responsible for ensuring that programs are consistent with the mission and goals of the centre. The type of relationship and degree of interactions with the director will vary, depending on the size of the centre and its internal structures. In the capacity of director, this person supports educators in their planning and monitors the programs. Although directors help educators plan, they do not plan for them.

There are a few points to keep in mind when dealing with the director.

- Purchasing and organizing materials.

- Use a professional and relaxed tone to communicate with the director.

- Recognize that the director is responsible to the children, the parents, and the board of directors.

Purchasing and organizing materials. If special materials are required for a project or supplies are running low, it is the responsibility of the educator to communicate this to the director. Give her or him adequate time to secure the materials—at least one week's notice. This does not eliminate spontaneity. It means that your spontaneity is limited by available resources. Sometimes many educators want certain materials at about the same time. The director, in conjunction with the educators, will have to prioritize these expenditures. The director is responsible for ensuring that the budget meets the demands of all the educators. As an educator you have the responsibility of communicating your needs to the director while recognizing that you are only one member of the team.

TOOL

Do an inventory of your classroom materials. Make a list of three special items that you would like to ask the director of the centre to purchase.

Item   **Price**

_____   _____

_____   _____

_____   _____

Prioritize this list. Look through catalogues for approximate prices. Verify the available budget with the director.

Use a professional and relaxed tone to communicate with the director. Respect the director's time when dealing with specific concerns. Make an appointment rather than catching him or her off guard in the halls. The director will be more receptive to your needs if the time to speak has been allotted. The notion of professionalism will be discussed in detail in Chapter 8. Remember, the director's role is to achieve harmony and avoid conflict, but he or she is often the agent for change (Meade-Robert, Jones, and Hillard 1993). To avoid conflict situations, be receptive to your director's needs and he or she will be more receptive to yours. Be open yet respectful when expressing differences of opinion.

Recognize that the director is responsible to the children, the parents, and the board of directors. It is easy to forget that as an educator you are not the only person who is placing demands on the director. He or she is often constrained by other demands, such as budgets, provincial regulations, and parents' demands. Try to see situations from more than one perspective.

Relationships with the Board of Directors

Generally speaking, you will not have much contact with the board of directors. Traditionally, one educator acts as the representative. He or she is invited to sit on the board as the liaison between the board and all the educators. It is important to note that this person is a representative and as such is there to voice the collective view of the group he or she is representing. This position does not invite a forum for the expression of personal biases and desires.

There are some things you can do to improve the level of communication between you and the board of directors. Use this checklist to prepare for board of directors meetings.

- Come prepared to meetings.   _____

- Read the agenda a few days before the meeting.   _____

- Ask the educators you are representing for input.   _____

- Submit topics in writing in advance.   _____

- Present yourself in a professional manner.   _____

Come prepared to meetings. If you will be speaking on a topic, ask for input from the other educators on the message they would like you to deliver. Make notes and review them before the meeting.

Read the agenda a few days before the meeting. Inform the other educators about the agenda items and discuss these with them. Clarify any items that are unclear to you.

Ask the educators you are representing for input. This means that you should go over the topic you are presenting with other staff members first. Get their input and opinions on the subject so that you can present a fair view of the situation. Often this can be done at a staff meeting prior to the board of directors meeting.

Submit topics in writing in advance. If there is one thing that your group wants discussed, submit it in writing to your director or to the chair of the board.

Present yourself in a professional manner. Dress appropriately and neatly. Use professional language. This is a business meeting.

Summary

- Interpersonal skills play a vital role in promoting meaningful relationships between the various stakeholders within the day-care system.

- Effective interpersonal interactions exist in an environment that accepts cultural pluralism.

- Numerous techniques of communication between you and other adults support meaningful interpersonal relations.

- You can relate to parents using informal or formal communication techniques. Both serve an important purpose.

- Get together with colleagues to share planning time as well as to discuss play anecdotes.

- For supervisory sessions to be effective, the student should come prepared with anecdotes for discussion.

- The supervisor provides feedback to the pre-service educator's emerging practice. The supervisor also outlines the intent of the training program to the cooperating agency.

- Communicate your needs and concerns with your director, giving him or her adequate time to react.

- An educator usually sits on the board of directors as a representative spokesperson for other educators. This person serves as the liaison between the board and the educators.

Questions and Activities for Further Reflection

1. During your fieldwork/practicum placement try and attend a social event at the day care. Compare your experience with that of the other students.

2. Discuss with your cooperating educator how he or she plans and prepares for parent interviews. See if you can observe the educator in a parent interview.

3. Speak to the director about attending a staff meeting.

Self-Test

Identify key factors for an effective interpersonal relationship with parents, the director, cooperating educators, and your supervisor. Make a separate list for each interpersonal relationship that you will engage in as an educator or pre-service educator.

References

Brock, D., and E. Dodd (1994). "A Family Lending Library: Promoting Literacy Development." *Young Children,* 49:6–21.

Creaser, B. (1993). "Teachers as Observers of Play: Involving Teachers in Action Research." In *Growing Teachers: Partnership in Staff Development,* ed. Elizabeth Jones 106–116. Washington, D.C.: National Association for the Education of Young Children.

Devito, Joseph. (1995). *The Interpersonal Communication Book,* 7th ed. New York: Harper Collins College Publishers.

Feeney, S., E. Moravcik and D. Christensen (1991). *Who Am I in the Lives of Children?* New York: Merrill.

Harris, Jane. (1995). "Is Anybody Out There Listening?" *Child Care Information Exchange,* 7:82–84.

Hendrick, Joanne. (1990). *Total Learning: Developmental Curriculum of the Young Child.* New York: Merrill Publishing Company.

Knowles, J.G., A.L. Cole, and C. Presswood. (1994). *Through Preservice Teachers' Eyes: Exploring Field Experiences Through Narrative and Inquiry.* New York: Macmillan College Publishing.

Meade-Robert J., E. Jones, and J. Hillard. (1993). "Change Making in a Primary School: Soledad, California." In, *Growing Teachers: Partnership in Staff Development,* ed. Elizabeth Jones, 106–116. Washington, D.C.: National Association for the Education of Young Children.

Spodek, B., O.N. Saracho, and M.D. Davis. (1991). *Foundations of Early Education, Teaching Three-, Four-, and Five-year-old Children.* Boston: Allyn and Bacon.

Wagg, Carol. (1995). "Team-Building in the Child Care Work Place." *Interaction,* 9:26–29.

Wilson, G.L., A.M. Hantz, and M.S. Hanna. (1995). *Interpersonal Growth Through Communication,* 4th ed. Madison, Wisconsin: Brown and Benchmark Publishers.

PART III

Defining Perspective: The System's Web

In this section, Chapter 6 explores the legal framework of a day care. We look at the impact of the federal, provincial, and territorial governments on the day-care system. Chapter 7 outlines the economic structure of a day care. The student will develop an understanding of financial management within the day care, the sources of income, and the importance of managing expenses. Chapter 8 identifies procedures on how to find a job within the field of early childhood education. We provide information on the job search, the interview, and starting your new job.

CHAPTER 6

Legal Framework

In this chapter you will:

- examine the role of the federal, provincial, and territorial governments in day care;
- identify the ministries responsible for day care in each province and territory;
- identify the provincial acts in each province and territory;
- examine the regulations in regards to educator qualification, educator/child ratio, and group size.

Advance motivator

Examine the following key terms before reading the chapter. Then, while reading the chapter, try to assign meaning to each one.

legal framework	Child Care Expense Deduction
day-care legislation and regulations	Training allowance
	Indian and Northern Affairs
bylaws	Child Care Initiative Fund (CCIF)
Canadian Assistance Plan	acts and laws

The Role of the Government in Day Care

All systems and organizations operate within a **legal framework**. The legal framework for day-care systems is bound by **day-care legislation and regulations** that determine the boundaries of the day-care system. The legal framework for day cares protects children, parents, and educators within the day-care environment. It establishes the limits or the parameters by which the system must abide. For example, the provincial regulations in Alberta do not permit a day-care centre to operate with more than sixty children in one building.

Canada does not have an established system of national day-care legislation or regulations. As a country, our organization and establishment of day-care systems vary. While some authors say that "existing child care programs cannot really be considered a system, since the delivery, availability, and the cost of child care vary so markedly from province to province and from city to city" (Cooke et al. 1986, 225), we believe in the importance of moving toward a common system in order to achieve professionalization in this field. Federal, provincial, territorial, and municipal levels of government all play a unique role in the development of the day-care's legal framework. Each province and territory has its own set of requirements that day cares must follow. However, most provinces share similar types of regulations, which we will explore later in this chapter. It is conceivable that these similarities could contribute toward the development of a Canadian day-care system.

Federal Government

As discussed in Chapter 1, the role of the Canadian government in child care began when it extended child support to families in need. Following the two World Wars, the federal government became actively involved in reviewing the child-care needs of children and families. Table 6.1 outlines the key commissions and task forces appointed by the federal government between 1970 and 1985. The federal government has influenced the day-care system and allocates funds to the provinces and territories based on studies, research, statistics, and task forces.

The Special Committee on Child Care appointed in 1985 had a larger mandate than some of the previous committees. This committee "looked at the care of all kinds of children in all types of care situations—at home and outside the home, by parents, neighbours and relatives or professional caregivers, in organized centres and in private homes" (Martin 1987, 3).

1970	The Royal Commission of the Status of Women reported on the changing needs of Canadian families. It identified that the demand for child care would increase and that this would lead to a crisis in the field of child care.
1984	The Task Force on Child Care studied child care across Canada and made recommendations to the federal government.
1984	The Royal Commission on Equality in Employment looked at the opportunities for women to improve or advance in the workforce. It was recognized that to accomplish those goals a child-care system was needed.
1985	The Special Committee on Child Care surveyed and reported on the child-care needs of Canadian families.

TABLE 6.1
Federal government commissions and task forces appointed to investigate child-care needs in Canada.

The results of these reports commissioned by the federal government have been consistent in their findings. They suggest that the lifestyles and the needs of the Canadian family are changing and that our present child-care system has not developed to meet the challenges. The 1980s and 1990s saw an increase in the numbers of mothers in the workforce. The present lack of quality licensed child-care services cannot meet the growing demand and this poses a greater and greater problem for Canadian families (Cooke et al. 1986). As we move toward the year 2000, changes are needed to meet these challenges.

In addition to federal commissions and reports, the federal government, since 1971, has been conducting national day-care surveys. The purpose has been to accumulate and publish statistics about various aspects of services available across Canada. The surveys are published in a report entitled *Status of Day Care in Canada*. Since 1971 the report has been updated each year. These reports provide valuable information on the

- total number of day-care spaces in Canada with a breakdown of the number of spaces in acentre versus the number of spaces in family day cares;

- number of children by age across Canada attending either day-care centres or family day cares;

- total number and percentage of day-care centres across Canada that are either profit or non-profit;

- breakdown of the total number of spaces across Canada that are either in profit or non-profit centres;

- number of day-care spaces occupied per province or territory;

- number of day-care centres per province or territory;

- percentage of children between 0 and 17 months who are in day cares;

- percentage of children between 18 months and 35 months who are in day cares;

- percentage of children between the ages of 3 and 5 years who are in day cares; and

- percentage of children between the ages of 6 and 12 years who are in day cares.

To obtain further information on the status of day care or to order a copy of one of the reports, contact the National Child Care Information Centre, Social Services Program Branch, Health and Welfare Canada, Ottawa, telephone: (613) 954-3959.

The federal government provides direct and indirect financial assistance for child care in Canada. The greatest source of child-care funding is the **Canadian Assistance Plan** (CAP), which is a cost-sharing plan between the federal, provincial, and territorial governments to provide day-care subsidies to low-income families. The **Child Care Expense Deduction** is an income tax deduction that allows parents to deduct the cost of child care from their income tax. **Training allowances** are paid to parents who require child-care arrangements while attending training courses through Employment and Immigration Canada. **Indian and Northern Affairs** provides support to child-care programs on reserves.

In 1988 the government introduced the **Child Care Initiative Fund** (CCIF), which remained in existence until March 1995. It was a program that allocated 100 million dollars to fund research and encourage innovative child-care programs. Its ultimate goal was to enhance and improve the quality of child care in Canada. CCIF placed a high priority on Aboriginal needs and over 21 percent of the total funding was allocated to Aboriginal groups. In December of 1994, with the termination of CCIF pending, the government established another initiative for the funding of child-care programs on reserves and for Inuit child-care programs. The government also proposed an initiative to provide funding for the Aboriginal/Inuit Head Start programs that would assist Aboriginal families living in urban centres or Inuit families living in large northern communities.

The federal government has an interest in Canadian families and child care across the country. With the accumulation of data and information collected through statistics and research, it has attempted to set directions for policies and financial assistance.

Provincial and Territorial Governments

The responsibility for day-care legislation, regulations, and standards in Canada lies with the provincial and territorial governments. The first task for these government bodies is to establish a definition of day care for their province or territory. Each defines what it considers to be a day-care centre. For example, in New Brunswick a day care is defined as a facility providing day-care services to seven or more children of the ages 5 and under and 6 and over. In Prince Edward Island a day care is defined as a "child-care facility," where facility means any place where child care is offered at any time to more than six children; or more than five children all of whom are less than 6 years of age; or more than three children all of whom are less than 2 years of age.

Provinces and territories also establish legislation and regulations that provide the legal framework for day cares. They pass **acts and laws** that outline the requirements for the establishment of day-care centres. The provinces and territories issue permits or licences that are good for a specified period of time. These time periods vary anywhere from one to two years. "Provincial and territorial legislative competence embraces licensing and enforcement of standards relating to the physical environment, program, and staffing requirements for child-care services, as well as training, employment standards and labour relations for employees in these programs" (Cooke et al 1986, 285). Permits or licences are renewed through a process that is outlined in the regulations. In general, the provincial and territorial governments are responsible for

- legislation for licensing a day-care centre,

- development of day-care regulations and standards,

- the enforcement of day-care standards, and

- arrangement and provisions for funding.

Legislation for licensing a day-care centre. Each province and territory is very specific in its definition of what constitutes a day-care centre and outlines in detail who is eligible to obtain a licence and the requirements for obtaining it.

Development of day-care regulations and standards. Each province and territory has departments in their respective governments that are responsible for establishing the day-care regulations and standards. The regulations range from the number of toilets required in the centre to the number of educators required. They may, for example, outline specifically that ratios must be maintained *during nap time*. It is during nap time that educators have their lunch break and often the number of staff in the building is lower, which would result in the ratios not being met. Day cares rely on volunteers or hire substitutes to work during the nap time in order to meet the government regulations.

The enforcement of day-care standards. The provinces and territories hire and assign inspectors who are responsible for visiting day cares and ensuring that each day care meets stated regulations. They also investigate complaints about day-care centres.

Arrangement and provisions for funding. Each province and territory establishes the amount and type of funding that it will provide to day cares. These amounts are often adjusted on an annual basis.

Each province and territory publishes these regulations in a document that is available through the government. Day cares could not function without knowing and understanding the implications of the regulations.

The time line for the development of regulations by the provinces and territories has varied, depending on their situation. British Columbia and Ontario were among the first provinces to institute provincial regulations—in 1943 and 1947 respectively. The Northwest Territories was the last to pass legislation in 1987. Following is a list of the provincial and territorial acts or regulations and the ministry responsible for that legislation.

- *Alberta*
  The Social Care Facilities Licensing Act and the Day Care Regulation (1987)
  Ministry: Family and Social Services

- *British Columbia*
  Provincial Child Care Facilities Regulations (1981) amended (1990)
  Ministry: Skills Training and Labour

- *Manitoba*
  Regulations Under the Community Child Day Care Standards
  Act (1987)
  Ministry: Family Services Child Day Care

- *New Brunswick*
  Day Care Facilities Standards (1985)
  Ministry: Department of Health and Community Services

- *Newfoundland*
  The Day Care and Homemaker Services Act (1990)
  Ministry: Department of Social Services

- *Northwest Territories*
  Child Day Care Standards Regulations (1987)
  Ministry: Department of Social Services Child Day Care
  Section

- *Nova Scotia*
  Day Care Act and Regulations (1990)
  Ministry: Department of Community Services

- *Ontario*
  The Day Nurseries Act (1990)
  Ministry: Community and Social Services
  Education and Training

- *Prince Edward Island*
  Child Care Facilities Act, the Child Care Facilities Act
  Regulations and Guiding Principles for the Development of
  Child Care Services (1987)
  Ministry: Department of Health and Social Services
  Child Care Facilities Board

- *Quebec*
  An Act Respecting Child Day Care (1992)
  Regulations Respecting Child Care Centres (1993)
  Ministry: Women's Issues

- *Saskatchewan*
  The Child Care Act (1989)
  Ministry: Social Services

- *Yukon*
  Child Care Act, Statutes of the Yukon (1990)
  Ministry: Department of Health and Human Services

It is interesting to note that currently several provinces are in the process of reviewing their provincial legislation. British Columbia, which was one of the first provinces to pass its provincial regulations, began in 1990 to review its child-care regulations and the Community Care Facility Act. This need for review and revision has occurred for various reasons. One current concern in British Columbia is that child care is limited to thirteen hours a day. This limitation poses difficulties for those parents who work twelve-hour shifts within a shorter workweek. New Brunswick is also in the process of reviewing its child-care regulations. The review was initiated when day-care representatives met with government officials to discuss their concerns. This process has led New Brunswick to develop a vision of child care for its children. "The vision for a child-care delivery system in New Brunswick is one which provides quality, affordable, accessible, centre-based, and home-based services for children needing non-parental care primarily because their parents are working/training/studying" (Government of New Brunswick 1994, 3).

Saskatchewan is also in the process of reviewing its day-care regulations and policies. As a result, Saskatchewan has instituted a new vision, The Circle of Family—Responsive Child Care Options, a circle model that approaches child care differently. This option "reflects a parent driven system that is supported by the community and government—with options and models available for enhanced flexibility for parents" (Government of Saskatchewan 1994, 12).

As we move toward the year 2000, it is conceivable that many provinces and territories will address the changes and challenges of day care and allocate time and resources to review their regulations in an attempt to improve and enhance services for our future generations.

Local and Municipal Governments

The provincial and territorial regulations specify that day cares must follow and implement municipal regulations and **bylaws**. The municipal governments can play an important role in the establishment of day-care facilities. Municipal zoning bylaws determine the possible location of a day-care facility. For example, day-care centres are not usually located in residential areas due to zoning laws. In order for a day care to locate in an area zoned for residential purposes, it would need to lobby the municipal government for a change in the zoning of that area. Local and municipal building codes and standards must be adhered to in order to obtain the provincial permit or licence. These standards usually relate to fire and safety concerns. For example, the number and often the location of exits that are required for a particular building are based on municipal bylaws.

There are some municipalities that operate their own day-care facilities. Ontario was known for having the most on-site municipal government day cares. Ontario's municipal governments allocate operating funds to these day-care centres (Friendly 1994; Yeates et al. 1994). Unfortunately, a new political era of government cutbacks will have a negative impact on this funding.

Internal Bylaws

Day cares also must define bylaws or internal regulations. These bylaws become the internal working framework of the day care and are usually determined prior to the opening of the centre. "They are the legal foundation of the organization and they explain how and by whom decisions are made" (Morissette 1994, 24). They include such information as the legal name of the day-care centre, who the members of the organization are, and when the organization must hold its annual general meeting.

The Influence of Specific Regulations

The day-care regulations of each province and territory are lengthy and quite inclusive. It is important that you become familiar with the regulations of your province or territory. Our discussion will focus on those regulations that will have the most impact on you as a student or educator within the day-care system. We will focus on qualifications for educators, educator/child ratios, the number of children per group and per day care, the size of a centre and its indoor and outdoor space requirements, and programming. Please note that these regulations were in force at the time of printing and may have changed by the time of your reading.

Qualifications for Educators

Qualifications for educators vary tremendously. Individuals can earn degrees, diplomas, or certificates, or qualify through in-service training and professional development. Early childhood programs range from one to three years at the college level and from three to four years at the university level. Students have the option in most provinces and territories to study part time, full time, or through distance education. Regulations regarding educator and director qualifications vary among the provinces and territories. For example, some require no formal training and others require a minimum of a college diploma. Regulations also differ as to how many trained educators are required in a centre. The regulations may require that only one out of three or one out of four educators be qualified. Some regulations are concise and specific, while others are more complex and integrate many factors. We will provide an overview of some of the specific regulations of each of the provinces and territories.

Alberta

The director needs a minimum of one year of early childhood education (ECE), and one out of every six educators needs a minimum of one year of ECE training.

British Columbia

British Columbia has no specified regulations for the qualifications of the director. The qualifications for educators vary, depending on the age group of children with whom they are working. For a group of educators working with children younger than 3 years of age, one of the educators must have a minimum of one year of ECE, plus special training for the age group with which they will be working. For example, an educator working with infants would need both ECE qualifications plus specialized training to work with infants. British Columbia is the only province that requires this specialized training.

Manitoba

In Manitoba the day-care director or supervisor is required to have a degree or diploma in the field of child care and at least one year of experience working with children in a day-care setting. The regulations for educators are detailed and specific to the year that someone began working in the field. The three levels of qualifications are Child Care Worker I, II, and III. A Child Care Worker II or III is an individual who has either a degree or diploma in child care from a recognized institution. In every day care, at least two-thirds of the educators must meet the requirements of either a Child Care Worker II or III.

New Brunswick

The regulations stipulate that the directors and the educators shall have minimum qualifications. These minimum qualifications are defined as having an understanding of children; participating in workshops and training; having an awareness of the resources in the community; possessing the ability to work with other professionals and parents; and having obtained first aid training recognized by the provincial government.

Newfoundland

Newfoundland has not instituted specific educator qualifications in its regulations. Instead, it has empowered its day-care boards to establish their own standards and policies for hiring directors and educators. However, these individuals must receive approval from the Daycare and Homemaker Services Licensing Board before they can be appointed to their positions. The regulations do indicate, though, that the board should hire individuals who are, in their opinion, suitable candidates. The regulations also suggest that staff be encouraged to participate in training programs.

Northwest Territories

There are no regulations stipulating required qualifications for directors or educators.

Nova Scotia

As of 1987 the director of a day-care centre was required to have completed an early childhood training program. By April 1989, a minimum of two-thirds of the educators were required to have completed an early childhood training program or its equivalent. The regulations stipulate the institutions and the three training programs that are recognized and what the requirements are for equivalence.

Ontario

The directors in this province need to have a minimum of a two-year ECE training program and a minimum of two years' experience working in a day care. These minimum qualifications for directors are the highest in Canada. One educator per group must have a minimum of a two-year ECE training program.

Prince Edward Island

In Prince Edward Island detailed and complex schedules specify the requirements. Schedule B in the regulations highlights the qualifications for the day-care director. There are six levels of recognized qualifications, which are a combination of training and experience.

For example, someone with a university degree in early childhood education does not need any experience in the field to be considered qualified. However, someone with a diploma in early childhood needs at least two years of experience to be qualified. Schedule C of the regulations highlights the necessary qualifications for educators. Qualifications range from ten university credit courses to a university degree in childhood development and child studies. There is less of an emphasis placed on experience in an educator's qualifications.

Quebec

Quebec does not have any regulations for the qualifications of a day-care director. One in three of the educators working with children must have some form of training. The regulations outline several categories of recognized qualifications. For example, an individual with a three-year diploma in ECE from a CEGEP (equivalent to a community college) is considered qualified, whereas an individual with an attestation in ECE from a CEGEP needs three years' experience in order to be considered qualified.

Saskatchewan

The director needs a certificate in child care from a recognized educational institution. The regulations for educators stipulate that all educators within six months of beginning to work at a child-care centre must complete 130 hours of an orientation course. This orientation must be taken with the Institute of Applied Science and Technology.

Yukon

There are no specified qualifications for either directors or educators. The regulations do provide a mandate that the director hire individuals who are competent in the areas of safety, communication, and programming for children.

Educator/Child Ratios

Educator/child ratios refer to the number of children for whom one educator is responsible. A low educator/child ratio refers to a small number of children with one educator; a high educator/child ratio refers to a large number of children with one educator. All provinces and territories have different regulations that apply to educator/child ratios. The similarity is that provincial and territorial ratios change depending on the age of the children. Table 6.2 outlines the provincial and territorial regulations for educator/child ratios in four age categories.

Province/Territory	Infants	2 years	3 years	5 years
Alberta	1:3	1:6	1:8	1:10
British Columbia	1:4	1:4	1:6	1:10
Manitoba	1:4	1:4	1:8	1:8
New Brunswick	1:3	1:5	1:10	1:10
Newfoundland	n/a	1:6	1:8	1:8
Northwest Territories	1:3	1:6	1:9	1:9
Nova Scotia	1:4	1:7	1:7	1:7
Ontario	1:3	1:5	1:8	1:8
Prince Edward Island	1:3	1:5	1:5	1:10
Quebec	1:5	1:8	1:8	1:8
Saskatchewan	1:3	1:5	1:10	1:10
Yukon	1:4	1:6	1:6	1:8

Note: The classification for infants in most provinces and territories ranges from 0 to 15 months to 2 years of age. Please check your provincial and territorial regulations for specific age classifications.

TABLE 6.2
Educator/child ratios of infants to 5-year-olds in provincial and territorial day-care centres.

Prince Edward Island appears to be the only province with separate ratios for day cares that have mixed age groups of children. They have developed a formula that allows the centre to calculate the number of educators it will require, depending on the age range of the children in the centre. For example, in a centre where there are three infants, three 2-year-olds, four 3-year-olds, five 4-year-olds, and six 5-year-olds for a total of twenty-one children, you would need three educators. This would give you an overall ratio of 1 to 7. This ratio exhibits a midpoint between the ratio of infants through to children 5 years of age.

Saskatchewan seems to be one of the only provinces that stipulates separate ratios for field trips. It requires a ratio of 1 to 3 for toddlers (18 to 29 months) and 1 to 5 for preschool age children (30 months to 5 years 11 months). This represents a ratio that is double to that which is normally required in a centre.

The Number of Children per Group and per Day Care

Group size refers to the maximum number of children that can be together in one age group in a day-care centre. The group size varies depending on the age of the children. Several provinces have six as the maximum group size for infants. The groups sizes for the other ages of children range from eight to thirty. Table 6.3 outlines group sizes in the provinces and territories.

Province/Territory	Infants	2 year	3 year	5 year
Alberta	6	12	12	16
British Columbia	12	25	25	25
Manitoba	6	8	12	16
New Brunswick	9	10	20	20
Newfoundland	N/A	25	25	25

Northwest Territories	9	12	18	18
Nova Scotia*	6–8	8–12	14	14
Ontario	10	15	15	15
Prince Edward Island	6	not specified
Quebec	15	30	30	30
Saskatchewan	6	10	20	20
Yukon	not specified

* These numbers are only the recommendations outlined by the province or territory.

TABLE 6.3
Group sizes of infants to 5-year-olds in provincial and territorial day-care centres.

An additional regulation relates to the maximum number of children per day-care centre. These numbers vary considerably across Canada:

Province and territory	Maximum number of children
Alberta	60
British Columbia	no maximum
Manitoba	70
New Brunswick	60
Newfoundland	60
Nova Scotia	60 (recommended)
Northwest Territories	30
Ontario	80
Prince Edward Island	50
Quebec	60
Saskatchewan	90
Yukon	no maximum

The Size of a Centre and Its Indoor and Outdoor Space Requirements

All provinces and territories seem to be consistent in the amount of regulated space that they require for children, both indoors and outdoors. Some provinces and territories, but not all, have clear regulations stipulating adequate amounts of indoor floor space. For example, in the Yukon the regulations clearly indicate that the floor space in the hallway, locker/cloakroom area, and washrooms cannot be included in the calculations of 4 square metres per child. Other provinces also stipulate the exclusion of kitchen and office area spaces from the calculations of the space per child. Table 6.4 outlines the indoor space required per child.

Province/Territory	Indoor square metres per infant	Indoor square metres per 2- to 5-year-olds
Alberta	2.5	3
British Columbia		3.7
Manitoba	4.6	3.3
New Brunswick	3.25	3.25
Newfoundland	n/a	3.3
Northwest Territories	2.75	2.75
Nova Scotia	2.75	2.75
Ontario	2.7	2.7
Prince Edward Island	3.5	3.5
Quebec	4	2.75
Saskatchewan	3.7	3.25
Yukon	4.0	4.0

TABLE 6.4
Indoor space requirements for provincial and territorial day-care centres.

In the Yukon a day care with thirty children would need 120 square metres of space for the children. Alberta is one of the few provinces that regulates the amount of space a child needs during nap time. Each child must have 2.3 square metres. Newfoundland, on the other hand, states that there must be 2.3 square metres dividing each child in the sleep room.

Provincial regulations also stipulate the amount of outdoor play space that is required per child. The regulations regarding outdoor play space are quite diverse. Table 6.5 outlines the outdoor space requirements in each province and territory.

Province/Territory	Outdoor square metres per infant	Outdoor square metres per 2- to 5-year olds
Alberta	2 for 50% of the licensed space	4.5 for 50% of the licensed space
British Columbia	7 per child	7 per child
Manitoba	7 per child for 50% of the licensed space	7 per child for 50% of the licensed space
New Brunswick	4.5 per child	4.5 per child
Newfoundland	no specification	no specification
Northwest Territories	5 per child	5 per child
Nova Scotia	5.5 per child	5.5 per child
Ontario	5.5 per child	5.5 per child
Prince Edward Island	7 per child	7 per child
Quebec	4 per child	4 per child
Saskatchewan	7 per child with 50% of the space located adjacent to the centre	7 per child with 50% of the space located adjacent to the centre
Yukon	5 per child	5 per child

TABLE 6.5

Outdoor space requirements for provincial and territorial day-care centres.

These regulations make it easy to determine the amount of outdoor space that is required. For example, in the Northwest Territories a day care with twenty-five children would need 125 square metres of outdoor space.

Saskatchewan is the only province that has a separate outdoor space requirement for infants. There must be 2.3 square metres exclusively available for infants adjacent to the day care. New Brunswick regulations state that children who are at a day care in excess of seven hours a day must have at least two hours of outdoor play per day (weather permitting). Generally, most provincial regulations allow centres the flexibility of using space in close proximity to their centres if there is not sufficient space located adjacent to the centre.

Programming

Another major component of regulations are the guidelines established for programming. The development of the program is a major role of the educator, so it is important to be familiar with your provincial and territorial regulations in this area. In brief, most provinces and territories state the importance of developing activities and opportunities that promote the child's physical, intellectual, language, emotional, and social development. Some of these are:

- develop a daily program that meets the needs of the *whole child;*

- provide suitable equipment and age-appropriate play materials;

- submit written plans;

- provide periods of free play time;

- ensure individual and group activities; and

- provide outdoor play.

These guidelines should be integrated with the curriculum and program planning discussion in Chapter 2.

Overview of the Additional Regulations

There are additional categories of regulations that are common to day cares across the country. These regulations apply to:

- nutrition,

- first aid,

- medication,

- organization of children's files,

- hours of operation, and

- ratio of toilets and sinks required per child.

Nutrition regulations include a variety of standards. They discuss the provision of nutritious snacks and meals and state that the menus need to be posted. Regulations prohibit withholding food as a form of punishment.

First aid certification is mandatory for most employees working in the day-care centre. Individuals must keep their certification valid by retraining every three years.

Medication regulations indicate that medicine for children must be kept in a locked container. A doctor's authorization is required in order to administer medication to a child. A prescription must be used and the centre must have parental consent to administer it to the child.

Organization of children's files must include the type of information stipulated in the regulations. For example, the information might include the names of those individuals authorized to pick up the child. The regulations sometimes indicate what should be done with the files once the child leaves the centre.

Hours of operation regulations in some provinces are very specific, stipulating that the centres can only be open twelve hours a day. A special permit is usually required to operate twenty-four hours a day. Most provinces state the maximum length of time that is recommended for children to be at the centre each day.

Ratio of toilets and sinks required per child by the governments outlines the minimum number of toilets and sinks that can be in a centre. The ratio is dependent on the number of children the centre is serving. You can often tell how many children are in a centre by quickly counting the number of toilets.

The provinces and territories also have some interesting regulations that we feel are worth mentioning.

- In Newfoundland the doorknobs must be located no higher than forty-eight inches from the floor or the bottom of the door.

- In Prince Edward Island, educators are not allowed to drink hot beverages while they are around or near the children.

- Manitoba has a regulation concerning night care. A centre may offer night care from midnight to 6 a.m. if the director feels that there is a need in the community.

- Saskatchewan requires that there be a parent board, a community board, or an advisory board in every day care.

- New Brunswick regulations state that children must have access to drinking water at all times.

Reflection

Which regulation strikes you as most important? Are there any regulations you would add?

Knowing and understanding the day-care regulations are important skills. It will help you understand the economics of the day care, search for a job, determine the quality of a day care, and advocate for day care. These topics are discussed in the following chapters.

Provincial Committees Responsible for Regulations

Each province and territory has its own committee that is responsible to its child-care community. The specific function of each committee varies with the different provinces and territories. In some cases the committee may be responsible for such tasks as granting permits and licences or enforcing day-care regulations. The following list is provided as a reference of the various committees across Canada.

Alberta
Day Care Programs
Family and Social Services
11th Floor–7th Street Plaza
10030–107th Street
Edmonton, AB T5J 3E4

British Columbia
Program Manager, Child Care
Community Care Facilities Br.
Day Care and Infant
  Development Program
Ministry of Health
7th Floor, 1515 Blanchard St.
Victoria, BC V8W 3C8

Manitoba
Dept. of Family Services
Child Day Care
114 Garry Street, 2nd Floor
Winnipeg, MN R3C 1G1

New Brunswick
Provincial Coordinator,
  Early Childhood Services
Office for Childhood Services
P.O. Box 5100
Fredericton, NB E3B 5G8

Newfoundland
Day Care and Homemaker
  Services
Dept. of Social Services
3rd Floor, Confederation
Building, West Block
P.O. Box 8700
St. John's NFLD A1B 4J6

Northwest Territories
Day Care Coordinator
Child Day Care Section
Family and Child Services
 Division
Dept. of Social Services
500–4920 52nd Street
P.O. Box 1320
Yellowknife, NWT X1A 3T1

Nova Scotia
Day Care Services
Family and Children's
 Services Division
Dept. of Community Services
Family and Children's
 Services Division
P.O. Box 696
Halifax, NS B3B 2T7

Ontario
Child Care Branch
Children's Services Division
Ministry of Community
 and Social Services
2 Bloor Street, 30th Floor
Toronto, ON M7A 1E9

Prince Edward Island
Early Childhood Services
 Co-ordinator
Early Childhood Services
Corporate Services Division
Dept. of Health and
 Social Services
P.O. Box 2000
Charlottetown, PEI C1A 7N8

Quebec
L'Office des Services de Garde
 a L'Enfance
100 Sherbrooke Street East
Montreal, QC H2X 1C3

Saskatchewan
Child Care Branch
Dept. of Social Services
11th Floor, 1920 Broad Street
Chateau Towers
Regina, SASK S4P 3L8

Yukon
Child Care Services Unit
Dept. of Health and
 Social Services
Yukon Territorial Government
P.O. Box 2703
Whitehorse, YU Y1A 2C6

Summary

- All day-care systems function within a legal framework.

- Day-care regulations are established at the provincial and territorial levels in each of the provinces and territories. At the time of writing this book, a national system of child care is not in place.

- Day cares must also respect the municipal bylaws.

- Day cares develop internal regulations referred to as bylaws.

- Regulations established by the provinces and territories differ from one another.

- The standards determined by each province and territory are also different.

Questions and Activities for Further Reflection

1. How will your knowledge about the regulations help you when you are working in the day-care environment?

2. Compare the licensing requirements of your province or territory to the examples provided.

3. After reviewing and comparing the regulations from many of the provinces and territories, are their any changes that you think your provincial government or territorial government should make?

4. Compare the national guidelines for educator/child ratio with the government regulations in your province or territory. How do they compare?

5. If you were working for the federal government, how would you try to influence the provinces and territories?

6. What type of further research would you want to see the federal government undertake?

Self-Test

Recall all the legal structures and existing policies that help define the day-care system in your province or territory.

References

Cooke, K., J. London, R. Edwards, and R. Rose-Lizée. (1986). *Report of the Task Force on Child Care.* Ottawa: Status of Women Canada.

Friendly, Martha. (1994). *Child Care Policy in Canada.* Don Mills, Ontario: Addison-Wesley Publishers Limited.

Government of New Brunswick. (1994). *New Directions Child Care Reforms, International Year of the Family.* Fredericton: Queen's Printer for New Brunswick.

Government of Saskatchewan. (1994). *Breaking New Ground in Child Care, International Year of the Family.* Regina: Saskatchewan Social Services.

Martin, S. (1987). *Sharing the Responsibility: Report of the Special Committee on Child Care.* Ottawa: Queen's Printer.

Morisette, Lucie B. (1994). *Starting and Operating a Native Child Day Care Centre.* Chisasibi, Quebec: Anjabowa Daycare Services Centre.

Yeates, M., D. McKenna, C. Warberg, and K. Chandler. (1994). *Administering Early Childhood Settings,* 2nd ed. Don Mills, Ontario: Maxwell Macmillan Canada.

CHAPTER 7

The Economics of the Day-Care System

In this chapter you will:

- define the economics of the day-care system;
- identify the components of an economic perspective;
- examine the relationship between elements in a systemic approach;
- examine the application of a systemic approach to early childhood education;
- define the day-care system.

Advance motivator

Examine the following key terms before reading the chapter. Then, while reading the chapter, try to assign meaning to each one.

economics	advisory committee
financial system	corporation
permit	suprasystem
licence	start-up budget
financial organization	operational budget
open system	fixed costs
closed system	variable costs
board of directors	provincial and territorial grants

An Economic Perspective

Economics is an integral part of society. "We live in a capitalist economic system" where business is considered to be at the centre of the economic system (Heilbroner and Thurow 1994, 11). Business, household income, and the government are institutions that are interdependent and create the economic system. What we produce, what we consume, and what services we provide are all factors of our economic system. From an economic perspective, day cares fall under the category of small businesses. A day care is a service provided to families and has financial obligations.

Economics is a central component of the day-care system. The day-to-day operations of the centre are influenced by the economic or financial aspects of the system. "Early childhood services are becoming a market commodity bought and sold according to principles of market demand and supply" (Culkin, Helburn, and Morris 1990, 9). The economics of a business, a community, or a government include the income and expenses of the operation. It is how the income and the expenses are managed that influences the economy. The economics of one system is often dependent on other economic situations. In a recession, or period with no economic growth, the economy of the day care can be affected if parents lose their jobs and no longer require child-care services.

Historically, the day-care economy was dependent on and driven by charitable organizations. As day care changed to meet the growing needs of families from varying socioeconomic backgrounds, so did its economy. The demand for day-care centres increases each year. The rate of growth of day cares in 1993 was 3.46 percent and in 1994 it was 8.67 percent (Human Resources Development Canada 1994).

•••

Reflection

How does the economic climate affect the demand for day-care services? Explain.

•••

The economic structure of the day-care system is based *on the number of children enrolled, fees, salaries, program costs, grants, and fundraising* (Halpern 1984). The central focus of the budget formulation is associated with the income and expenses within each day care. Because a day care operates on the principles of a small business that provides a service, it must be responsible for managing its finances.

This chapter focuses on the economic and financial structures and examines the expenses and income of both profit and non-profit centres. We discuss licensing, channels of communication, and funding in profit and non-profit centres.

Influence of the Financial System

In some centres the economy is managed by the stakeholders within the system—the parents, director, and educators—**provincial and territorial grants**, and by elements outside the system—subsidies, and fundraising. In other centres the economy is controlled strictly by the owner. Examining the **financial system** of a day care is a complex task. All stakeholders must be knowledgeable about the income and the expenses of the system. Understanding the perspective of the different stakeholders and the complexities of the financial system is pivotal in understanding how and why certain decisions are made. The perspectives of different stakeholders often vary in regards to the economic and financial situations.

For example, all stakeholders want the cook to prepare nutritious food for the children. Most stakeholders want the cook to try and provide these nutritious meals based on economical considerations. They want the cook to be frugal and to organize his or her shopping around the weekly specials available at the supermarkets or to buy in larger quantities in order to save money. These expectations influence the cook's job and may require more preparation time and creative menu planning. Since all stakeholders have the same goal, it is the responsibility of the cook to achieve this goal within the approved budget.

Permits and Licences

The economic structure of all day-care systems begins when a day care receives a **permit** or **licence** from its respective province or territory. While this topic appears to be part of the legal framework of the day care, it is also what designates a day care as a **financial organization** or business.

Our present discussion provides an overview of the initial steps required in order to obtain a licence. Tables 7.1 and 7.2 provide examples of the initial procedures required to obtain a licence in Prince Edward Island and Saskatchewan respectively.

Prince Edward Island

1. Complete an initial application form for a fee of $25.00.

   1.1 The first part of the form requires the name, location, mailing address, and telephone number of the centre.

   1.2 Information on who will operate the facility, whether a private owner or a community or other organization, is required. If it is a community organization, then the application must indicate the name of the organization, the president, and the secretary of the organization. If the application is from a non-community group or organization then the name of the organization, and the name of two officers of that organization must be included.

   1.3 These organizations also must indicate their legal status, i.e., are they a non-profit organization.

   1.4 The application must also include the:
   a) type of services and the hours of operation of the centre
   b) number and ages of the children anticipated by the centre
   c) name of the supervisor or day care's director
   d) name of staff members

---

2. Additional information may be required by the child care facilities board. [The additional information may include a comprehensive business plan and a comprehensive service plan.]

3. Copies of permits and/or reports from specific provincial authorities are required. These might include information related to fire safety, hygiene, or liability insurance coverage.

TABLE 7.1
Summary of Prince Edward Island's Child Care Facilities Act Regulations (EA475/87, pages 2, 11, 12).

Saskatchewan

1. Complete an application form that is supplied by the ministry.

2. Provide a report from the health officer or the municipality that indicates that the facility meets requirements related to:
   - sanitation
   - ventilation
   - lighting
   - general health and safety standards

3. Provide a report outlining the fire safety standards of the facility.

4. Provide a proposed budget.

5. Provide information on the zoning of the property and the facility's location.

6. Corporations and cooperative associations need to provide a copy of the incorporation of the corporation or the association and a copy of the bylaws.

or

A business corporation needs to provide the names and addresses of the shareholders; a partnership needs to provide the names and addresses of the partners.

7. Provide a detailed floor plan of the facility.

TABLE 7.2
Adapted from Government of Saskatchewan, *Child Care Regulations*, September 1992 (pages 5, 6). Used by permission.

The licence and permit application process is similar in most provinces and territories and in all cases is lengthy and requires a remarkable amount of documentation. A licence is essential in order for a day care to become operational. It also enables the majority of centres to access grants and subsidies and to provide essential tax and charitable receipts to parents and other donors.

Open and Closed Systems

The concepts of **open** and **closed systems** were first introduced in Chapter 1. They were discussed in terms of the types of boundaries that day-care systems function within and how relationships and interactions can differ within these boundaries. Whether a system is open or closed in nature has an influence on the economics of the day-care system. An open system is non-profit and involves several stakeholders in the financial decision-making of a centre, whereas a closed system is a profit centre whose financial decisions are usually made by fewer stakeholders with the owner as principle decision-maker.

The centre must also recognize itself as an open or closed system when applying for a licence. In the licence application examples provided in tables 7.1 and 7.2, both Prince Edward Island and Saskatchewan require explicit information on who is seeking to operate or manage the day care. The same is true for other provinces. The terminology used by provinces, however, is often different. Prince Edward Island makes a distinction between private owner and community and group organizations. In Saskatchewan a distinction is made between corporate or cooperative association and business or partnership cooperation. Day cares can fall under two classifications and provincial terms place them into open or closed systems. Table 7.3 lists the terms that describe open and closed systems.

Profit or commercial centres function within the context of what can be described as a closed system, while non-profit centres function primarily within the context of an open system. Our discussion in this chapter examines what this means and identifies the factors that

private owner business partnership corporation	CLOSED SYSTEM (profit)
community organization group organization cooperative association corporate association	OPEN SYSTEM (non-profit)

TABLE 7.3
Terms that describe open and closed day-care systems.

distinguish an open system from a closed system. The terms open and closed should not be equated in any way with the concepts of positive or negative. The channels of communication and the decision-making process are some of the distinguishing factors that help define the nature of the system. The source of and access to funding are key elements in defining whether a particular day-care system is profit or non-profit, closed or open.

Making the Distinction between Profit and Non-Profit Centres

In Canada both profit and non-profit centres are in existence. Our provincial, territorial, and federal governments have made a distinction between non-profit and profit day cares. For example, some provinces only subsidize non-profit day cares for their ongoing operational expenses. This can be considered as a statement of political preference.

For many years now there has been an ongoing debate around the pros and cons of profit and non-profit centres. The issue of profit versus non-profit is an emotionally charged one in many provinces (Christian 1990). It is a debate that often divides the profession (Kagan and Newton 1989). It is sometimes felt that the debate is grounded more in ideology than in fact. The non-profit advocates argue that profit day cares benefit financially from the children attending the day care. They believe that a centre will be of higher quality if all finances remain in the system (ibid.). Advocates of non-profit daycare "argue that, when maximizing profits is the bottom line, the quality of care suffers as corners are cut to ensure continuing profits" (Cooke et al. 1986, 49). They also believe that a greater amount of the centre's financial resources can go toward salaries since profit is not a driving factor in the day care's existence. To meet a bottom line often means to cut costs and salaries.

Those individuals in favour of profit child-care arrangements believe that increased competition will lead to higher standards. "Advocates of for profit care claim that their dependence on parent satisfaction forces them to manage efficiently" (Kagan and Newton 1989, 4). They also believe that there is less red tape in making and achieving decisions (Cooke et al. 1986). Others feel that the issue of profit in centres is really a misnomer (Christian 1990). They believe that the expenses related to the operation of day-care centres are enormous and therefore it would be very difficult to earn a profit.

The question that is often asked is: Has this debate had any impact on the growth of non-profit or profit centres? "In 1968, seventy-five

PHOTO 7.1
Both profit and non-profit centres enjoy versatile, inexpensive equipment such as the parachute.

percent of all daycare spaces were under commercial auspices" (Health and Welfare Canada 1990, 3). By 1979, 50.59 percent of all day-care spaces in Canada were non-profit, the remaining 49.41 percent were for profit. According to a 1990 study, there was a shift whereby 65.76 percent of day-care spaces were non-profit as compared with 34.07 percent for profit (ibid.). This shift continued in 1994, 70.63 percent of day-care spaces were non-profit and 29.37 percent were profit (Human Resources Development Canada 1994). These changes may be indicative of circumstances that prevailed from 1979 to 1990. During this time, many provinces and territories established regulations and standards providing guidelines and resources for parents to organize non-profit centres. In several provinces the new regulations made a monetary provision for start-up grants and operating grants for non-profit centres.

Today, the actual number of profit and non-profit centres vary in the provinces and territories, as shown in Table 7.4.

Profit Centres

Profit centres or commercial centres are owned and operated by individuals, groups, or franchises. In a profit centre the decision-making is more likely to be hierarchical and made by those who are members of the system. This approach is indicative of a closed system structure. The individual owner, group, or franchise has a vested interest. There is an emphasis on functioning in accordance with the mission statement.

In a profit centre that is individually owned there are several structures that can exist for decision-making. A common arrangement is one where the owner of the centre is also the director or administrator of the centre. In this situation the owner/director is responsible for the total operation and makes decisions that reflect the mission statement. This structure can be advantageous as the owner/director works directly with the educators, children, and parents of the centre and would be aware of their needs when he or she makes decisions about the centre.

Interprovincial Comparison of Day Care Centre Spaces by Auspice

Provinces/Territories	Non-Profit	Commercial	Total
Newfoundland	1 027	1 956	2 983
Prince Edward Island	1 371	898	2 269
Nova Scotia	4 067	2 919	6 986
New Brunswick	4 329	3 402	7 731
Quebec	71 728	14 524	86 252
Ontario	97 484	26 626	124 110
Manitoba	10 353	1 223	11 576
Saskatchewan	4 342	67	4 409
Alberta	21 962	36 202	58 164
British Columbia	16 563	4 512	26 075
Northwest Territories	825	48	873
Yukon	548	197	745
National totals	234 599	97 574	332 173

From *Status of Day Care in Canada: Employment Ability and Social Partnership Ability,* Health and Welfare Canada 1994, p. 6. Reproduced with permission of the Minister of Supply and Services Canada, 1996.

TABLE 7.4
Numbers of profit and non-profit day-care centres in Canada.

Situation 1

Budget

The owner/director is responsible for the organization, development, and implementation of the day-care budget. The owner/director knows that the day care could benefit from new tricycles. He or she knows that these will be used during the day and will not be highly visible to the parents. The owner/director is aware that the only way to find funds for these tricycles would be to limit the number of field trips. Wearing an owner's hat he or she is aware that field trips provide positive interactions with parents and are a good marketing tool. Wearing a director's hat he or she is aware that the tricycles will have long-lasting use. Which hat would you wear? On what would you base your decision?

Where the director is not the owner but an employee of the centre, she or he is responsible to the owner. In theory, within these centres, the owner makes the decisions and the director has the responsibility of implementing them. In reality, however, decision-making depends on the particular individuals involved, their relationship with other staff, and the length of time they have been working at the centre. For example, in Situation 2 the owner could consult with the director before asking the director to implement the budget.

Situation 2

Budget

The owner informs the director of the budget. The director has the responsibility of following and implementing the budget according to the guidelines established by the owner. The director has not asked the owner for his or her advice before finalizing the budget. The director knows that they will need to replace several of the tricycles this year and would have liked to reduce the amount of money to be spent on field trips. How would you suggest that the director approach the owner with the request?

The decision-making structure will differ in a franchise system. The owner and director may be one and the same person who is accountable to the franchise's head office. Directives can be imposed upon the owner/director that he or she must implement. The owner/director must maintain standards that are established by the larger system (the franchise) through the mission statement. Often decisions that influence the day-to-day operations and functions of the centre, which influence the educators, children, and parents, are made by the head office. For example, a franchise may require its centres to order all their paper products from a particular supplier. With all franchise centres ordering from the same supplier, the bulk ordering will result in lower prices. The owner/director needs to know the budget guidelines before developing the centre's budget.

....

Situation 3

Budget

The owner contacts the head office for guidelines regarding the budget. The owner then establishes the budget. A franchise might impose a central buying office. The head office requires that the centre buy its tricycles from their central buying office. The cost imposed by this supplier will necessitate limiting the number of field trips for the centre. You know that the tricycles can be purchased second hand at a much better price leaving enough financial resources for field trips. How would you handle this situation?

....

Most provincial and territorial regulations do not require that profit centres have an elected **board of directors**. However most provinces and territories require that profit centres have an **advisory committee**. The guidelines for advisory committees vary. However, their main purpose is to provide parents with a vehicle for sharing and exchanging ideas and expressing concerns with the owner/director of the centre. The initiation of these advisory committees was a conscious effort on the part of the provincial and territorial governments to encourage constructive communication between centres and parents. In addition, in Newfoundland all centres are required to establish an admissions committee, which is responsible for the selection of children to the day care.

Types of Profit Centres

Profit centres are usually located within residential communities and are often referred to as *neighbourhood day cares*. Neighbourhood day cares have certain advantages. They serve parents who either work or live in a particular community and can reduce the amount of travel time for the children. Downtown and industrial locations of profit centres also exist. They usually accommodate parents who work in those areas.

Profit centres come in many models, designs, and sizes. Their physical design and layout vary and reflect the amount of space available, the size of rooms, and the philosophy and goals of the centre. Profit centres either rent or own their facility and can be located in storefronts, old school buildings, or in houses on residential streets. In one city, for example, two day cares are located in the same residential area on neighbouring streets. The centres are linked through a common backyard. The architectural design of the centres resembles the homes in the area and the common backyard blends the centres in with the community. From an economical perspective, the centres share the cost of purchasing equipment for the common outdoor play area.

Non-Profit Centres

A non-profit day care is a **corporation**. One of the fundamental requirements of a non-profit corporation is that they are required to reinvest or keep all profits in the corporation. The majority of provincial and territorial regulations require that non-profit centres have a board of directors. The board of directors operates under the guidelines of the internal bylaws. "The Board of Directors carries out all actions necessary for the accomplishment of the corporation's goals and purposes in compliance with letters patent and by-laws of the corporation" (Morissette 1994, 50). In New Brunswick, for example, all non-profit day cares must have a board with a minimum of five members who are elected at an annual public meeting. Of these five members at least two must be parents of children enrolled in the day-care centre. The organization of boards depends on the guidelines outlined in the provincial and territorial regulations.

Board of Directors

The board of directors is a group of elected individuals who play a significant and important role in the economic well-being of the day-care system. The board of directors meets on a regular basis, usually once a month, to oversee and govern the functioning of a day-care centre. These members are elected to their positions at a centre's annual general meeting (AGM). A day care's board of directors will have an executive and members at large. The executive positions are a chairperson, vice-chairperson, treasurer, secretary, and registrar. Each member of the executive has particular responsibilities. For example, the chairperson and the director are responsible for the preparation of agendas for the meeting. The members at large can be parents, educators, or other stakeholders.

Depending on the size of the centre, the board may have anywhere from six to ten members in total. Voting procedures vary between centres and must be stipulated in the bylaws. The chairperson does not usually have a vote except in instances where there is a tie. The voting rights of the day care's director and educators differ from centre to centre and are stipulated in the centre's bylaws. In some day cares the director and educator participate as full and active members with all voting rights and privileges. At other day cares the educator's role may be strictly that of an observer and reporter of current issues in the day care. All other members and executive of the board of directors have an equal vote in the decisions that are made about day-care fees, salary scales, salary increases, major purchases to the day care, such as large swing sets, or budget allotments for repairs to the facilities.

In a neighbourhood day care the board consists of parents with children attending the centre. They would make up the executive and membership of the board. A neighbourhood centre renting space within a church would be fairly autonomous in its operation. In this case the centre would need only to consult with the church on what would be considered normal tenant/landlord circumstances. A member of the church executive might sit on the centre's board of directors to facilitate the channels of communication between the two systems. On the other hand, a neighbourhood centre within a synagogue usually has to follow certain operational regulations of the synagogue. The day-care centre would be required to follow all holidays and dietary laws associated with the religion. It would, however, have an independent board of directors.

Situation

Day care A was renting space from a church and had been doing so for about five years. During that time, the day care had grown in size, requiring more classroom space. This was easily accommodated by the church.

A problem occurred concerning the outdoor space. The centre had a small outdoor area that was fenced in adjacent to the church parking lot. With the increased number of children, this space was no longer adequate. The only available space was the parking lot.

The day care's board of directors approached the church executive about the possibility of using one section of the parking lot for the children to ride their tricycles.

The church seemed to be empathetic toward the needs of the parents but explained that they needed those parking places for Sunday services. They would allow the day care to put up barriers during the day but they had to be removed at night.

The centre tried this solution for awhile. It did provide the extra space that was needed for the children to move around. However, this area required a tremendous amount of adult supervision on the part of the educators, which created a very stressful situation.

The board of directors went back to the church and explained how they appreciated being allowed to use the extra space but that the educators found it very unsafe. The church board then proposed a solution wherein the day care would have a fence built with two very large gates that could be closed when the day care was in operation and opened for the church members when they needed to use the space.

This situation demonstrates the flow of communication between one system and another—the day care and the church. When the roles of each player and each system are clearly identified, the flow of communication is effective. Problems can be resolved.

A board in a workplace day-care centre will be made up of parents, the director, and at least one or two representatives from the workplace. In this type of system the board of directors and the company strive to meet the needs of the parents as well as those of the company. "The most stable and longest-running employer-supported facilities to date are those that encourage significant involvement on the part of all parties concerned" (Andre and Neave 1992, 49). One of the best illustrations of this is a day care's hours of operation. In a workplace environment, shift work for parents is common. It is extremely important that the centre accommodate these hours. Some hospital day cares operate 24 hours a day to accommodate all the hospital shifts.

There are centres that operate within larger organizations or **suprasystems**. These structures reflect the mission statement of both the centre and the suprasystem. The structure and mandate of a board of directors of a day care within a community centre would again be based on this model. The day care itself would have a board that would be made up of parents using the day care. This board would be responsible to the board of the suprasystem and therefore may not be as autonomous in the decision-making process as some of the other day-care boards. The day care often appoints a representative to the board of the suprasystem who acts as a liaison between the two systems.

Types of Non-Profit Centres

Non-profit centres are located in neighbourhood centres, community-based centres (which are day cares within suprasystems), churches or synagogues, workplace day cares, in colleges, universities, hospitals, and companies. Some provinces and territories have municipal child-care centres. When a day care is part of a suprasystem, both the day care and the suprasystem can benefit from the situation. For example, churches and similar institutions do not pay municipal taxes on the land that they own. In order to keep this status they can only rent space to non-profit corporations. If they were to rent space to a for profit business, they would then be required to pay taxes on that portion of their property. The money from non-profit rentals is put back into the facility to help keep it in good condition.

Components of the Budget

Regardless of whether a centre is profit or non-profit, it operates within a budget. The first budget that a centre develops is a **start-up budget**. This is a budget that is only done once to determine the costs necessary to set up or start the day care. An **operational budget** is a budget that is done on an annual basis to determine the income and expenses of the centre. The development of a day-care budget includes the determination of the fees, the anticipated enrolment, and the anticipated costs. There are both **fixed costs** and **variable costs**. Fixed costs are determined for the year and do not fluctuate—the rent is a good example of a fixed cost. Variable costs relate to those items with costs that can fluctuate during the budget period—a good example of this is food costs. Field trips and the amount of money allocated for this type of expense can be increased or decreased, depending on the funding available. The budget process involves the projection of income and expenses.

Income

Day cares receive their income and funding from different sources: parent fees, subsidies, grants, fundraising, and donations. Sources of and access to grant funding and subsidies vary across Canada in relation to profit and non-profit day cares, and it is these sources that define how a day care can deal with its surplus income. For example, a non-profit centre is mandated to reinvest or leave its funds within the day-care system. In other words, if at the end of a fiscal (financial) year the centre has a surplus, it can leave the money in the budget as operating expenses for the upcoming fiscal year. Such a decision might allow the centre not to increase the fees, the board of directors may choose to spend the money in a variety of ways. They might decide to purchase new equipment, increase the educators' salaries, or complete some renovations. At a time when sources of funding are being reduced and abolished, a goal of all day-care centres is to manage their income efficiently and effectively.

···

Situation

The board of directors at the Magic Day Care were very happy with the educators at the centre and wanted to increase salaries to reflect a recognition and appreciation of their work.

They had agreed to increase the day-care fees to help cover some of the costs of the increase in salaries.

The afternoon of the meeting, the day care's furnace died. The result was that the centre needed to purchase a new furnace. With this unexpected cost, the board was forced to decrease the amount of the projected salary increase.

The board had to make a very difficult decision.

···

Parent Fees

The process for determining parent fees is based on the organizational structure of the day-care system. A day care's fees are established by the board of directors in a non-profit centre and by the owner in a profit centre. However, some provinces and territories set a maximum daily fee that profit and non-profit centres must not exceed. For example, in Manitoba in 1993 the maximum daily fee per child in a day-care centre was $16 per day.

Table 7.5. provides an overview of the average weekly fees charged to parents in 1995 for children attending day care on a full-time basis. These fees differ slightly for day cares in an urban or rural area.

Province/Territory	Weekly fee
Alberta	$85
British Columbia	$96
Manitoba	$88
New Brunswick	$74
Newfoundland	$86
Northwest Territories	$129
Nova Scotia	$95
Ontario	$137
Prince Edward Island	$90
Quebec	$102
Saskatchewan	$87
Yukon	$110

TABLE 7.5
Average weekly fees of day-care centres by province and territory in 1995.

All centres, whether non-profit or profit, rely heavily on the parents' fees as their major source of income. In reality, parent fees do not cover the full cost of operating a day-care centre. These fees usually make up about 80 percent of the total day-care budget in a non-profit centre and up to 100 percent in a profit day care.

Most centres have a fee policy that outlines:

• when the fees are to be paid,

• deduction for sick days,

- deduction for vacation time, and

- reduced-fee payments.

When the fees are to be paid varies from one centre to another. Fees can be paid on a weekly or monthly basis. They are usually paid in advance. Many centres require that post-dated cheques be submitted either bi-annually or annually.

Deduction for sick days differs extensively throughout the day-care system. Some centres do not require parents to pay for the days when the children are sick and do not come to the centre. Others require payment whether the child is there or not.

Deduction for vacation time in some centres is deducted from the cost of the fees if the centre knows in advance when the child will be away. Other centres only allow parents to deduct vacation time during the summer months.

Reduced-fee payments are offered by most day-care centres to parents for their second and third child attending the centre. Many centres provide reduced fees to educators who have their children attending the day care. Some centres offer a reduced fee to a select number of parents who are in need of financial aid.

Financial Aid

Many parents, depending on their personal income, may be eligible to receive financial aid to help defray the cost of child care. Financial aid, or subsidy is organized by the provincial and territorial governments, which determine the net income level at which parents will be subsidized and the amount per day of that subsidy. This figure also depends on how many adults and children are in the family.

In Quebec the maximum net income depends on the makeup of the family. For example, a single-parent family with only one child with a net income of $20,000 per year would receive $6.67 per day in subsidy. A family with two adults, two children in day care, and a net income of $23,000 would receive $19.74 per day in subsidy. As of March 1994, in New Brunswick, families with a net income of less than $15,000 per year were entitled to a maximum day-care subsidy of $17 per day for infants and $15 per day for preschool-age children. New Brunswick projected that approximately 1,070 families would use the available subsidy in 1995.

Provincial and Territorial Grants

Provinces and territories that provide direct grants to centres recognize that day cares need to be kept affordable for parents. Direct grants help keep the parent fees lower. The dollar amounts of grants differ because they depend on the age group of the children. Grants for infants and toddlers are usually higher, reflecting the additional costs incurred in these types of services.

Grants from the provincial and territorial governments for non-profit and profit centres are not standardized throughout the country. Sometimes licensing is the only criteria required for day cares to receive grants. The size of the grants varies extensively as well. In Newfoundland the government provides a one-time grant of $1,000 upon licensing. Manitoba provides a variety of grants with an annual operating grant of $1,846. New Brunswick has reduced its day-care grants considerably. In April 1994 it eliminated its start-up grants to workplace centres and reduced the annual operating grants by 50 percent. It plans to eliminate these grants in its 1995–96 budget. Quebec also put a freeze on the granting of new permits in its 1994–95 budget and has not provided funding for new non-profit centres since April 1994.

On December 13, 1995, the Canadian government announced a grant program that would provide up to $630 million to day cares across the country. To be eligible for the grant, provinces and territories will have to match funds dollar for dollar. It will be interesting to see how this effects the current day-care situation in Canada.

Table 7.6 provides a sample of some of the grants that exist within the provinces and territories.

Operating grant	Annual money based on a predetermined formula
Emergency repair grant	In case of an emergency, money is available to the day care.
Equipment grant	This is often for centres that have been in operation and need to replace equipment.
Infant grants	Some provinces offer additional money to those centres that operate an infant room.
Maintenance grant	This grant assists in the maintenance of the centre.
Special Needs grant	These grants are available to centres that have children with special needs in attendance.
Start-up grants	These grants are available for the establishment of new centres.
Salary enhancement grant	This grant goes directly to educators to improve salaries.
Training grants	These grants are available for educators to upgrade their training.

TABLE 7.6
Sample provincial and territorial grants.

Fundraising and Other Sources of Income

Centres in Canada rely heavily on fundraising as a valuable source of income. Depending on the types of grant a centre receives, some may have a greater need to fundraise than others. Fundraising involves a tremendous amount of work by the parents and the day care's staff. Parents and staff alike realize the advantages and benefits of fundraising. This endeavour helps keep the day care's fees affordable and often provides salary enhancements for the staff. There is probably no other profession where workers fundraise to enhance their salaries.

Centres have become very creative in the types of fundraising events that they organize. Ideas include raffle tickets, fairs, spaghetti dinners, and garage sales. Other sources of income include donations. Nova Scotia provides information to centres on how to request donations from various organizations. The Canadian Centre for Philanthropy will do computer searches to locate those organizations that donate to day-care centres.

Expenses

Salaries

Salaries are by far the largest expense that day-care centres incur. Seventy to eighty percent of the budget goes to the educators' salaries. The majority of centres have implemented salary scales that reflect the educators' training, educational background, and years of experience in the field of early childhood. Table 7.7 provides the average hourly rate, based on 1995 figures, in the provinces and territories.

The range of salaries is interesting and reflects a profession that is still growing and developing. It is difficult to make comparisons across provinces and territories as the cost of living varies and salary requirements are different.

Province/Territory	Hourly rate
Alberta	$6.76
British Columbia	$8.94
Manitoba	$9.29
New Brunswick	$6.19
Newfoundland	$6.03
Northwest Territories	$11.34
Nova Scotia	$7.64
Ontario	$11.51
Prince Edward Island	$7.25
Quebec	$10.25
Saskatchewan	$7.52
Yukon	$9.58

TABLE 7.7
The average hourly rate for day-care workers in the provinces and territories. Rates are based on 1995 figures.

Additional Expenses

Additional expenses for a day care are the children's food and equipment, the programming costs, the rent or mortgage payments, and maintenance costs of the facility. The sample operational budget provided in Table 7.8 highlights the expenses of a day-care centre. This budget is designed for a day-care centre with forty-five children, ten infants and thirty-five children, between the ages of 18 months and 5 years. There are eight full-time educators, a director, a part-time secretary, and a cook.

Income	1995–96
Fees	$213,840
Operational Grant	$65,776
Infant Grant	$30,000
Special Needs Grant	$5,000
Fundraising	$4,000
Donations	nil
Total	$318,106

Expenses	1995–96
Salaries	$224,000
Professional Development	$4,200
Food	$28,500
Rent	$24,000
Equipment	$5,000
Office Supplies	$1,200
Office Expenses	$1,500
Maintenance Contract and Supplies	$8,000
Insurance	$3,200
Equipment	$6,000
Art Supplies	$3,000
Other	$4,500
Total	$313.100

TABLE 7.8
A sample operating budget of a day-care centre listing its income and
expenses.

Regardless of whether a centre is for profit or not, it will rely on some form of fundraising to supplement its budget. In both instances it is common practice to put the money back into the day care to enhance facilities or purchase materials and equipment. In a non-profit centre the money may also be used for salary enhancement.

In summary, understanding the economic structure of the day-care system is important. The income, expenses, and budget design significantly influence the decisions that the centres make. For example, far too often day-care centres are forced to make unfavourable decisions that are purely a result of financial constraints. We may not like the decisions that are made, but we can better understand why they are made when we understand the economic factors behind the decision.

Summary

- Economics of the day care refer to the expenses and income of the centre.

- All centres, whether profit or non-profit, need to have a provincial or territorial licence in order to operate legally.

- Each province or territory has its own licensing procedures.

- Profit centres are referred to as a closed system.

- Non-profit centres are referred to as an open system.

- Non-profit day cares have a board of directors.

- Profit day cares generally have an advisory committee.

- A day care's funds come from a variety of sources (fees, subsidies, grants, fundraising, and donations).

Questions and Activities for Further Reflection

1. What grants and subsidies does your province or territory offer?

2. How would you feel about helping the centre where you work fundraise in an effort to increase your salary?

3. Do you feel that parents should be paying the full cost of child care?

Self-Test

Discuss the organizational and economic structure of a profit centre versus a non-profit centre. Describe the funding of each type of centre.

References

Andre, Therese, and Cheryl Neave. (1992). *The Complete Canadian Day Care Guide.* Toronto: McGraw-Hill Ryerson.

Christian, C. (1990). "Going Non-Profit in the Yukon." *Vision,* Number 11: October.

Cooke, D., J. London, R. Edward, and R. Rose-Lizee. (1986). *Report of the Task Force on Child Care.* Ottawa: Status of Women Canada.

Culkin, M.L., S.W. Helburn, and J.R. Morris. (1990). "Current Price Versus Full Cost: An Economic Perspective." In *Reaching the Full Cost of Quality in Early Childhood Programs,* ed. Barbara Willer. Washington, D.C.: National Association for the Education of Young Children.

Government of Prince Edward Island. (1987). *Prince Edward Island's Child Care Facilities Act Regulations.* R.S.P.E.I. Cap. C-5. Charlottetown: Acting Queen's Printer.

Government of Saskatchewan. (1990). *The Child Care Regulations 948/90.* Cap. C-7.3 REG.1 Section 27. Regina: Saskatchewan Social Services.

Halpern, R. (1984). "Surviving the Competition: Economic Skills and Arguments for Program Directors." In *Administering Programs for Young Children,* ed. Janet Brown. Washington, D.C.: National Association for the Education of Young Children.

Health and Welfare Canada. (1990). *Status of Day Care in Canada.* Ottawa: Health and Welfare Canada, National Child Care Information Centre.

Heilbroner, Robert, and Lester Thurow. (1994). *Economics Explained.* New York: Touchstone.

Human Resources Development Canada. (1994). *Status of Day Care in Canada.* Ottawa: Employability and Social Partnerships Division, Department of Human Resources Development.

Kagan, S.L., and J.W. Newton. (1989). "For-Profit and Nonprofit Child Care: Similarities and Differences." *Young Children:* 4–10.

Morissette, Lucie B. (1994). *Starting and Operating a Native Child Day Care Centre.* Chisasibi, Quebec: Anjabowa Daycare Services Centre.

CHAPTER 8

Employment

In this chapter you will:

- know what to look for in an advertisement for the position of early childhood educator;
- learn to design your own curriculum vitae;
- examine the value and implication of a job description;
- describe the types of educator positions that exist in a day-care system;
- identify different workloads in a day care;
- learn about the value of record keeping in a day care;
- identify various educator benefits.

Advance motivator

Examine the following key terms before reading the chapter. Then, while reading the chapter, try to assign meaning to each one.

résumé	shifts
curriculum vitae	peak hours
cover letter	record keeping
interview	benefits
contract	salary scales
job description	

Seeking Employment

Knowledge of the provincial and territorial regulations and an understanding of the economic framework of day cares will assist you in your search for employment. Finding employment is a concern for all who are training to be educators in the field of early childhood. Where do you start and how do you prepare yourself?

Job Advertisements

Short advertisements for positions in early childhood education can be found in local newspapers and professional magazines and are posted at colleges and placement services. These advertisements provide minimal information about the available positions and the desired qualifications. Job postings tend to include information concerning the starting date, the age group that the position is for, and perhaps the starting salary. A job posting provides information related to whether there is full-time or part-time employment available. Table 8.1 gives an example of what an advertisement for an early childhood educator might stipulate in terms of qualifications. Notice that in this sample a diploma and bachelor's degree are considered to have more weight than a certificate or attestation. This explains the additional years of experience required with the certificate or attestation.

Day-care educators required to start immediately. We have an opening for one full-time and one part-time position.

Qualifications: Must have diploma or bachelor's degree in early childhood education, or certificate or attestation in early childhood education plus three years of experience.

T A B L E 8 . 1
Sample job advertisement stipulating required educator qualifications.

An effective way to respond to an advertisement is by mailing or sending a fax of your **résumé** or **curriculum vitae** to the prospective employer.

Job Application

Résumé or Curriculum Vitae

A few months before completing your early childhood training program you should prepare a professional curriculum vitae (CV) or résumé. (In this book we use the terms résumé and curriculum vitae (CV) interchangeably.) Then keep this document up-to-date throughout your professional career.

A résumé is a summary of an individual's educational background, work experience (for example, summer jobs, fieldwork placements), volunteer projects, and special achievements. It outlines an individual's professional history for a potential employer. Your résumé is a good place to record your professionally related accomplishments. Any information you give does provide a bias whether favourable or not. So include only and all the information that you want people to know.

There are two points to keep in mind when preparing your CV.

- Keep your résumé clear, concise, and truthful.

- Remember that one résumé may not be suitable for all job applications. Although the basic information stays the same, you may choose to highlight different aspects of your accomplishments for different jobs.

Table 8.2 provides a guideline for you to use in creating your own CV. Fill in the personal details and you will be well on your way to having a completed résumé.

YOUR FULL NAME

FULL MAILING ADDRESS

TELEPHONE NUMBER WITH AREA CODE

- Specialized areas of interest (these should be written out as short phrases of one or two words).

- Educational background (written in reverse chronological order).

- Work and work-related experience (written in reverse chronological order).

- Volunteer positions that you have held.

- Relevant memberships and special accomplishments that will set you apart from other applicants.

TABLE 8.2
Guidelines for a personalized CV.

Information such as your date of birth, marital or religious status is not required by law. This information is protected by the Privacy Act and need not be included in a curriculum vitae. It is common practice today to omit items that imply a religious affiliation. However, we believe that this is an individual choice. Base your decision on how much you want a potential employer to know. Provide social insurance numbers only once you are hired. This is because in our modern age of information a social insurance number can provide a potential employer with a great deal of information about you.

Cover Letter

A **cover letter** is used to accompany all applications and it is specifically tailored to the particular job for which you are applying. There are some basic guidelines you can follow in designing a cover letter. Generally, begin by paraphrasing what the job requires.

- I am writing for the position of...

Then, highlight the points in your CV that reflect the skills being sought after. For example:

- My college training in the field of ... qualifies me for the job. I feel I would be an asset to your centre because...

Summarize by saying:

- I look forward to setting up an interview with you at your earliest convenience.

Keep the following points in mind when you write a cover letter. Do not state anything more than once. Cover letters should be short, clear, and concise. Mention that you are available and willing to travel. Include your return address and telephone number on the cover letter, although it is already on the CV. This makes it convenient for the reader to contact you. You want to make it easy for the person who is evaluating and eliminating many candidates. Allow one week for the letter to arrive and be read. Then, follow up the application with a phone call to verify that the potential employer is in receipt of your CV. Ask when you can expect to hear from them regarding your application.

References

It is common for potential employers to ask you to supply two to three references. These references do not need to be provided as a part of your application, unless specifically requested in the advertisement. You should bring references with you to the **interview**. Before sending in your application or going to the interviews, be certain that you have contacted the people you plan to use for reference purposes. It is important that you receive their permission to give out their names and phone numbers. Use professional references rather than personal references. Professional references can include previous employers, teachers, or supervisors.

As a recent graduate include at least one reference from a cooperating educator, teacher, or professor. Your supervisor is the teacher that knows your practical work best. If you have any work experience, provide one reference from a previous employer.

Interview

You have now responded to an advertisement for the position of educator in a day care. Your CV has been read and you are invited for an interview. Here are a few tips about the interview:

- be punctual,

- present yourself confidently and politely,

- dress appropriately, and

- prepare some questions.

Be punctual. If the day care is in a location that you are unfamiliar with, it is advisable to go the evening before to find out how much time you will need to get there. Arriving late with the excuse "I got lost" does not present a professional or positive image.

Present yourself confidently and politely. Look directly at the individual who is speaking to you. When responding, focus first on the individual asking the question and then on the other people who may be present in the room. Take time to think about your answers.

Dress appropriately. Keep in mind that your appearance is the first impression you make. Someone who shows up for an interview dishevelled gives the impression that this is the type of classroom they will have. Appropriate dress includes clean clothes. You could wear slacks or a skirt (for women), either is acceptable. Avoid jeans and leggings for interview purposes. A neat shirt or sweater is appropriate. Hair should be brushed neatly or tied back.

Prepare some questions. Before going for the interview, think of some questions that you might like to ask about the job. Write these questions on a piece of paper so that you do not forget them.

TOOL

Here are some questions you can use in your interview.

1. What will the educator/child ratio be for this position?

2. Do the hours for this position remain consistent or do educators rotate their shifts?

3. Is there a board of directors at this centre?

4. What types of benefits are available to the educators?

The individual responsible for carrying out the interview may be different in a profit centre than in a non-profit centre. In a non-profit centre the responsibility for hiring is usually part of the mandate of the day care's board of directors. Typically, the board of directors forms a subcommittee that is responsible for hiring the director and the educators. This subcommittee, along with the day-care centre's director, reviews all candidates for the available position. The initial interview usually consists of the subcommittee, the director, and the candidate. Sometimes a few candidates are asked to spend some time at the centre with the children. This situation provides the director with the opportunity to observe the candidates' interactions with the children. It also helps candidates assess whether this is a suitable place of employment for their needs and beliefs.

Once the subcommittee has made a decision about which candidate to hire, they will present this information at a meeting of the board of directors for final approval. Then, one member from the subcommittee, not necessarily the director, will contact the candidate to offer him or her the position of employment. This is when a **contract** will be offered.

In some non-profit centres the responsibility for hiring educators is delegated solely to the director. When this is the case, hiring and staff supervision fall under the director's work mandate as outlined by the board of directors. The director keeps the board informed of the interviews and the candidates and makes recommendations directly to the board.

The interview process in the profit centre is similar to that of the non-profit centre. Again, the process reflects the internal structure of the particular system. In the case where the director is also the owner, this person alone will be responsible for the hiring process. In a situation where the owner is not the director, several scenarios might unfold. The owner may do all the hiring, or the owner and the director may work together to do the hiring, or the director may do an initial screening and then present only the finalists to the owner who may make the final decision.

We can see the systemic nature of day care in the interview and hiring process, which is designed to meet the structure of a particular day-care centre. Each day care is a self-contained system that has common elements with other day cares.

Job Description

A **job description** in any field helps define and provide an outline of the general tasks and responsibilities that an employee will be asked to carry out. In the field of early childhood education, the job description is usually defined by the centre's owner or board of directors. An early childhood educator's job description often reflects the complexity and variety of the job.

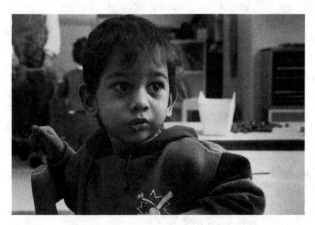

Photo 8.1
Children represent an important part of the clientele and educators are hired to meet their needs.

Job descriptions vary from centre to centre. Each day care's job description, like other day-care documents, relates to the centre's mission statement. The job description effects the day-to-day functions of the educator within the context of the specific day care for which it is written. The dynamic nature of the day-care system suggests that the job description will endure amendments and changes over time to reflect developments in the field of early childhood education and the changing needs of a particular centre. The unique nature of each centre's job description is influenced by the clientele that the day care serves, the location of the day care, and the resulting specificity of the mission statement. A comparison of job descriptions in the field of early childhood education will reveal both similarities and differences.

It is important for a centre to develop a job description that is accurate and complete (Taylor 1989). Job descriptions that are vague and misleading often lead to confusion. As a potential educator within a centre, you should take the responsibility of requesting a complete and well-articulated job description before accepting a position at a particular centre. You have a right to know what the work entails and what your responsibilities will be. Of course, you should retain a degree of flexibility, keeping in mind that job descriptions can change over time. It is useful to record any changes and amendments to the job description. This helps avoid potential misunderstandings.

The ability to translate the job description into its day-to-day tasks is important. When you are hired to work in a day care, it becomes your job to translate the job description from paper to action. Table 8.3 represents a sample job description. It delineates the work expected of you as an employee. It details what is involved regarding the care and education of the children that will be entrusted to you. In this example the job description includes a mandate that you continue to participate in activities that will further your professional growth and development. This particular addition to the job description indicates that this day-care centre wants its staff to remain informed about current changes and developments in the field of early childhood education.

Types of Educator Positions and Workloads

There are several positions within any day care. The combination of positions that any day care may rely on also can vary. You may be hired for one of a variety of positions in the day care, such as assis-

GENERAL RESPONSIBILITIES OF A
DAY-CARE EDUCATOR:

- Work effectively with other members of the system; that is, the director, other educators, and support staff.

- Develop a curriculum in collaboration with the director and other educators. This curriculum should be indicative of the centres mission statement.

- Design and plan opportunities and activities that are considerate of the children's interests and developmental level.

- Provide an environment that is safe and secure.

- Supervise the children both indoors and outdoors and know where each child is at all times.

- Plan and organize routines and transitions in harmony with other members of the centre.

- Communicate with parents regarding the needs and interests of their children.

- Participate in professional development sessions/workshops.

- Keep an inventory of materials and equipment in your room.

TABLE 8.3
Sample job description for an educator in a day-care centre.

tant educator, educator, head educator, or, eventually, director. There are also different work schedules and shifts that may be applicable to your situation. It is important to be familiar with these positions as they affect the day-to-day routines and responsibilities. Table 8.4 provides an overview of four different staffing models that might exist in any centre.

Employees of a day care can work a variety of hours and **shifts**. With a majority of day cares open at least ten hours a day, shifts are established to cover these hours. The term shift is used to describe

model one	model two	model three	model four
director	director	director	director
head educator	assistant director	educators	educators
educators	educators	assistant educators	

TABLE 8.4 Types and combinations of positions in a day-care centre.

blocks of time that employees are expected to work. Shifts vary from one centre to another. They may be staggered in some centres, which means that one shift may start at 7:00 a.m. and run for eight hours, while another starts at 9:00 a.m. and also runs for eight hours. This staggering enables day cares to have more staff on duty during **peak hours**. We discussed peak hours in Chapter 3 in relation to the centre's orientation. As you may recall, peak hours refer to the hours of the day where the greatest number of children are attending on a regular basis. Peak hours may vary from centre to centre. As an educator in the day care, the peak hours of the centre can influence the type of shift that you may be required to work. For example, in a university- or college-based centre, peak hours tend to begin as late as 10:00 a.m., while in a hospital day care peak hours tend to start at 8:00 a.m.

A day-care centre bases its decisions about shifts on the needs of the centre. Usually, the director is responsible for making these decisions. Here is a description of several commonly used combinations of shifts.

- One educator works alone with one group of children for an eight-hour block of time. Children who stay longer than eight hours join another group at the end of the day.

- Team teaching: One or two educators work with the same group of children. One educator comes in at 7:00 a.m. as described earlier. This educator leaves at 3:00 p.m. The second educator comes in at 10:00 a.m. and leaves at 6:00 p.m. In this way the entire day is covered. Educators can keep this schedule for the whole year or rotate early and late shifts on a weekly basis.

- Shift work: Early morning shift, a designated educator(s) opens the day care. All children who arrive early are organized in a family grouping for the beginning of the day. At 9:00 a.m., when the other educators arrive, the children switch to a same-age grouping. At 5:00 p.m. all but one or two educators leave. Children are regrouped into a family grouping for the remainder of the day.

- Shift work: Late shift—closing the centre. The designated educator(s) begins later in the day working with a single-age group of children. At the end of the day the children are placed in a family grouping as in the above example. The designated educator(s) works with them until closing. One educator is designated to close the day care and ensure that all windows and doors are properly locked.

- Half-day shift: This could be a morning or an afternoon shift.

- Mid-day shift: This goes from mid-morning to mid-afternoon. The purpose of this is to maximize supervision during the hours of the day when there is the largest group of children present and awake.

Some centres combine a few of these positions and shifts. Many centres have educators rotate their shifts so that all the educators have an opportunity to greet the parents in the morning and say goodbye to them in the evening.

Situation

A day-care centre has forty children who are 2 years to 5 years of age. There are three classrooms with ten children in the youngest room and sixteen children in the 5-year-old's room. Each room operates with three educators. One educator works all day while the other two educators work a half day each. Their shifts overlap at lunch time. What are the advantages to this type of shift work for the educators?

. . . .

Your position within a day-care system and the shift that you work will influence your responsibilities and the specifics of your job description. The type of centre and the age group of the children also influence your role as an educator. As a student you can get the most out of your experience by varying your schedule and shift. We recognize that as a student you are registered in courses at your college or university and this ideal situation may not always be possible.

Record Keeping

An important part of a professional early childhood educator's job is to have a useful system of **record keeping**. Be sure that the time spent in record keeping is not overwhelming. It should not take away from your interactions with the children. Records are kept about child information, toy and materials inventory, attendance, child observations, curriculum planning, maintenance, and professional development.

An important factor in maintaining records is to consider where these records will be kept. These records are usually kept in a file drawer in the centre's office, but it is worthwhile having a backup copy of this vital information. These could be stored in a place that is easily accessible. This information should be kept in the strictest confidence.

Child information should include family data, health information for each child, and the parents' emergency phone numbers. Health information should include information about allergies and the phone number of the child's pediatrician.

....

Reflection

What information do you feel is essential to record as a part of your recordkeeping. Generate a list and compare it with a colleague's list. Keep the list detailed enough to be of value and short enough not to be burdensome.

....

Inventory is another record that should be maintained. An inventory is a list. An inventory of toys and materials is usually carried out on an annual basis. There should be a record of each toy in the classroom and of all books, dramatic play materials, and art supplies. At the end of each year it is useful to verify the condition of these materials to identify what needs to be repaired, replaced, or gotten rid of. Some supplies need to be checked more than once a year. These include consumable materials such as paint, plasticine, crayons, and paper. Table 8.5 provides a sample inventory checklist that can be used for general purposes.

This list is meant as a sample and should be adjusted to meet the particular needs of your day care centre. As a pre-service educator you might find it useful to do a material inventory. As an educator it is part of your job description to maintain and update the inventory. Inventories can be more detailed by making a specific information card for each item. For example, it is wise to keep an information card for each board game, listing the quantity on hand, the last known vendor (in case replacement is needed), and the storage location. It is often difficult to remember where we keep all the materials unless we update our storage location inventory.

Salaries and Benefits

In order to attain professional recognition in the field of early childhood education, educators should be able to work in environments that respect and recognize them as professionals. Salaries and **benefits** provide one source of recognition. You have a right to know what your salary and benefits will be before starting the job. Satisfaction in this area will provide positive motivation to stay with the job.

___ manipulative tabletop toys

   ___ peg boards

   ___ lace-up toys

   ___ puzzles

   ___ plasticine

___ gross motor manipulatives

   ___ balls

   ___ hoops

   ___ bean bags

   ___ music area

   ___ record player/cd player or tape recorder

___ push/pull toys

___ art materials

   ___ paper

   ___ finger paints

   ___ easels

___ instruments such as tambourines, shakers, and xylophones

   ___ sound boards

___ planting area

___ computer

___ building blocks

   ___ wooden

   ___ plastic

   ___ floor size

   ___ tabletop size

___ books

   ___ paint brushes of different sizes

___ dramatic play area

   ___ dress-up clothes and other props

___ woodworking or carpentry area

TABLE 8.5
Sample inventory checklist for toys and materials.

Salaries

Research by the Canadian Child Care Federation and the Canadian Day Care Advocacy Association (1992) found that the national average salary varied. Salaries in the municipal centres were highest at $13.88 per hour. This compared to salaries of $10.07 per hour for educators working in non-profit centres and an average rate of $8.07

per hour for profit or commercial centres. It should also be noted that salaries vary from province to province and in the territories.

Educators begin working in centres with varying degrees of training. Many early childhood professionals believe that salaries should reflect training. In other words, centres should develop **salary scales** that represent the type of education or training and experience that the educator has.

Salary scales are advantageous in two ways: they recognize the training accomplishments and they create an incentive for educators to continue their training because they know it will be recognized. Having salaries that reflect training is a step toward quality child care. Table 8.6 provides an example of how day cares can implement a sliding salary scale based on an educator's years of experience and training.

Years of experience	Training			
	certificate	diploma	bachelor's degree	master's degree
1 year	$7.25	$8.25	$9.50	$11.00
2 years	$7.97	$9.07	$10.45	$12.10
2–3 years	$8.60	$9.61	$11.07	$13.58
3–4 years	$9.11	$10.18	$11.73	$14.25
4–5 years	$9.56	$10.68	$12.31	$14.96

Note: Many centres also add a cost of living percentage to the figures in the salary scale.

TABLE 8.6
Sample of a sliding salary scale based on experience and training.

Centres can reduce educator turnover by providing comparable salaries. It is the responsibility of the stakeholders to be up-to-date on educators' salaries within their community and province or territory. Salaries paid to educators also must reflect the market value. Low educator turnover is an important criterion for quality, which will be discussed in the next chapter.

Traditionally, early childhood professionals are highly valued, have an enormous responsibility, and are underpaid. "Given the tremendous responsibility inherent in the job, child care advocates long have suspected that child care staff have been subsidizing the entire child care system through low wages and few benefits" (Canadian Child Care Federation and the Canadian Day Care Advocacy Association 1992, xvii).

Benefits

Benefits are important features. In some cases they are as important as salaries. Educators should be aware of what benefits exist in other centres. Centres should try and offer comparable benefits. Benefits are truly an individual and personal concern. All educators will need to consider for themselves those benefits that they feel are most important. Some common benefits are:

- paid sick days
- medical plan
- dental plan
- disability insurance
- professional development funds

- professional days
- varied work schedules
- paid time for planning
- staff facilities
- vacation time

....

Reflection

What other benefits can you think of? Which benefits are important to you?

....

You will need to closely examine salary and benefits before you accept a position. Accepting a position that you feel meets your needs will make you more likely to stay on the job. You are more likely to have a sense of job satisfaction.

Situation

Irene was finishing off her final early childhood courses and was ready to graduate. She had been doing her fieldwork at a centre very close to her home and had been fairly happy with her experience. A week before her fieldwork was over, the director offered her a position with the toddlers. The educator in the toddler room had left unexpectedly and the centre needed a replacement very quickly. Irene was very unsure as to what to do, she had never worked with toddlers before and was uncertain if she would enjoy that position. The other problem was that the director needed to know Irene's decision by the end of the week. Feeling very flattered that she had been asked to take this position, Irene decided to accept it.

What Irene had not done was to investigate the salaries and benefits of the centre in comparison with other centres in the area. Within a month Irene realized that most of her friends had found positions in day-care centres and were earning more money.

Two months after she had begun her position, Irene's friend told her about a position in her centre. Irene was very torn between applying for the new position that would pay a higher salary and staying with the children who had come to know and trust her.

What would you do in a situation like this? If Irene decides to take the second position then the first centre continues its trend of high staff turnover. What is her responsibility to herself and to the children with whom she is working?

Work Environment

Salaries and benefits are an important part of the job. They may be what initially attracts an educator to a particular centre. However, once employed the work environment is also extremely important. Components of a good work environment are friendly staff, a staff room or lounge stocked with books to facilitate planning, and access to a phone when needed.

Educators are expected to provide appropriate programming for the children and they need to have the material and resources to fulfil this responsibility. Philips, Howes, and Whitebook (1991) found a correlation between educators who were not satisfied with their job and their failure to provide appropriate programming.

....

Situation

Frank had been working at the day-care centre for four years and was finding that his job was becoming more difficult each year. In the first two years at the centre the educators were given time and salary for program planning. With budget cutbacks in the last two years, there were no longer resources for planning and preparing the programming. During the same period the educator/child ratios increased.

With this change in the work environment, Frank was finding it very difficult to motivate himself to plan and program in the same fashion that she had in the past.

This situation has notable consequences for the quality of care in that day-care environment. The feelings of the educators and the consequences of monetary cutbacks must be discussed by all stakeholders so that everyone is aware of the repercussions of certain decisions. As more and more centres are faced with monetary issues, we will all be expected to do more with less. This may give all of us the opportunity to ensure open communication, to brainstorm, and to be creative in the way we work with less resources.

....

The quality of your work environment is important to the maintenance of high standards in the field of early childhood education. There are many factors that influence quality standards in day care. These are addressed in detail in the next chapter.

Summary

- A job description provides a framework that outlines the responsibilities of an employee.

- The main positions within a day care are the director, the assistant director, the educators, and the assistant educators.

- Shifts refer to the hours of a day that an individual works.

- A résumé or curriculum vitae (CV) is a summary of educational and professional experience.

- Early childhood educators require salaries and benefits that value and reflect their professional status.

- The educators' work environment is essential to the attainment of high-quality early childhood education.

Questions and Activities for Further Reflection

1. Write a letter of application for a job as an educator with the age group with which you would like to work.

2. Collect five advertisements from your local paper for the position of educator. Identify the similarities and differences in each.

3. Get together with a colleague. Have them pick out one job advertisement from your collection. Ask them to interview you for that position. What have you learned from the experience of being interviewed?

4. Once you complete your training in one province or territory, find out to what extent your qualifications are recognized in another province or territory. Some of the addresses provided in Chapter 10 will be useful.

Self-Test

Write a curriculum vitae. Compare it with the sample provided in this chapter. On a separate sheet of paper list the records that you will be responsible to keep as an educator.

R e f e r e n c e s

Canadian Child Care Federation/Canadian Day Care Advocacy Association. (1992). *Caring for a Living*. Ottawa: Canadian Child Care Federation.

Phillips, D., C. Howes, and M. Whitebook. (1991). Child Care as an Adult Work Environment. *Journal of Social Issues,* 47(2):49–70.

Taylor, Barbara. (1989). *Early Childhood Program Management: People and Procedures.* Columbus, Ohio: Merrill Publishing Company.

PART IV

Quality Counts

The objective of this book is to provide a historical and theoretical foundation to child care. This is one step that enhances training in the field. It is a step toward reaching the ultimate goals of establishing quality care for all children and ensuring professional status within the field.

CHAPTER 9

Achieving Quality Care

In this chapter you will:

- define quality day care;
- discuss the research indicators of quality;
- identify the components of quality;
- examine the importance of quality;
- identify the elements of a quality work environment;
- examine the process of improving quality child care.

Advance motivator

Examine the following key terms before reading the chapter. Then, while reading the chapter, try to assign meaning to each one.

quality child care   educator qualifications

quality   educator/child ratio

global perspective   group size

indicators of quality

Quality

Quality child care and achieving quality are current and important issues in the field of early childhood education. As the services of child care have evolved and as the provinces and territories have established regulations, day care has become an integral part of our society. We are no longer asking, *Do we need day care? Is day care good for children?* We are now asking, *What constitutes quality child care and how do we achieve it?* **Quality** is an essential component of the day-care system. Early childhood educators need to

243

understand quality, quality child care, and their implications in working with children.

Quality at one time was seen as a luxury rather than as a component of child care. It is still a subject with a variety of interpretations. A tremendous amount of research has been conducted and continues to be conducted in this area. Most of the research in the past focused on educator/child ratios and health standards. Recent research is focusing on supervision and training of pre-service educators. Achieving quality is an essential requirement for all day cares.

Defining Quality

Quality day care is a combination of many interconnected and inter-related attributes and features that influence one another. It is about the type of care and education that children receive. It is about the calibre of the centre's administration. The way in which stake-holders in the day care define and implement quality is influenced by their beliefs and values. Quality reflects and encompasses all elements that affect the day-care system. "The term 'high-quality' suggests something that is desirable or meets more than minimal standards" (Doherty-Derkowsky 1995, 3).

We can examine the quality of a day-care centre from many perspectives. This chapter will define those parameters that influence and determine the quality of the day-care centre in particular and the day-care system as a whole. We also discuss the issue of responsibility and look at the questions *Who is responsible for quality care?* and *Why is quality care so important?* The discussion on quality focuses on the elements of quality child care that directly affect the children.

Global Perspective

Defining and establishing quality is a complex task. Our description and definition of quality provide a **global perspective** and reflect general guidelines and principles that are universally agreed upon as elements of quality. It is also important to recognize that there are additional elements of quality that will be unique to provinces, territories, regions, communities, and individuals. A discussion about quality and what it means to your day care begins as part of the discussion about the development of a mission statement. Constructing and determining the parameters for quality must reflect the viewpoints of all stakeholders in the system.

....

Reflection

From your experience thus far, what do you think would be or is an important indicator of quality?

....

Who Is Responsible for Quality Day Care?

Everyone within society is responsible for quality day care. Each individual has a vested interest in the future of our children and the system of child care. All stakeholders are responsible for ensuring that there is quality child care and all stakeholders are entitled to quality child care. The educators, directors, support staff, and the parents are responsible for providing quality child care. The members have a right to receive quality from the program and the centre. Stakeholders must interact and establish relationships with other systems in order to improve quality. For example, stakeholders must work closely with funding agencies to access all possible funds for the day care.

Building and establishing a quality day-care centre is like assembling a tent. A tent, like a day-care centre, needs to provide safe and secure shelter, and in order for the tent to be functional it must be assembled correctly. There are many pieces that fit together and these pieces, when fitted together correctly, hold or support one another. It is when the pieces are all connected and working together that the tent will provide a good source of shelter. If one piece of the tent is missing, the tent may still provide cover, but it may be leaning to one side. Eventually, if too many pieces are missing or have difficulty fitting together, the tent will collapse. These same principles apply to the establishment of a quality day care. The components need to be assembled and function in harmony with one another in order to provide quality care and service. In order to appraise and judge the quality of any day-care centre, numerous components of the system needs to be examined. First and foremost, the quality of the interactions among everyone involved in the system need to be surveyed. "The maintenance of these relations is of primary importance. The process by which these relationships are maintained is the system's regulation—the rules of the game and the limits within which these rules can be sustained are the conditions of the system's stability through time" (Banathy 1992, 14).

All of the components of a day-care centre are equally important and each should strive to be of the highest quality. However, your perception of the priority of a particular component may vary, depending on your position in the system. The cook, for example, is concerned with the provision of nutritious food. Quality from this perspective includes proper kitchen facilities, access to quality produce, and funds for healthy foods. An educator, on the other hand, is more concerned with the educator/child ratio, room size, and materials and equipment. Parents, like the educator, are concerned with educator/child ratio, and, like the cook, are concerned with nutritious food. The director is concerned with these items in relation to quality and has the added responsibility of maintaining quality within the budgetary framework. The work of all members of the system will overlap and this should compel members to work together in their attempt to provide quality care.

The responsibility to oversee the quality of the day-care environment and program varies between profit and non-profit centres. In profit centres the owner usually sets the standards for the various components. In a non-profit centre, the board of directors is responsible for ensuring quality child care. In either centre the mandate and daily responsibility of accomplishing the goals and objectives deemed important to ensure a quality centre for children are given to the centre's director.

The Importance of Quality Child Care for Children

The importance of quality care cannot be underestimated. It is crucial and essential as children attending day-care centres represent the future citizens of our society. Children spend many hours a day away from their home and family in day care.

What Does the Research Tell Us?

The inquiry into quality day care is relatively recent and is related to the increase in the demand for day-care services over the last quarter of a century. As day care has become embedded into our daily lives, questions arise as to whether day care is good for children. Does day care have any long-term negative effects on them? These and other similar questions triggered the beginning of many years of research that attempted to determine the **indicators of quality** day care.

The research is highly conclusive and implies that high-quality day care is essential for children and that poor-quality day care can have an adverse affect on children (Phillips 1987; Doherty-Derkowski 1995; Caldwell 1984). The most significant research was children at the center:*Final Report of the National Day Care Study* carried out in the United States by Ruopp, Travers, Glantz, and Coelen and published in 1979. This study has had a tremendous influence on subsequent day-care studies. Its results identified those indicators that foster quality care: the size of the group, the educator/child ratio, plus the educational training and background of the educator (Phillips and Howes 1987).

In surveying the research it appears that the findings of the *National Day Care Study* were used in the design of subsequent studies and influenced those areas to be researched, namely **educator qualifications, educator/child ratios, group size**, and the environment, and how these influence quality child care (Vandell and Corasaniti 1990; Howes and Marx 1992; Howes 1990; Phillips 1987; Caldwell 1984). Vandell's (1988) extensive longitudinal study began with observation of children at 4 years of age and again at 8 years of age. In the first part of the study, it was found that "children in the better quality programs had more positive interaction with their teachers, while children in poorer quality programs spent more time in unoccupied behaviours and in solitary play" (1290). In a study by Howes (1990) it was found that children entering poor-quality day cares as infants had greater difficulty with their peers as preschoolers. These same children seemed to be distracted more easily, less task-oriented, and were generally less considerate of others. Schliecker, White, and Jacobs (1991) conducted a study to determine if there was any correlation between children's understanding of vocabulary and the type of day-care centre they attended. Their study found that "those who were in high-quality settings had significantly higher vocabulary scores than those in low-quality settings" (22). The findings of these studies and of other research clearly demonstrate the benefits of high-quality child care.

Canadian research into quality is increasing and has focused on indicators similar to that of American studies. Some of the most current Canadian research is listed here.

- 1986—SPR Associates Inc/National Mail Surveys Inc. *An Exploratory Review of Selected Issues in For-profit Versus Not-for Profit Child Care.* SPR conducted research in 927 centres across Canada. The study rated non-profit and profit centres on twenty-seven different items related to quality. In general, the study found that non-profit centres ranked higher. However, profit centres "ranked higher on their flexibility of hours" (Doherty 1994, 32).

- 1988—DeGagné and Gangée. *Garderies a but lucratif et garderies sans but lucratif subventionnées vers un évaluation de la qualité.* The authors conducted a study in Quebec involving all licensed day-care centres. The initiative for the study was a result of the number of complaints that had been filed against profit centres.

- 1988—West conducted a study in Ontario. *A Study on Compliance with the Day Nurseries Act at Full-Time Child*

Care Centres in Metropolitan Toronto. This study involved 431 day-care centres.

- 1992—Friesen. *A Sociological Examination of the Effects of Auspice on Daycare Quality.* This study, conducted in Alberta, involved forty-five day-care centres. The research focused on the quality of care infants and toddlers received in both profit and non-profit centres.

In general, the Canadian research has focused on the components of quality and how they compare in profit and non-profit centres.

Quality Child Care

Understanding the implications of the research is crucial in working toward and developing high-quality child care. It is extremely important to understand that a provincial or territorial licence does not assure quality. The provincial and territorial laws and regulations provide for minimal standards rather then optimal quality. The provincial and territorial governments establish regulations that determine standards for health and safety rather than components for quality child care. Usually, quality child care necessitates going beyond the provincial and territorial regulations and government norms. Meeting the provincial and territorial norms and regulations is only the first step toward the establishment of a quality centre.

Quality child care begins with the educator. Our discussion will reflect the research findings that identify educator qualifications, educator/child ratios, and group size as key indicators of quality. Additionally, we will examine staff turnover, the physical environment, and the curriculum, and how these influence quality. The same components of quality that affect the well-being of the children also significantly affect the quality of the work environment for the educators.

Figure 9.1 highlights quality child care in terms of educator training, educator/child ratios, and group size.

F I G U R E 9 . 1
Important components of quality child care.

Educator Training

Educator training and qualifications are critical indicators in ensuring quality care. The *National Statement on Quality Child Care* developed by the Canadian Child Care Federation (CCCF) states, "Quality child care employs graduates in early childhood and care as primary care providers" (1991, 3). Ideally, to ensure quality, all educators within a centre should be graduates of early childhood education; however, many centres still hire untrained individuals as their provincial and territorial regulations do not require them to hire qualified individuals. Given the reality of the profession, CCCF has also stated that minimal training includes the study of child development, knowledge about developmentally appropriate practice, and supervised fieldwork experience (CCCF 1991). From a global perspective it is evident that knowledge about child development is pivotal in the study of early childhood education. "Without that background, it is too easy for teachers and caregivers to fall back on making decisions based only on vague notions that are part personal values, part memories, part expediency, and part images of desirable future behaviour" (Gestwicki 1995, 6).

A review of the research (Howes 1983; Clarke-Stewart and Gruber 1984; Berk 1985) shows that educators with child-related training are educators who:

- are more positive in social interactions with the children;

- are less negative and punitive in their interactions with the children;

- show more encouragement and less restrictions;

- help children experience more positive social interactions; and

- demonstrate increased levels of cooperation.

Educator Interactions

In Chapter 4 we discussed educator/child interactions as part of your early childhood training. Learning how to effectively interact is an integral part of early childhood training and practicum experiences. Supervisors often spend considerable time discussing and modelling appropriate interactions.

Educator interactions are important indicators of quality. It is the calibre of the interactions that establishes quality. For example, as pointed out earlier in this book, an appropriate interaction is to talk to a child at his or her level and to stay close to a child when you are communicating with him or her, rather than shouting or calling from across the room.

The evidence overwhelmingly concurs that the educators' qualifications and the quality and consistency of their interactions are important determinants of the overall quality of an early childhood program. Knowing that training is an indicator of quality implies that you have a professional responsibility to meet and maintain appropriate standards. You can participate in professional development and in-service training to remain up-to-date with current research and pedagogical developments.

PHOTO 9.2
A one-to-one educator/child ratio is effective in promoting the child's self-help skills.

Educator/Child Ratios

Educator/child ratios influence quality child care. For example, it is generally considered important for infants to be in situations with low educator/child ratios. Research studies indicate that educator/child ratios significantly affect both children and the educator in the day-care centre (Howes 1983; Field 1980; Howes and Rubenstein 1985). Appropriate educator/child ratios have a positive effect on:

- the type of verbal interactions between the educator and the child;

- how children engage in play;

- the nurturance and care provided on the part of the educator;

- the increase in the frequency of interactions between the children and educator; and

- individualized care and attention.

When the educator is responsible for a small group or small number of children, he or she has more time to join children in their activities and is able to have quality conversations with them (Doherty-Derkowski 1995). When the educator is responsible for a large number of children, there is greater concern with group management and it becomes difficult for the educator to provide individual attention (Essa and Young 1994).

Appropriate national standards for educator/child ratios for different age groups of children have been recommended by the CCCF. Unfortunately, the ratios in many provinces and territories do not reflect the position taken by either the American National Association for the Education of Young Children in their *Developmentally Appropriate Practice* (Bredekamp 1987) or the CCCF's *National Statement on Quality Child Care* (1991). Table 9.1 outlines the CCCF's recommended educator/child ratios for Canada.

Age of children	Ratios
0–12 months	1:3
12–24 months	1:4
2 year olds	1:4–1:5–1:6
3 year olds	1:5–1:6–1:7
4 and 5 years olds	1:8–1:9

TABLE 9.1
Recommended educator/child ratios. From *National Statement on Quality Child Care,* Canadian Child Care Federation 1991, p. 9. Reproduced with permission of the Canadian Child Care Federation, 1996.

···

Reflection

Compare the recommended national ratios with your provincial or territorial ratios. How do these discrepancies affect you as an educator?

···

As an early childhood educator, whether training or working in the field, it is extremely important that you are aware of this information because it will affect your day-to-day performance. If you are working in a day-care centre with ratios that are above the norm, your abilities to conduct yourself in the fashion in which you were trained and in which you believe to be important will be inhibited. Chances are you will not be as effective as you would like to be.

Group Size

Group size is influenced by the physical environment, the actual physical space available, and the philosophy of the centre. For example, some centres believe in the importance of team teaching and therefore organize their groups around this concept. Other centres have larger groups to optimize the use of their rented space.

The organization and size of a group, the amount of space per child and the number of children in one given space influence quality care. One indication of quality care is to have children in small groups (CCCF 1991). Educators who are working with smaller groups of children spend more time in meaningful interactions rather than just supervising them (Yeates et al. 1994; Friendly 1994). Research (Howes 1983; Field 1980; Clarke-Stewart and Gruber 1984) suggests that children who are in smaller groups:

- participate more actively in the classroom;

- are less aggressive;

- demonstrate more cooperative skills and behaviour;

- are more talkative; and

- engage more in dramatic play.

Table 9.2 outlines recommended group sizes as outlined in the *National Statement on Quality Child Care*. As in educator/child ratios, group sizes for infants need to be smaller than group sizes for older children. Many centres try to create an appropriate balance for the children by providing them with a variety of group size experiences.

Age of children	Group size
0–12 months	6 infants
12–24 months	6–8 toddlers
2-year-olds	8–12 children
3-year-olds	10–14 children
4- and 5-year-olds	16–18 children

TABLE 9.2
Recommended group size. From *National Statement on Quality Child Care*, Canadian Child Care Federation 1991, p. 9. Reproduced with permission of the Canadian Child Care Federation, 1996.

Reflection

Compare the national group sizes with your provincial or territorial regulations. How do they compare? Are there differences?

Situation

Ayesha had just graduated from an early childhood training program and was beginning her first job in a day-care centre. When she began looking for a job she was uncertain as to whether she wanted a position where she would work alone with a group of children or whether she wanted to team teach with another educator. She saw both situations as having positive and negative possibilities. She felt she would be less nervous if she was on her own and yet, on the other hand, team teaching would provide support during her initiation into the field. She was thrilled when she was hired by a centre to work with another educator in the two smaller classrooms, which were divided by a sliding wall. This situation offered both possibilities. During free play, the sliding wall was pulled open and the children and the educators worked together, and at other times of the day the wall was closed and Ayesha worked on her own with her group of children.

This situation reflects how the needs of a novice educator were met and how the classroom arrangement provided the children with an ideal situation: they had a combination of large and small group size experience with appropriate educator/child ratios.

Low and High Educator Turnover

Low educator turnover plays a key role in the quality of child care. Low educator turnover refers to a centre where the educators who are working there remain for many years. Centres with low educator turnover provide the children with the opportunity to become comfortable and familiar with many of the educators. High educator turnover refers to centres where there is a frequent change or turnover in the educators. A centre with a high educator turnover could result in the children having to adjust to many different educators during a short period of time. High educator turnover is a problem and concern for children, parents, and administrators.

Physical Environment

The organization and set-up of the environment reflect the quality of the child-care centre. "Studies have found that both child development and adult behaviour are influenced by the organization of the early childhood program's setting and the materials available in it" (Doherty-Derkowski 1995, 59). These components create a quality environment.

- Appropriate indoor and outdoor space for the number of children enrolled in the centre.

- Indoor space or indoor facilities at another location for gross motor activities.

- An environment that is safe and clean.

- Material that is organized and accessible so children can self-select activities.

- An environment that is organized for both individual and group play.

- The materials and equipment are appropriate for the ages and developmental levels of the various groups of children at the centre.

- The materials and equipment are rotated on a regular basis.

The Curriculum

In Chapter 2 we discussed a variety of curriculum models and how to use them in personal planning. Overall, the curriculum and programming must ensure a balance between the children's self-initiated activities and the educator guiding and instructing them

(Doherty-Derkowski 1995). To achieve this, the curriculum will reflect the mission statement; be based on a sound curriculum model; incorporate the educator's observations of the children; pursue the development of the goals and objectives of the centre; plan opportunities and activities based on the interests and needs of the children; and provide a schedule that is flexible and that offers a balance between active and quiet periods and individual and group times.

Quality of the Work Environment

High-quality child care would not exist if it were not for the professionals working with the children. It is therefore extremely critical that the stakeholders ensure a high-quality working environment in the day care.

A quality work environment will reflect the quality care that has been established for the children. For example, a centre that establishes quality educator/child ratios and appropriate group sizes provides a high-quality situation for the children. It also provides an appropriate work environment for the educator. Appropriate and quality educator/child ratios allow educators to effectively do their jobs.

How Can Quality Day Care Be Improved?

Within Canada, the governments of the provinces and territories are responsible for the licensing of child-care centres. Each province and territory is responsible for setting standards that will ensure quality child care: suitability of environment, adequate space, appropriate educator/child ratios, and adequate training for educators. However, the government bodies do not always enforce these standards or incorporate research findings that would improve these standards—for example, the CCCF's recommendations for educator/child ratios. Howes and Marx (1992) found that when it comes to advocating the need for higher level training in educators, it is the individuals involved in the centres (directors, educators, and parents) rather than the policy-makers who are the advocates.

Quality care is costly. In order to improve day care or maintain current standards, funding should be available. Salaries for educators should reflect the professional training and level of responsibility.

In order to improve quality child care we need to bridge the gap between the ideal and the real. All stakeholders and professionals involved in day care must work together to create and sustain quality environments for the children. This may require difficult decisions, but these decisions must be made. We know that early childhood educators are professionals and their salaries should reflect this. This is the ideal! However, we do not live in an ideal world! Expecting to have quality child care with professional educators requires salaries higher than minimum wage.

Unfortunately in the day-care environment, the educators' salaries are often closely linked to the fees that parents pay and this is often a difficult dilemma for all those involved. This situation works toward depressing the cost of child care, so that the fees parents pay are much lower than what the actual cost of child care should be (Willer 1990). Some provinces and territories have implemented salary enhancement programs that provide direct grants that supplement educators' salaries.

So how do we bridge the gap? Are there any government initiatives in the provinces and territories working toward this goal? Is government funding a thing of the past? The financial challenges will determine the future of day care. How will day cares maintain or enhance their services without additional cost to the centre and how will they raise the money to meet their high-quality standards?

Regardless of where we find the extra funds, the goal of quality should be maintained. We must not forget that quality child care will benefit children now and shape our future society (Willer 1990). This goal may not be attainable all at once, but steps to its attainment should exist. All stakeholders in the system have a vital role to play in establishing quality child care and it is through their interactions that this goal can be achieved.

Keep in mind that the day care's main goal is to provide quality care for the children. The people directly responsible for this are the educators. Part of the director's role is to support the staff in order to ensure this quality care, but it is not the only role he or she plays. Managing a day-care centre requires the director to wear many hats. There are times that one role will dominate over others.

Gina Gasperini, daycare director and educator

Summary

- Quality child care is about the type of care and education that children receive.

- The three major principles that contribute to quality care are educator qualifications, the educator/child ratios, and group size.

- Low educator turnover is essential for quality child care, high educator turnover negates the quality of centres.

- Physical environment is a component of quality.

- The curriculum and programming must be developed and strive for quality.

- Provincial and territory regulations are minimal and do not reflect quality.

Questions and Activities for Further Reflection

1. How will you respond to a situation where you are asked to work with more children than is considered appropriate? Who will you talk to in this situation?

2. How can you work toward developing quality care?

3. How can you, as an educator, encourage parents to help bridge the gap between the need for higher salaries and lower fees?

Self-Test

Provide definitions and examples for the key terms that were identified at the beginning of the chapter. Identify and describe indicators for quality child care.

References

Andre, T., and C. Neave. (1992). *The Complete Canadian Day Care Guide.* Toronto: McGraw-Hill Ryerson.

Banathy, Bela H. (1992). *A Systems View of Education.* Englewood Cliffs, N.J.: Educational Technology Publications.

Berk, L. (1985). "Relationships of Educational Attainment, Child Oriented Attitudes, Job Satisfaction, and Career Commitment to Caregiver Behaviour Toward Children." *Child Care Quarterly,* 14;103–129.

Bredekamp, S. ed. (1987). *Developmentally Appropriate Practice in Early Childhood Programs Serving Children from Birth Through Age 8.* Washington, D.C.: American National Association for the Education of Young Children.

Caldwell, B.M. (1984). "What is Quality Child Care?" *Young Children,* 40:3–8.

Canadian Child Care Federation. (1991). *National Statement on Quality Child Care.* Ottawa, Ontario.

Clarke-Stewart, K.A., and C. Gruber. (1984). "Daycare Forms and Features." In *Quality Variations in Daycare,* ed. R.C. Ainslie, 35–62. New York: Praeger.

Doherty, Gillian. (1994). "Quality Child Care Contextual Factors." *Interaction,* Winter 1994:32–39.

Doherty-Derkowski, Gillian. (1995). *Quality Matters.* Don Mills, Ont.: Addison-Wesley.

Essa, E., and R. Young. (1994). *Introduction to Early Childhood Education.* Scarborough, Ont.: Nelson Canada.

Field, T. (1980). "Preschool Play: Effects of Teacher-Child Ration and Organization of Classroom Space." *Child Study Journal,* 10:191–205.

Friendly, Martha. (1994). *Child Care Policy in Canada.* Don Mills, Ont.: Addison-Wesley.

Gestwicki, C. (1995). *Developmentally Appropriate Practice Curriculum and Development in Early Childhood Education.* Albany, N.Y.: Delmar Publishers.

Howes, Carollee. (1983). "Caregiver Behaviour in Centre and Family Day Care." *Journal of Applied Developmental Psychology,* 4:99–107.

Howes, Carollee. (1990). "Can the Age of Entry into Child Care and the Quality of Child Care Predict Adjustments in Kindergarten?" *Developmental Psychology,* 26(2):292–303.

Howes, C., and E. Marx. (1992). "Raising Questions About Improving the Quality of Child Care: Child Care in the United States and France." *Early Childhood Research Quarterly,* 7:347–366.

Howes, C., and J. Rubenstein. (1985). "Determinants of Toddlers' Experience in Day Care: Age of Entry and Quality of Setting." *Child Care Quarterly,* 14(2):140–151.

Phillips, D. A. ed. (1987). *Quality in Child Care: What Does Research Tell Us?* Washington, D.C.: National Association for the Education of Young Children.

Phillips, D., and C. Howes. (1987). "Indicators of Quality in Child Care: A Review of the Research." In *Quality in Child Care: What Does the Research Tell Us?* ed. D. Phillips, 1–19. Washington, D.C.: National Association for the Education of Young Children.

Ruopp, R., J. Travers, F. Glantz, and C. Coelen. (1979). *Children at the Center: Final Report of the National Day Care Study.* Cambridge, M.A.: Abt Associates.

Schliecker, E., D.R. White, and E. Jacobs. (1991). "The Role of Day Care Quality in the Prediction of Children's Vocabulary." *Canadian Journal of Behavioral Science,* 23:12–24.

Vandell, Lowe D. (1988). "A Longitudinal Study of Children with Day-Care Experiences of Varying Quality." *Child Development,* 59:1286–1292.

Vandell, D.L., and M.A. Corasaniti. (1990). "Variation in Early Child Care. Do They Predict Subsequent Social, Emotional, and Cognitive Differences?" *Early Childhood Research Quarterly,* 5:555–572.

Willer, B. Ed. (1990). *Reaching the Full Cost of Quality.* Washington, D.C.: National Association for the Education of Young Children.

Yeates, M., D. McKenna, C. Warberg, and K. Chandler. (1994). *Administering Early Childhood Settings,* 2nd ed. Don Mills, Ont.: Maxwell Macmillan Canada.

C HAPTER 10

Professionalism, Advocacy, and Ethics

In this chapter you will:

- identify the meaning of professionalism in the field of early childhood education;
- distinguish between various stages of professional growth;
- define advocacy;
- examine the meaning of ethics in relation to a professional early childhood educator.

Advance motivator

Examine the following key terms before reading the chapter. Then, while reading the chapter, try to assign meaning to each one.

professional	consolidation
advocacy	renewal
ethics	maturity
survival	

The Early Childhood Educator

As an emerging educator you are a member of the profession of early childhood education and care. This is a profession that includes individuals from the various levels of professional development (Vander Ven 1988). What does it mean to be a **professional** early childhood educator? How do you become involved in child care **advocacy**? What are the **ethics** inherent in the field of early childhood.

Professionalism

According to Morrison (1995), the early childhood profession is faced with an identity crisis. It is in the process of redefining itself as a profession with professional status. What does it mean to *professionalize* early childhood educators who are embedded in the system of early childhood care and education? It means that educators need to develop a new professional identity, to establish a mission statement, and to identify goals suitable for the 21st century. Educators are not baby-sitters, they should not be hired to work with young children without adequate training and an "early childhood knowledge base" (Morrision 1995, 17).

There are many definitions for the term professional. There is relative agreement that a professional is an individual who carries out work that is essential to the functioning of society (Katz 1987; Schön 1983) or a person with exceptional skill, experience, and competence in a given field (Isenberg 1995). Generally, a professional carries out his or her work with a certain degree of autonomy. The day care "does not dictate the nature of practice but hires the professional to exercise judgment based on specialized knowledge, principles, and techniques" (Katz 1987, 5).

To be a professional in the field of early childhood education is a challenging task. Currently, we do not have a "coherent and coordinated system of professional development in early childhood education" (Goffin and Day 1994, 4). With a system of professional development managed by the profession itself, we will be in a better position to counteract externally imposed policies and regulations that are developed by groups who have a limited understanding of the scope and purpose of early childhood education (Goffin and Day 1994). These facts suggest that advocacy is an important and inseparable element of professionalism. The issue of advocacy is covered later in this chapter.

It is difficult to raise the public's perception of you as a professional when there are inconsistencies within the profession. For example, some day cares continue to hire individuals who do not have any relevant training or education in the field of early childhood education. Another problem is that early childhood education began as custodial care for children from disadvantaged families and child-care workers were seen as baby-sitters. While the past twenty years have seen a tremendous improvement in the status of early childhood educators, the **baby-sitter** stigma has clung to the profession throughout the years.

As a professional it is your responsibility to elevate the status of the field of early childhood education. It is important to recognize that to have optimal environments for children, the environment must also be optimal for the educators who work with the children (Katz 1987). This can be achieved in part by acting in a competent, knowledgeable, and skilled manner. Your teacher training program can only bring you to an initial level of competence and professionalism. It prepares you to begin an ongoing process of professional growth.

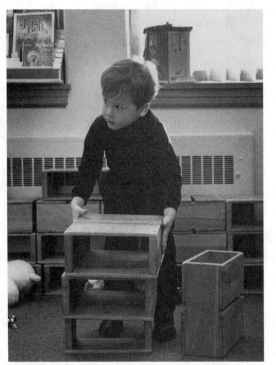

PHOTO 10.1
The materials educators make available for children encourage them to learn through exploration.

Knowledge, Skills, and Attitudes of a Professional Early Childhood Educator

Knowledge

"Knowledge is frequently identified as one of the defining characteristics of a professional" (Morrison 1995, 18). In the field of early childhood education the core of knowledge that constitutes the definitive base for professional educators is still unclear. We advocate that each educator needs to complete a training program in the field of early childhood education. This basic training provides an important part of the necessary expertise needed to work effectively in the field of child care. Degrees in early childhood can be achieved through relevant studies and teacher-training programs. You can refer to Chapter 3 for a review of the various training programs and degree categories available in Canada.

Once you have obtained your preliminary training in the field it is important to keep current. You can achieve this by subscribing to journals and attending conferences. You may want to share this knowledge with parents. For example, read journal articles that might be of particular interest to the parents and select one or two that can be copied and posted on the bulletin board. Or you can provide a short summary of an article or an annotated bibliography of articles so that parents can easily select the ones that are of interest to them.

Good educators also use their knowledge to help children make everyday connections. For example, building with blocks helps a child make connections about concepts, shapes, size, balance, and weight of objects. They know how to enrich children's learning as well as their own learning. Some of the best educators are themselves avid learners (Isenberg 1995).

Reflection

> With a group of classmates or colleagues, generate a list that reflects what should constitute a knowledge base for the early childhood profession.

Skills

Professional early childhood educators need to translate knowledge into skills. Essentially, knowledge forms the theoretical foundation for practice. Skill proficiency is reflected in practice. There is an emerging body of research (Goffin and Day 1994; Morrison 1995; Stremmel et al. 1995) that is studying the link between theory and practice, knowledge and skill.

A skilled practitioner uses observation skills as a tool for planning. The skills needed to carry out observations are taught in many training programs. This knowledge helps the educator plan situations with skill and take informed action.

With appropriate knowledge you will have the skill to plan a curriculum that works over time. Plan programs that meet the needs of children on an individual and group basis. As a skilled educator you will be abe to handle routines with fluency and efficiency. As your skill level increases, you will find yourself becoming more relaxed in day-to-day situations.

Communication skills are important for success as an early childhood educator. Techniques used to develop these skills were discussed in chapters 4 and 5. Refer to these chapters to focus on the development of communication skills.

Attitudes

The approach or outlook you have in dealing with your role as an educator is important. It is not enough to project a positive attitude, you should feel it within you. You need to model this positive attitude with the children since you influence the development of their attitudes. A professional attitude includes being punctual and prompt for work. It means recognizing the importance of arriving early to set up and organize materials for the children. Whether a student or practitioner, if your shift starts at 8:00 a.m., then you need to be set up and ready for the children at 8:00 a.m. and not arriving at 8:00 a.m. Being ready for the children shows an attitude of respect.

Whether you are a student or graduate educator you should present yourself cheerfully. Be kind to your profession and support it. You can support your profession by "joining local organizations and being an active member, supporting and lobbying for principles and ideals of early childhood education" (Taylor 1989, 160).

Stages of Educator Development

Gradually, the practitioner moves along a continuum acquiring knowledge, perfecting skills, and developing appropriate attitudes. Katz (1977) identifies four stages of development that an educator experiences as he or she pursues his or her career: **survival**, **consolidation**, **renewal**, and **maturity**. How you progress through these stages of development will be influenced by the quality of the centre(s) where you work and the relationships that you will develop with other early childhood professionals.

Survival, the first profesional stage of development that you will experience, is the time in your career when you question all that you have learned and question how to apply it. Depending on you as an individual and on the experiences you have had in your practicum placements, this survival period can last between one and two years. We suggest that, as a professional, you acknowledge this survival period and to help yourself move through it find a colleague to whom you can comfortably ask some of your many questions. Do not wait until you encounter your first question or dilemma. Rather, when you begin your new job, ask your director if he or she can suggest a colleague who would be willing to work closely with you and answer your questions. This establishes an open line of communication between you, your director, and your co-workers. This technique will guide your development and help you to become a professional educator.

Preparing your curriculum and daily teaching plans provides a good opportunity to seek advice and assistance. For example, you might ask an experienced educator or the director to come in and see your room arrangement. Try some of the ideas that other stakeholders in your day-care system might suggest. You need not follow every bit of advice, but be open to hearing it. Recognize that you are human and you need to experience your own ideas to know if they will work. When practice does not work, do not regard it as a failure. Try to assess how to change it so that it will work.

Another strategy to use during this period is to stay in touch with a few of your classmates. Arrange monthly meetings to share anecdotes and experiences. This provides a support network and helps you broaden your understanding of situations. This is also a good step toward the development of reflective practice.

The second stage of development is consolidation, which begins anywhere from the end of the first year and lasts into the third year. During this stage you will feel better equipped to deal with children's specific behaviours. Your focus will shift from trying to keep up with daily routines and planning to attending to specific children. You will become more comfortable looking into children's individual needs and behaviours.

As in the first stage, draw on your fellow practitioners for support. This is a time when attending conferences and workshops can provide useful support.

The third stage is called renewal. This stage occurs somewhere between the third and fourth year. At this point you will find yourself ready to develop your own techniques in the field. You are now comfortable with your established program and routines and are ready to adapt and use them with a greater degree of flexibility in developing your program ideas. In this stage you begin to accept yourself as an educator and as a professional in the field of early childhood.

The fourth stage is called maturity, which you enter after three to five years of practical experience in the field. While you may be mature in dealing with colleagues, parents, and children from the beginning of your career, this stage refers to a professional maturity that develops with experience. In this stage your self-acceptance as an educator will grow stronger. You will find it useful to engage in activities that encourage your search for insight and perspective and may want to pursue greater depths of knowledge by seeking an advanced degree.

Experienced and mature educators have the ability to act on what appears to be instinct. This is sometimes referred to as a sixth sense. In fact, it comes from repeatedly thinking about what you have done after you have done it. Gradually, you begin to think about what you are doing during, rather than after, you have done it. This simultaneous thinking and action is what Schön (1983) refers to as "reflection-in-action." It is in fact a part of reflective practice. It means that as a practicing educator you are aware of your actions and behaviours at all times.

Another feature of this stage is a readiness to become involved in advocacy. While it is positive to become an advocate while you are a student, it is only at this mature stage of professional development that you are equipped to respond to the professional rhetoric. You are able to inform others about the field of child care and explain the type of formalized training that is required to work in the field.

Advocacy

Advocacy enhances professionalism. An advocate is someone who becomes actively involved to promote or support a cause. Advocates of child care help link services and needs. This link is needed for systemic reform. Canada is an affluent country that, at present, does

not have a national child-care system. Educators who act as advocates can positively influence the development of Canadian child-care programs and services. The main purpose of advocacy in early childhood is to ensure that all children have access to high-quality services.

There are many good day-care and child-care facilities in Canada, all of which operate through a variety of

PHOTO 10.2
Advocating for good quality child care ensures that children are provided with environments that will help them develop self sufficiency and independence.

initiatives. Most day-care centres are regulated through provincial groups, while others like family day care may be completely unregulated. The lack of a national program is indicative of the low priority status that child care has in the eyes of the Canadian government. "Canada is one of only a few Western industrialized countries that does not have a national child care policy" (Friendly 1994, 10). Government responds to social pressure. This is where the role of advocacy enters.

To be an advocate in the field of early childhood education is to support your profession. The early childhood profession is concerned with the well-being of children. So, by definition, as an advocate you will promote programs and actions that improve the lives of children and families (Hildebrand 1993). Canadian child-care advocates make a difference. In the 1980s a demand for more and better day-care and child-care facilities led to an "emerging perception of child care as a national issue" (Friendly 1994, 145). The result was a rise in public awareness of the key issues surrounding child-care needs.

Relying on a systems approach implies that you will be concerned with more than just the day-to-day environment of your day-care system. As an advocate in the field of early childhood education, it is your responsibility to be in touch with the other systems that affect your day-care centre. For example, the system of government agencies and services is an important resource that affects the day care and the child's well-being. When there are federal, provincial, or territorial cutbacks in day-care funding, the quality of your day-care system is affected. For child care to be available and affordable to all, government needs to offer such things as accessible subsidies and tax benefits.

The Role of an Advocate

An advocate actively joins in discussions that promote and support a cause that will benefit from community attention (Hildebrand 1993). In promoting a particular cause, you must view it from the perspective of the individual(s) on whose behalf you are advocating. If you are advocating on behalf of children, then you must come to understand what is best for them. If you are lobbying for yourself, as in demanding better wages, then you must see the situation from a personal perspective. As in any system, perspective plays an important role.

Join forces with other advocates rather than working alone. Networking provides ideas and strength. Join relevant groups and organizations that support the same cause. There are ten important things that any advocacy group or individual can do (adapted from Hildebrand 1993).

1. Wake up complacent agencies. Write to your member of Parliament. Identify specific needs. Invite her or him to visit your day care. Get local newspapers to write stories about some positive event at your day care and how the children and community benefit from your day care.

2. Forge links among systems on behalf of children. Get together with other day cares in your area. Work together to contact municipal services and to maximize service benefits to all the child-care facilities in your area.

3. Resolve all conflicts peacefully. Avoid alienating any group. Deal with issues in open conversation.

4. Provide or locate pertinent information. Keep a list of provincial or territorial agencies at your day care. Provide the appropriate addresses or contact person(s) to parents who express concern over issues and who could lobby on your behalf.

5. Encourage people to work together. Advocacy has little result when you work alone. Join forces with other educators, parents, directors, or local community groups.

6. Uphold the constitutional and legal rights of children. This refers to a maintenance of the rights of children as governed by the legal code. It also refers to upholding a moral and ethical code of conduct when working with children and their families.

7. Demonstrate an enjoyment of children and foster this in the families with whom you work. This profession requires that you like what you are doing and that you

believe in the merit of child care. When you can no
longer enjoy the work, it is time to look elsewhere for
work.

8. Encourage the development of related new services,
    such as community libraries or parks. Government
    understands needs that are based on statistical
    information. To encourage the development of
    community facilities, you can go to the municipal
    offices to find out the population within the area of a
    given age group. If you can show that there are enough
    people who can benefit from a service, you may receive
    help from your municipality to develop the facility.

9. Provide publicity on child-related issues. Again, go to
    local newspapers. They are always ready to publish
    human interest stories. An example of an issue is the
    low pay that child-care workers receive. It is also one
    of the few jobs where individuals can become employed
    without training. These two factors undermine the
    professionalism of the field.

10. Improve children's lives today for a better tomorrow.
    Today's children are tomorrow's adults. Provision of
    quality child care will give children a greater sense of
    themselves.

Who Listens to Advocates?

Your task is to be heard by the right group. Advocates direct their
lobbying toward decision-makers. Decision-makers can range from
heads of government agencies to parents to boards of directors to
child-related business executives. Politicians are decision-makers.
They need to hear your voice in order to put your needs at the forefront of policy. "Advocacy can enhance the evolution of an early
childhood profession that designs itself, speaks for itself and
demonstrates a continuing dedication to the needs of its members
and the children and families they serve" (Fennimore 1989, 23).
Policy can be changed through pressure applied by large groups of
the voting public. When politicians recognize an issue as important
to a large group of the voting public, they are inclined to make
policy changes.

Canada at the present time has a fragmented system of child care. Advocacy toward the promotion of national unity in the field of day care is a valuable goal. The Canadian Day Care Advocacy Association began in 1982 and has been active since then in pursuing their goal of a Canadian child-care system that is both accessible and of the highest quality. "A comprehensive childcare system should respect the right of the child, the role and rights of the parents and would result in social and economics benefits for all Canadians" (Canadian Day Care Advocacy Association 1995, 13).

Ethics

Along with relevant knowledge, ethical standards represent another fundamental characteristic required for the identification of a profession. "The ethics of a profession reflect its obligations to its clients and to society" (Feeney, Christensen, and Moravcik 1991). The recent establishment of a code of ethics by the National Association for the Education of Young Children (NAEYC) is a positive and important step toward the professionalization of early childhood education. You can obtain a copy of this code of ethics by writing to NAEYC at the address provided under the section Associations at the end of this chapter. In Canada several provinces have established a code of ethics. At the time of publication these provinces are Ontario, British Columbia, Nova Scotia, Manitobia, and Saskatchewan. The Canadian Child Care Federation is in the process of drafting a Canadian Code of Ethics, which they anticipate presenting at their annual general meeting in 1997. To obtain copies of the provincial or territorial code of ethics contact those associations at the addresses provided under Associations.

To maintain ethical standards is a challenging task that requires personal attention and practice throughout one's life. Ethics involve reflection on personal behaviour and moral judgment based on a personal belief system. Ethical behaviour considers beliefs, moral decisions, and knowledge of basic skills and educational principles underlying your chosen profession.

In the field of early childhood education you can practice ethical behaviour by demonstrating appropriate responsibility to the families, children, and society you serve. NAEYC's code of ethical conduct assumes that ethical decisions are based on core values. Some of these values are personal and others are rooted in the history of child care. Some standards of behaviour identified in NAEYC's position on ethical conduct are:

- appreciating childhood as a unique and valuable stage of the human life cycle;

- basing our work with children on knowledge of child development;

- appreciating and supporting the close ties between the child and family;

- recognizing that children are best understood in the context of family, culture, and society;

- respecting the dignity, worth, and uniqueness of each individual; and

- helping children and adults achieve their full potential in the context of relationships that are based on trust, respect, and positive regard.

Each of us faces ethical dilemmas in our work. A dilemma does not have a clearly defined right or wrong answer. The term dilemma infers an impasse, a situation where the resolution is not obvious or clearly identifiable. When faced with ethical dilemmas, we are required to act in "accordance with high moral standards" (Feeney 1995, 13).

Some moral principles that you can draw on as part of an ethical process of decision-making include respecting the children and families you are working with, upholding the moral code of confidentiality, being honest and fair when dealing with children, and being supportive toward children and their families. "Teachers shape children's sense of themselves and the world.... Because young children are so vulnerable, unethical behaviour in early childhood programs can be very damaging" (ibid.).

Reflection

One ideal according to the ethical code of conduct is for an educator to build support networks for families. In the following example, how would you do this? Parent A divulges that parent B is verbally abusive toward their child. You have never witnessed this abusive behaviour. What responsibility do you have in this situation? What action can you take?

Concluding Remarks

To be deemed a professional in the field of early childhood education requires that you have an educational foundation and certain basic skills. This book has provided you with the foundations of your educational knowledge and the reflections and activities have been designed to help you develop your basic skills. In addition to these, professional educators must develop positive attitudes and outlooks that will enhance their career and contribute to the well-being of the children under their care. "Being a member of the teaching profession goes beyond an accumulation of methods, course work, and teaching experiences. Being a professional teacher suggests an attitude about teaching.... Teachers are called to the profession when they believe they can indeed make a difference in the lives of children" (Gordon and Browne 1985, 122).

"Doing what is right becomes difficult at times; knowing what is right may be illusive" (ibid., 123). The interdependence of your educational knowledge, experiences, skills, and commitment to your profession will serve to make you a qualified professional in the child-care system.

When you finish this textbook you are ready to begin a new stage of learning. Use Appendix A to review what you have learned and to guide you in launching your career as an early childhood educator.

Reflection

Now that you have completed this book ask yourself once again why you would like to become an educator of young children.

Summary

- A professional refers to an individual who carries out work that is essential to the functioning of society. An early childhood professional carries out work that is essential to families with young children. This work is in the form of care and education.

- Fundamental knowledge, skills, and attitudes are essential for the professional early childhood educator.

- An educator goes through four stages of professional development: survival, consolidation, renewal, and maturity.

- An advocate is an individual or group of individuals who supports or promotes a specific cause. A professional educator should advocate for the improvement of all aspects of child care and education.

- Ethics of a profession refer to the obligations that an individual within a profession has to his or her clients and to society.

Questions and Activities for Further Reflection

1. Contact your local associations for information on your profession. Find out how you can become an involved advocate.

2. Contact one of the provinces or the Canadian Child Care Federation to review a copy of a code for ethical conduct.

3. Why do you want to be an early childhood educator? Identify some professional values that will guide your practice.

Self-Test

Think of an ethical dilemma that has happened to you or to a colleague. Using an ethical code of conduct as your guide, how would you attempt to solve this ethical dilemma?

Associations

The following list is by no means complete. Contact your local agencies for a more comprehensive listing in your area or the Canadian Child Care Federation, which has a comprehensive listing of associations across Canada.

National

Canadian Child Care Federation
120 Holland
Ottawa, Ontario
K1Y 0X6
(613-729-5289)

Canadian Day Care Advocacy Association
323 Chapel Street
Ottawa, Ontario
K1N 7Z2
(613-594-3196)

Canadian Association for
Young Children
5417 Rannock Avenue
Winnipeg, Manitobia
R3R 0N3
(204-831-1658)

Provincial/Territorial

Alberta

Alberta Association for Young Children
7340–78th Street
Edmonton, Alberta
T6C 2N1

Early Childhood Professional Association of Alberta
P.O. Box 3631
Spruce Grove, Alberta
T7X 3A9

British Columbia

Early Childhood Educators of BC
1675 W. 4th Avenue, Suite 201
Vancouver, British Columbia
V6J 1L8

Manitoba

Manitoba Child Care Association Inc.
364 McGregor Street
Winnepeg, Manitoba
R2W 4X3

New Brunswick

Early Childhood Coalition Petite Enfance
123 York Street, Suite 201
Fredricton, New Brunswick
E3B 3N6

New Brunswick Daycare Association
200 Newman Street
St. John, New Brunswick
E2K 1M4

Newfoundland

Association of Early Childhood Education
of Newfoundland and Labrador
P.O. Box 21462, 14 Torhay Road
St. John's, Newfoundland
A1A 4J7

Northwest Territories

N.W.T. Child Care Association
5004, 54th Street
Yellowknife, Northwest Territories
X1A 2R4

Nova Scotia

Association of Early Childhood Educators
60 Thornehill Drive
Dartmoth, Nova Scotia
B3B 1S1

Child Care Connection NS
1200 Tower Road, Suite 100
Halifax, Nova Scotia
B3H 4K6

Ontario

Association of Early Childhood Educators of Ontario
40 Orchard View Boulevard., Suite 211
Toronto, Ontario
M4R 1B9

Ontario Coalition for Better Child Care
500A Bloor Street W., 2nd Floor
Toronto, Ontario
N2B 2T1

Prince Edward Island

Early Childhood Development Association of P.E.I.
c/o The Park Day Care
West Royalty Industrial Park
Charlottetown, Prince Edward Island
C1E 1B0

Quebec

Association of Early Childhood Educators
828 Decarie Boulevard, Suite 201
Montreal, Quebec
H4L 3L9

Saskatchewan

Saskatchewan Child Care Association Inc.
#1-3002 Loise Street
Saskatoon, Saskatchewan
S7J 3L8

Yukon Territory

Yukon Child Care Association
Box 5439
Whitehorse, Yukon
Y1A 5H4

United States

National Association for the Education of Young Children

1834 Connecticut Avenue, N.W.
Washington, D.C.
20009-5786

International

World Organization for Early Childhood Education
Canada (OMEP)
Laval University
Quebec, Quebec
GiK 7P4

United States (OMEP)
Eastern Michigan University
Early Childhood Education Department
Ypsilanti, Michigan
48197

R e f e r e n c e s

Canadian Day Care Advocacy Association. (1995). *Child Care— the Set of Principles*. Ottawa, Ont.

Feeney, S. (1995). "Professionalism in Early Childhood Teacher Education: Focus on Ethics." *Journal of Early Childhood Education,* 16:13–15.

Feeney, S., D. Christensen, and E. Moravcik. (1991). *Who Am I in the Lives of Children?* New York: Macmillan Publishing Co.

Fennimore, Beatrice. (1989). *Child Advocacy*. New York: Teachers College Press.

Friendly, M. (1994). *Child Care Policy in Canada*. Don Mills, Ont.: Addison-Wesley.

Goffin, S., and D. Day. (1994). *New Perspectives in Early Childhood Teacher Education: Bringing Practitioners into the Debate*. New York: Teachers College Press.

Gordon, A.M., and K.W. Browne. (1985). *Beginnings and Beyond: Foundations in Early Childhood Education*. New York: Delmar Publishers Inc.

Hildebrand, V. (1993). *Management of Child Development Centers,* 3rd ed. Toronto: Maxwell Macmillan.

Isenberg, J. (1995). "Professionalism in Early Childhood Teacher Education: Who? What? Why?" *Journal of Early Childhood Education,* 16:11–13.

Katz, L.G. (1977). *Talks With Teachers*. Washington, D.C.: National Association for the Education of Young Children.

Katz, L.G. (1987). "The Nature of Professions: Where is Early Childhood Education?" *Current Topics in Early Childhood Education* 7:1–15.

Morrison, G. (1995). "Early Childhood Professionals: Toward a New Identity." *Journal of Early Childhood Education,* 16:17–19.

Schön, D.A. (1983). *The Reflective Practitioner: How Professionals Think in Action*. New York: Basic Books.

Stremmel, A., V. Fu, P. Patet, and H. Shah. (1995). "Images of Teaching: Prospective Early Childhood Teachers' Constructions of the Teaching-learning Process of Young Children." *Advances in Early Childhood Education and Day Care,* 7:1–40.

Taylor, Barbara. (1989). *Early Childhood Program Management: People and Procedures*. Columbus, Ohio: Merrill Publishing Company.

Vander Ven, Karen. (1988). "Pathways to Professional Effectiveness for Early Childhood Educators." In *Professionalism and the Early Childhood Practitioner.* New York: Teachers College Press.

APPENDIX A

The Educator Emerges

This appendix highlights the many tools throughout the book that can be used by the practitioner. As a student it is important to learn techniques and understand the theory behind them. As a graduate it is valuable to draw on these techniques and find them quickly when the need arises.

The first column describes a need or concern that an emerging educator might have. The second column describes when and why you might use this tool. The third column identifies the textbook chapter or other resource where you can find this information.

Educator resources	When can I use this?	Location
Curriculum vitae	**When:** To write a CV when applying for any job?. **Purpose:** To provide data on your professional and educational qualifications.	Chapter 8
Cover letter for job applications	**When:** To apply for a job. **Purpose:** To provide concise information that sets you apart from other applicants.	Chapter 8
Salaries	**What** can I expect?	Chapter 7 and Chapter 8 provide a salary scale.

Educator resources	When can I use this?	Location
Job description	**When:** Once you have been accepted for a job, you should look back at sample job descriptions. **Purpose:** To establish if your job description reflects what you understand your role will be. Look at the sample job description to determine if you wish to ask for any modifications to the one provided. Remember, the job description is a personal contract between you and the day care.	Chapter 8
Educator/child ratios by province and territory	**When:** Important to know before beginning your day-care employment. **Purpose:** To compare local norms with those of the day care where you are or will be working.	Chapter 6
Who am I?	**When:** After you have been hired and before you start you job. **Purpose:** This tool is intended to help new practitioners identify their position and function within the day-care system.	Chapter 8

Educator resources	When can I use this?	Location
Communicating with children	**When:** At all times. **Purpose:** To use techniques of communication that will provide a high quality of interaction between the practitioner and the children.	Chapter 8
Establishing a mission statement	**When:** As a member of a centre working on a mission statement. A centre that has a mission statement should review it on an annual basis. A centre that does not have a mission statement should establish one. **Purpose:** To provide direction and purpose to the day care.	Chapter 3
Which curriculum approach best reflects my beliefs as an educator, and how can I use it?	**When:** Before beginning to plan for your group of children, it is important to establish a curriculum approach. You may select from more than one curriculum area, but you should be clear as to what you like about each one. **Purpose:** To provide consistency in your planning as an educator.	Chapter 2

Educator resources	When can I use this?	Location
Observations	**When:** These are carried out when you begin working with a group of children. Observations should be carried out on a regular basis. **Purpose:** To establish the developmental level of each individual child and his or her interest needs. This facilitates program planning and ensures that the plans meet your goals and objectives.	Chapter 2
Program plans	**When:** This is an ongoing task that all educators are required to fulfil. Begin planning after you have selected a curriculum approach, met your group of children, and carried out some observations. **Purpose:** To set objectives for you and the children you work with. Program plans also provide an organizational structure to experiences, routines, and activities.	Chapter 8

Educator resources	When can I use this?	Location
Purchasing materials	**When:** Consumable materials are purchased three to four times a year while equipment is usually ordered annually. **Purpose:** To anticipate needs (consumable, and to revitalize equipment and materials.	Chapter 7
Assessing the design of the environment and the available materials	**When:** After you have been hired and before you start planning. **Purpose:** To identify the materials available to you both in your room and throughout the day care.	Book: Harmes and Clifford. (1980). *The Environment Rating Scale.* New York: Teachers College Press.
Improving interpersonal interaction	**When:** Ongoing as a practitioner. **Purpose:** To have positive and effective relations with co-workers, parents, and children.	Chapter 4
Parent conferences	**When:** At least once or twice a year. **Purpose:** To inform parents and guardians about the development of and daily lives of their children during the hours when they are not present.	Chapter 5

Educator resources	When can I use this?	Location
Parent information meetings	**When:** Two or three times a year. **Purpose:** To guide the practitioner in selecting and planning relevant meetings for parents and guardians.	Chapter 4
Board of directors meetings	**When:** After your first year working in the field you may be ready and willing to take on the responsibility of representing your colleagues on the board of directors. **Purpose:** To make the points of view of educators heard by other stakeholders in the day-care system.	Chapter 6
Provincial or territorial regulatory offices	**When:** Contact as soon as you become a practitioner in the field. **Purpose:** To become aware of the rules governing the early childhood profession and the system of day care in your province or territory.	Chapter 6

Educator resources	When can I use this?	Location
Early childhood associations	**Purpose:** To continue your professional growth and development and become an advocate within your field.	Chapter 10
Provincial and territorial legislations governing day care	**When:** You begin working in a new day care or when you relocate to another province or territory. **Purpose:** To become knowledgeable and familiar with regulations and legislations that will influence and impact on your job.	Chapter 6

APPENDIX B

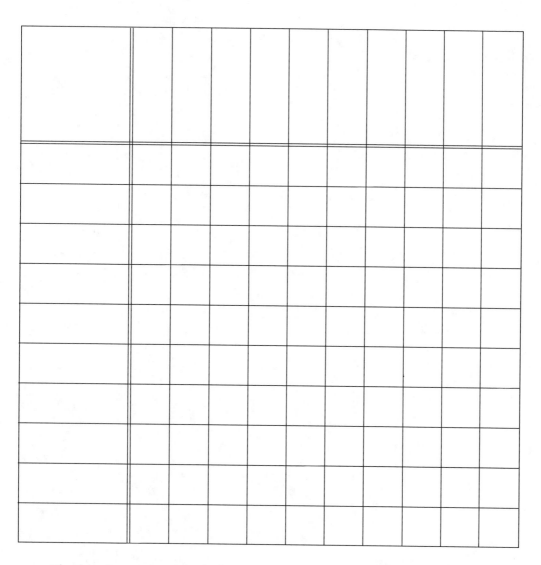

The blank matrix provided in Appendix B can be used as a starting point to begin creating a grid to develop a mission statement for your day-care centre.

GLOSSARY

accommodation—is a process where we change the way we think in order to incorporate new knowledge.

acts and laws—outline the requirements and regulations that the provincial and territorial governments establish for day-care centres.

advisory committee—a committee of parents which assists in the operations of the day care.

advocacy—the act of advocating for the betterment of an identified cause.

advocate—is an individual or group who lobbies for a particular cause.

anti-bias curriculum—an integrated curriculum that strives to avoid and eliminate bias.

assimilation—is a process where by we filter or modify information in order to fit it into the knowledge we already have.

Bank Street/developmental interactionist—the goal of this educational program is the development of the child through a process of stages.

behaviour modification—changing the behaviour of an organism through a system of reward or punishment.

behaviourist theory—individual behaviour is shaped by the environment through a system of reward or punishment.

benefits—relate to the different advantages that centres offer their employees.

board of directors—group of elected individuals who have decision-making power.

boundaries—are parameters that define a system. Boundaries vary in each organization and are system-specific.

brainstorming—a process where two or more people provide as many ideas as possible to solve a problem or come up with ideas.

bylaws—internal regulations of the day care.

Canadian Assistance Plan—a cost-sharing plan between the federal and provincial and territorial governments to provide day-care subsidies to low-income families.

child care—a system of care and education provided for children whose parents are unavailable to care for them for parts of the day.

Child Care Initiative Fund (CCIF)—a fund set up by the federal government to provide funding to new and innovative child-care projects.

Child Care Expense Deduction—is a tax deduction available to parents on their federal income tax.

clientele—refers to the individuals who are served by a particular system, for example, the parents.

closed system—in a closed organization the decision-making process involves fewer individuals than in an open system.

cognitive dissonance—is when we have a conflict in our thinking.

cognitive-developmentalist theory—is a stage-related theory of child development that sees children passing from one stage to the next in a spiral formation.

components—are the numerous elements within a given system that work together and are related to each other to help it function as a unit.

consolidation—is the second stage of professional development during which time an educator becomes more comfortable working with individual children. It begins around the end of the first year of work in a given profession and generally lasts into the third year.

constructivist approach—is a child-centred approach to early childhood education.

contract—the legal document that exists between an employer and an employee.

convergent thinking—taking many ideas and narrowing them down to a few ideas.

cooporation—when individuals work together to achieve a common goal.

cover letter—a letter sent in reply to a job advertisement.

cultural pluralism—the co-existence of many cultures.

curriculum—involves a decision-making process of why to include certain elements, a planning of these elements, a decision of how and when they should happen, and finally an assessment of how and when the children learned. All curricula emanate from goal setting.

curriculum content—is developed through a variety of perspectives and helps to generate ideas for the development of activities and opportunities.

curriculum framework—the organizational framework that sets the direction for the development of the curriculum.

curriculum vitae—contains information that is deemed pertinent in the application of a job. It provides a summary of educational background, work experiences, and other relevant achievements. It is often referred to as a résumé.

day care—a physical place where children are left for parts of a day for care and education.

day-care legislation and regulations—are the legal framework established by each province and territory under which day cares operate.

disposition—is the temperament of your actions.

divergent thinking—the ability to see many possibilities or solutions to any one situation.

dynamic—implies that there is constant adjustment or change to a particular situation. In a dynamic system there is active learning and shared decision-making.

eclectic approach—this approach to curriculum involves borrowing ideas from a few models to create a new approach.

ecological model—this model asserts that there is an inseparable relationship between any organization and the environment in which it is situated. An ecological view is based on an assumption that there is an interdependence between the environment and any given system.

economics—the financial system of the day-care system.

educator training—the educational background of the educator.

educator/child ratio—the number of children per educator in a group of children.

educator qualifications—the type of diploma or degree required by the provincial or territorial government in order to work in a day care.

elements of a system—the elements refer to people, materials, or surroundings that might have an influence on a system.

embedded—when a smaller system is completely a part of a larger one it is said to be embedded in it. For example, a day-care system that exists within a hospital system is said to be embedded.

ethics—the study of right and wrong. Professional ethics involve a reflection on professional responsibility.

facilitator—is an individual who helps guide an individual's learning. A facilitator generally focuses on listening more than talking.

family grouping—a system of grouping children of different ages together. Programming is geared toward this mixed age group.

family notebooks—a notebook in which parents and educators can leave informal comments, ask questions and receive answers, or read an anecdote about the child and his or her day.

family structure—a system that includes the child, other siblings, and the parents or guardians of the children in question. Today's family structure is diverse and may not necessarily include a mother and a father in the traditional sense.

financial organization—is an organization that operates with income and expenses.

financial system—the income and expenses of the day-care system.

fixed costs—items on the budget where the cost or expense does not change during a specific budget year, for example, the day care's rent is a fixed cost.

flexibility—the ability to adapt one's communication style to fit the needs of a situation.

formal communication techniques—these are planned and organized events in which educators and parents communicate and share ideas.

global perspective—an overall general outlook on a topic.

goal orientation—the agreed-upon direction that a system strives toward. It is an orientation that helps drive the system.

group size—number of children per group.

high/scope curriculum—a curriculum approach that focuses on the plan, do, review concept.

holism—information about an organization is examined from a variety of perspectives. It involves examining the whole picture and not just part of it.

holistic—an integrated approach to curriculum development that takes into consideration the development of the whole child.

Indian and Northern Affairs—a division of the federal government that provides support to child-care programs on reserves.

indicators of quality—educator training, educator/child ratio, and groups size are all indicators of quality.

informal communication techniques—are not planned and often occur at the beginning or at the end of the day.

inquiry-oriented practice—a process that is driven by an individual's conscious desire to ask questions and seek answers in order to improve her or his practice.

integrated—when one event is within another and cannot happen in isolation.

intercultural awareness—to become aware of one's personal values and assumptions with respect to culture.

interdependence—the concept that there is a synergistic relationship between elements of a system. That is to say, when people work alone the result is not as great as when people work by relying on each other.

interpersonal competence—competence in relating to and interacting with ourself is enhanced through the development of interpersonal and intrapersonal skills.

interpersonal skills—involve those skills that an individual draws on in order to communicate effectively with others. They stem from an aptitude to understand and communicate with people.

interview—where an applicant for a position is asked questions by one or more individuals to assess if they would meet the qualifications of the position.

intrapersonal self—this refers to the inner-self and the ability to look within to understand personal beliefs and values. An understanding of the intrapersonal self involves self-reflection.

intrapersonal skills—involve skills that an individual draws on in order to understand themselves.

job description—is a portrait of the general parameters of responsibility that an individual will have in a given job.

knowledge—refers to the information about a given subject. It can be a theoretical paradigm or simply facts about a certain subject.

legal framework—all day cares operate within a legal framework, which is established by the province or territory.

licence—each province and territory establishes the licensing requirements for day-cares.

maturationist view—suggests that the course of human development is based on a genetic predisposition.

matrix—a grid used to develop and organize ideas.

maturity—this is the fourth stage of professional development when self-acceptance as a professional educator becomes stronger. One generally enters this stage somewhere after three to five years of practical professional experiences.

mentor program—a program where a new educator is assigned a mentor who is available to answer questions and help her or him become familiar with the centre.

mission statement—a statement of purpose that drives an organization or a system.

mixed grouping—grouping children of the same age together for some parts of the day and with children of different ages for other parts of the day.

modelling—demonstration and practice of a behaviour that others can learn from by seeing or experiencing it.

Montessori—this is a curriculum approach based on individual instruction.

newsletters—bulletins put out by either the educator or the day care that provide useful information to the parents of the children at the day care.

non-profit centre—a day care that must keep all its assets and profits within the centre.

open system—in an open system the decision-making process involves the influence of many of the stakeholders.

operant conditioning—controlling behaviour by increasing or decreasing the presence of that particular behaviour.

operational budget—an annual budget that includes the income and expenses of an organization.

outcome—this is an action or objective toward which the educator plans. The educator does the planning and the child demonstrates the outcome.

parent conferences—meetings organized between an educator and the parents to discuss details that are of interest to both parties about a child. These meetings are private and confidential.

parent information meetings—are meetings set up for the parents of children enrolled in or planning to enrol in a particular day care. They provide a forum for information on specific topics and for social interaction between parents.

participative management—a style of management that involves employees and clientele in relevant decision-making.

peak hours—hours in a day care when the greatest amount of children are present.

permit—after receiving a licence, a day care receives a permit to operate.

process—the experiences that an individual goes through in order to achieve an outcome. It does not refer to the result but the way one gets to the result.

professional—an individual who works to meet a societal need. A professional tends to have clients rather than customers.

profit centre—a day care that is run as a business and is financially able to make a profit.

program content—includes the knowledge, skills, and attitudes that are a part of professional practice.

program plans—the day-to-day activities and opportunities provided to the children.

program planning—the process of organizing the schedule, routines, activities, and opportunities during the day.

provincial and territorial grants—grants available to licensed day cares by the provinces and territories.

psychodynamic theory—a developmental theory related to the personality development of individuals.

quality—refers to the high standard and excellence of a facility or situation.

quality child care—refers to standards of training, health, safety, and educator/child ratios that are considered important to the provision of good care and education for young children.

record keeping—is a system that is useful for keeping track of information and resources.

reflective practice—refers to an individual's ability to question and reassess decisions and actions with the intent to make positive changes.

regulations—are the conditions that a day care must following to be able to obtain a permit or licence.

reinforcement—the process of modifying a behaviour through some sort of reward system.

relationships—there are many relationships within a system. Relationships affect the way the system functions.

renewal—this is the third stage of professional development when an educator gains greater confidence in developing and applying his or her program techniques. This stage occurs somewhere between the third and fourth year following a professional training program.

resources—the day-care system is dependent on a variety of resources.

résumé—contains information that is deemed pertinent in the application of a job. It provides a summary of educational background, work experiences, and other relevant achievements. It is often referred to as a curriculum vitae.

salary scale—a scale indicating the salary an individual can expect based on educational qualifications and experience.

same-age grouping—a situation where children of the same age are grouped together for the whole day. Programming is based on this grouping arrangement.

separation anxiety—the apprehension that is experienced by some children when their parents leave them at the day care.

shifts—refers to an employee's working schedule. Shift work scheduling usually implies that a worker shares the working hours with another employee.

skills—competencies required to carry out a specified task.

stakeholder(s)—refers to an individual or group of individuals who has a vested interest in a system.

start-up budget—is the budget that determines the costs necessary to set-up a day care.

suprasystem—is a larger system that has one or more smaller systems embedded within it.

survival—this is the first professional stage of development. It is a time of questioning all that you have learned and how to apply it. Depending on the individual and on the experiences you have had in your practicum placements, this can last between one and two years.

system—is an organizational framework that includes people, materials, and surroundings.

systems approach—is a way of looking at an organization. It asserts that an organization is goal oriented, can function on its own, yet has an inseparable relationship with the outside environment. The outside environment may include a number of larger systems that encompass the system under study.

theoretical foundations—serve as a framework to provide direction and focus for curriculum and program planning.

Training allowances—money that is provided to individuals in federal training programs to cover the cost of child care while they are studying.

variable costs—items on the budget where the cost or expense changes during a specific budget year.

zone of proximal development (ZPD)—term used by Vygotsky to describe the independent achievement of a task. It is an educator's responsibilty to set up a ZPD for each child. Once the ZPD is reached the educator sets a new one which becomes the new goal for that child.

INDEX

To the owner of this book

We hope that you have enjoyed *Emerging Educator,* and we would like to know as much about your experiences with this text as you would care to offer. Only through your comments and those of others can we learn how to make this a better text for future readers.

School _____ Your instructor's name _____

Course _____ Was the text required? _____ Recommended? _____

1. What did you like the most about *Emerging Educator?*

_____
_____
_____

2. How useful was this text for your course?

_____
_____
_____

3. Do you have any recommendations for ways to improve the next edition of this text?

_____
_____
_____

4. In the space below or in a separate letter, please write any other comments you have about the book. (For example, please feel free to comment on reading level, writing style, terminology, design features, and learning aids.)

_____
_____
_____

Optional

Your name _____ Date _____

May ITP Nelson quote you, either in promotion for *Emerging Educator* or in future publishing ventures?

Yes _____ No _____

Thanks!

You can also send your comments to us via e-mail at
college_arts_hum@nelson.com

 **I T P® Nelson**
an International Thomson Publishing company

 **MAIL POSTE**
Canada Post Corporation
Société canadienne des postes
Postage paid   Port payé
if mailed in Canada   si posté au Canada
Business Reply   Réponse d'affairess

0066102399   01

0066102399-M1K5G4-BR01

ITP NELSON
MARKET AND PRODUCT DEVELOPMENT
P.O. BOX 60223 STN BRN 8
TORONTO ON M7Y 2H1